China and Japan—
Emerging Global Powers

Peter G. Mueller
Douglas A. Ross

Published in cooperation
with the Canadian Institute
of International Affairs

The Praeger Special Studies program—
utilizing the most modern and efficient book
production techniques and a selective
worldwide distribution network—makes
available to the academic, government, and
business communities significant, timely
research in U.S. and international economic, social, and political development.

China and Japan— Emerging Global Powers

Praeger Publishers   New York   Washington   London

PRAEGER SPECIAL STUDIES IN INTERNATIONAL POLITICS AND GOVERNMENT

Library of Congress Cataloging in Publication Data

Mueller, Peter G
   China and Japan, emerging global powers.

   (Praeger special studies in international politics
and government)
   "Published in cooperation with the Canadian Institute
of International Affairs. "
   Bibliography: p.
   1. China—Foreign relations—1949-   2. Japan—
Foreign relations—1945-   I. Ross, Douglas A. ,
joint author. II. Title.
DS740. 4. M83   327. 51   74-33039
ISBN 0-275-05400-4

PRAEGER PUBLISHERS
111 Fourth Avenue, New York, N.Y. 10003, U.S.A.

Published in the United States of America in 1975
by Praeger Publishers, Inc.

Printed in the United States of America

The origin of this study was a profound concern of two young Canadian scholars with the strategic issues their country would face in the next decade. Their search led them inevitably to the less calculable factors on the Pacific frontier, to the great Asian nations whose more recent transformations are challenging the assumptions of early generations. To see China and Japan as challenges, but not inevitably as threats, requires a fresh perspective. It is perspective, along with zealous curiosity and intellectual integrity, that gives this study its special quality. As the authors make clear, they are not Old China or Old Japan hands. They have examined diligently the evidence of those who are and looked at that evidence whole from our distance. This is not at all intended to replace the studies of specialists; it looks at them--and incidentally provides a useful survey of what the specialists are saying. The authors have the additional advantage of being young enough to look clear-headedly at these "strategic" phenomena without the preconceptions either of cold war or of detente, neither of which provides any longer a valid framework for a world outgrowing them.

I had the good fortune to be associated with Peter Mueller and Douglas Ross in their graduate studies and to commend their research to the Defence Research Board (DRB) in Ottawa. It is evidence of the foresight of DRB that it encouraged a strategic study of this nonmilitary kind by young scholars and recognized the value of their perspectives. The intensive work involved was made possible by a grant for this purpose to the Canadian Institute of International Affairs, under whose sponsorship the work was carried out. Those associated with the study are particularly grateful to the Atlantic Council of the United States for its recognition of this work by two Canadians. It may be that Canadians have some advantage of detachment from subjects in which Americans have been more painfully and responsibly involved. The issues raised by these two emerging powers have few particular Canadian dimensions, however; and this treatment of them is of interest to all interested readers in the Atlantic and other communities.

John W. Holmes
Director General
Canadian Institute of
International Affairs

This study of the People's Republic of China and Japan is intended to provide an overview of the changing political and strategic balance of power in Asia, especially as it is seen, experienced, and influenced by the leadership of these two nations. The sheer scope of such a study was the source of our most difficult problems and the root cause of our own "protracted struggle" in completing the text. Begun in May 1972 as a short paper commissioned by Canada's Defence Research Board, the work grew into a report well beyond the scope of the original undertaking--in both size and complexity.

We wish to express our gratitude to the Defence Research Board for having provided us with the original opportunity to undertake this study. Second, we would like to thank the Atlantic Council of the United States for their interest; and finally, we are most grateful for the assistance and encouragement extended to us by the Canadian Institute of International Affairs. We would like to thank in particular John W. Homes, director general; Robert W. Reford, executive director; Jane Barrett, librarian; and Marion Magee, our indefatigable editor. Responsibility for any shortcomings in the work is, of course, ours alone.

CONTENTS

LIST OF TABLES

He who has many enemies is like a pigeon among kites:
whichever way he turns he faces attack

                                        Hindu proverb

Our purpose in writing this book was to attempt to define the roles
of the People's Republic of China and Japan in the course of political
evolution in east Asia over the next decade. As newcomers to the
study of the Asian political-strategic calculus, it was hoped that, at
the very least, a fresh perspective could be gained in the continuing
effort to discern and analyze the principal motive factors in the Asian
balance of power. The structure and method of the study is eclectic
and aggregative. There is no attempt to build a broad systematic
theory of the regional political system in Asia.

Research and analysis has served to confirm our initial opinion
that the Asian region will be dominated by the two nascent superpowers,
Japan and the People's Republic of China. The United States gradually
is going to relinquish its position as the prime molder of the political
and social structures of east Asia. In the most probable scenario,
China and Japan will continue to prosper economically and socially.
They will continue to increase their influence on the nations of Indochina and the southeast Asian archipelago--the Japanese through continued capital investment and technical assistance and the Chinese
through a new cycle of foreign aid and skillful diplomacy.

The Japanese as homines economici could expand and deepen their
hold on the economies of Thailand, Indonesia, Malaysia, North and
South Vietnam, and the Philippines. But this increased involvement
abroad, whether it is through direct control of industries overseas
or joint ventures with foreign nationals, will make Japan's dependence
on maritime trading routes even greater than it is now. Given a
modicum of prudence and circumspection on the part of the Russians
and the Chinese, however, the Japanese likely will not be driven to
the acquisition of a strategic deterrent to safeguard these lifelines.
Their security will be assured through maintaining a favorable balance of power among the four other actors in the global pentarchy
and by promoting and stabilizing the present atmosphere of compromise and detente.

In effect this implies that there will be a quadrapartite balancing
act in Asia (Western Europe being left without a significant role to
play in Asian affairs), but that the balancers will not be totally free

to shift their alignments to and fro as immediate political-strategic interests might dictate. It is difficult to imagine either Japan or China sharing very much in common with the USSR for the foreseeable future, even should the Russians be successful in wooing Japanese investors to exploit Siberian gas, oil, and metals. Neither the Japanese nor the Chinese are likely to trust the Russians. If Japan is going to look for new allies, or at least seek to move closer to former enemies, the beneficiary of Japanese insecurity and diplomacy is likely to be Peking, not Moscow. The Chinese are eager to achieve more direct contact with decision makers and industrialists, eager because they seek to neutralize politically any potential military threat from Japan and because increased contacts could mean a greater inflow of valuable technology and complex capital goods, particularly in the fields of electronics and computer science. For the medium term, the Chinese also may be thinking in terms of a political understanding with the Japanese whereby the two nations would pressure the superpower duopoly to leave "Asia for the Asians." Neither the Japanese nor the Chinese will be thinking in terms of an imperialist or even quasi-imperialist policy. Both governmental elites are sincere in their advocacy of greater autonomy for Asian states.

In considering the possibilities for meaningful coordination between China and Japan, it is imperative to realize that the situation in east Asia is shot through with contradictions and anomalies. A serious attempt by Japan and China to minimize American and Soviet influence in Asia necessarily will require at least the tacit and probably the explicit coordination of their respective foreign policies. But resistance to such coordination probably would be stiff from opposition groups in both nations. Moreover such a goal, if achieved, would be at the expense of Japanese security, since a further disengagement of American forces in the western Pacific could only leave the Japanese with an even less credible nuclear guarantee from the United States. For Japan, at least, there would be a trade-off between the goal of Asian autonomy and that of national security.

Similarly, though the cultures of Japan and China are inextricably interwoven by a common historical and intellectual experience, the two contemporary societies are irrevocably split apart by the fact that Japan is committed to an essentially bourgeois, corporate, capitalist economy and an open, representative and democratic polity; but China relies on a one-party dictatorship and, of course, is bent on achieving a fully socialist system of production as soon as is humanly possible. Furthermore, it is virtually certain that the the post-Mao collective leadership of China will be indifferent if not antagonistic to multidimensional social and intellectual contacts with either the Japanese or the Americans. For China the united front policy of detente may mean that the Chinese must share temporarily the imperialists' beds, but the situation does not require any lovemaking. The Chinese will remain deeply concerned about maintaining the ideological purity of their revolution.

The past five years have been ones of rapid reorientation for foreign policy planners in both Peking and Tokyo. Japan has had to adjust psychologically to the loss of an automatic American commitment to Asian security. China has had to come to grips with the stark reality of the military menace posed by its socialist mentor, the USSR. For the Japanese and Chinese this half-decade and especially the last 18 months has been a time of intense, vigilant searching for new buttresses to their respective security systems. The Japanese and Chinese have been led to scrutinize each other more closely and with more hope and mutual respect than at any time in recent history. But both the problems and goals of these societies are so markedly different that an effective entente between them seems improbable. The Sino-Japanese relationship is nearly devoid of social and economic complementarity. China, in the midst of its drive toward "autarky if necessary but not necessarily autarky," is intent on setting an example of political autonomy through economic self-sufficiency in the hope that many Third World nations will emulate it. Japan, however, is dedicated to an even wider expansion of international economic activity. The watchword for the Japanese is interdependence, not independence. The central thrust of both domestic and foreign policy in Japan is the maintenance of a high rate of economic growth and the promotion of stable social and political relationships with the external environment, which will be conducive to increasing trade and investment flows. The desire for stability, growth, and an evermore complex but reliable set of economic links to other Western nations necessarily imposes on Japan the role of apologist for the status quo. In no way would the Japanese align themselves to a policy of revolutionary social development. Here is the one fundamental obstacle in the way of a closer rapport between China and Japan.

In terms of direct strategic questions there is, however, a substantial area for consensus and accord. First, both China and Japan prefer a slow retrenchment of the American military presence. Peking would be gravely concerned if a peremptory American pullback prepared the way for an expansion of Soviet influence on Taiwan or the Indochinese peninsula. The Japanese are concerned equally about the expansion of the Soviet navy and its recently acquired amphibious capability. Second, neither the Chinese nor the Japanese themselves wish to contemplate Japan's accession to the nuclear club. For Japan the material costs and the probable political risks are not appealing, and the Chinese could only view such a move with deep apprehension. For this reason the Chinese necessarily are going to try to project a cordial, even sympathetic, image to the Japanese.

The Liberal Democratic Party (LDP) government under Premier Kakuei Tanaka does not at present seem to have any clearly defined long term goals for Japanese participation in the east Asian political system. In part, this is because Japanese national interests (perceived in economic terms) may be best served by a policy of minimal commitments in relation to the other three Asian powers. Detente with the People's Republic of China in 1972 rectified what had become an embarrassing situation for the LDP government, but as yet Tanaka and his cabinet do not appear to have any clear idea of the role that their country ought to play in the hierarchy of the states system. In theory it is possible for Japan to remain a great economic power, without committing itself to acquiring and maintaining a much larger (and possibly nuclear-equipped) military establishment. But theory is often too simplistic. Were it not for the peculiarities of the Japanese experience in World War II (namely, Hiroshima and Nagasaki), it surely would be only a few years until Japanese public opinion evolved sufficiently to press for a constitutional revision enabling the government to arm itself with the full panoply of modern weaponry. If the U.S. nuclear guarantee, as embodied in the Treaty of Mutual Cooperation and Security and the Nixon Doctrine, can maintain its credibility for the Japanese people, then Japanese leaders will content themselves with maintaining great-power status in the economic dimension alone. In political and strategic terms, the Japanese would follow a middle-of-the-road policy of no antagonism with respect to both China and Russia. But although this would not be a disagreeable outcome for the Western Alliance system, it seems a relatively improbable scenario for security relations in the late 1970s since it is a static projection of a volatile system of variables.

Various analysts have raised the possibility that within the next five to ten years China may have developed a mature nuclear establishment, comprising a large number of first-strike intercontinental ballistic missiles (ICBMs) capable of hitting North American targets and a much more modest (but nevertheless psychologically critical) second-strike force of hardened missiles. Should this occur, the Japanese leaders would then be faced with a predicament similar to that of General Charles de Gaulle in the early 1960s: as the American homeland becomes vulnerable, can the American nuclear guarantee remain credible?

This may be a spurious question since the issue of Sino-Japanese security relations is not even the predominant one for Japanese leaders. In reality, Japan has been confronted with this kind of problem ever since the mid-1960s when the Soviet Union achieved a firm second-strike capability against the United States. Yet this did not provoke severe doubts within the Japanese polity. Why should a similar development in China precipitate a crisis in trust? One certainly can sympathize with Japanese anxiety concerning nuclear proliferation, but it seems at best a doubtful proposition that the Japanese will feel menaced by a technologically and industrially third-rate power, which in all likelihood will be adhering to a conservative profile in strategic matters over the next decade.

Basic structural changes in the east Asian balance of power will not be initiated by the sudden foreign policy realignments of any of the great Asian powers. We foresee Japan preserving the ability to go nuclear--but not needing (or desiring) to exercise this option. We foresee a continued strategic standoff between the Soviet Union and the United States as a comparatively reliable parameter in the equation of power. The United States will not be so foolish as to retreat to fortress America. The trauma of Vietnam may be great, but it will not be strong enough to inspire a period of isolationist withdrawal. China will continue to support "revolutionary praxis" in Africa, the Middle East, and Indochina; but it will be, for the most part, a muted, rhetorical support as far as east Asia is concerned. National liberation movements probably will continue to enjoy considerable success, but they also will be relatively independent of Peking's policies. Sino-American detente has undermined China's credibility in the eyes of fellow Asian revolutionaries, but this is a cost that will be willingly borne by the Chinese as long as they face a severe military threat along their northern border. The Sino-Soviet rift and its concomitant military confrontation should remain a stable parameter in the east Asian configuration of power.

Although it is true that, of the four great Asian powers, China is the nation most committed to overturning the balance of power, the Chinese ultimately may provide a key buttress to global stability by creating a viable model, albeit totalitarian-communist, for social and economic progress for societies caught in the vicious and apparently unending grip of unchecked population growth.

In extreme situations usually only extreme means suffice to remedy grave crises. The dual processes of representative democracy and a technologically progressive oligopoly economy within our present pluralistic Western societies required generations of social and cultural preparation before the various component elements of each nation could mesh to provide a continuing source of ordered progress through tacitly structured monopolistic competition and a muted struggle between labor and the management-ownership hierarchy in the private sector. Asian nations do not have generations to evolve similar structures and processes to meet the present challenges to their very survival as sovereign political entities. What is therefore a probable outcome of the social-political dynamics of Asia is a phase of proliferating authoritarian government. Such a pattern of development ought not be construed in the West as a threat. The initiative for technical progress and long term material improvement will continue to be with the West. This fact must not be overlooked. It is the trump card that gives cause for optimism concerning humanisitc reform in the communist nations and permanent reconciliation with the West in terms of the creation of a viable world order. But of course the West's hand must be played carefully, prudently, and with confidence. The greatest threat to Western liberal-democratic states is an internal one: a crisis in public morale, in maintaining a commitment to a rational, ordered, and effective response to authoritarian rule.

The chapters that follow attempt to elucidate the broad array of forces activating the Asian political system as it pertains to China and Japan. The book is concerned particularly with the way that the Chinese and Japanese decision makers see the world and such major developments as the Nixon Doctrine, the U.S. departure from Vietnam, and the Soviet military buildup. Policy should flow from a sound appreciation of all the fundamental operative parameters in the international arena. We hope that this study will contribute in some measure to such understanding.

I

THE PEOPLE'S
REPUBLIC OF CHINA

Make peace with the powerful,
War with the equal;
And make quick raids against the timid.

Hindu proverb

1

SINOCENTRISM AND THE
MIDDLE KINGDOM COMPLEX

Generally in war the best policy is to take a state in-
tact; to ruin it is inferior to this. . . . For to win one
hundred victories in one hundred battles is not the acme
of skill. To subdue the enemy without fighting is the
acme of skill.
Sun Tzu, The Art of War, c. 500 B.C.

BASIC STATISTICS

The People's Republic of China (P.R.C.) is a nation that encom-
passes roughly 3.7 million square miles of territory. Its population
of approximately 750 million must extract a living from a comparatively inhospitable geography, for less than 15 percent of China's
land is suitable for cultivation. Most of its agriculture is carried
on in the drainage basins of the three principal rivers (the Hwang Ho,
the Yangtze Kiang, and the Si Kiang). And the technologically primitive nature of the Chinese economy means that most of the population must inhabit these regions to work the farmland in a labor-in-
tensive fashion. Because of China's sheer size, the massive administrative problems of governing a population nearly four times that
of the United States, and the low level of economic development, the
Chinese inevitably are going to focus most of their physical and intellectual efforts on their own domestic problems. Although it may,
on occasion, prove conceptually fruitful to envision the Chinese nation as a cohesive, potentially aggressive, or expansionary empire
confronting an equally if not more impressive imperial power to the
north, a prudent observer of the Chinese political system cannot
justify easily a predatory conception of the People's Republic.

One of the central theses of this work is that the Chinese are not an overt military threat to their Asian neighbors. First, the Chinese, unlike the Russians, do not now have, nor in the foreseeable future could they acquire, sufficient physical resources to undertake an imperialist policy toward Southeast Asia, India, the USSR, or Japan (see Table 1.1). Second, they lack the requisite ideological program to justify such a policy. Maoist theory and practice is by nature antiimperialistic. The creation of satellite states on its borders is not a goal of China's foreign policy. Control of another nation's revolutionary project is an anathema to both China's declaratory foreign policy and its operational program for promoting the communist global strategy of division and encirclement.

This is not to imply that the P.R.C. is no threat whatsoever to the Western Alliance system, although the menace of the "red tide" seems to have lost most, if not all, its compelling urgency in the context of the new U.S. multipolar balancing act. The illusory struggle to "save the free world" at last has been seen for what it was--Western (primarily American) paranoia. Nevertheless, in a world of finite resources and growing appetites, the People's Republic will create serious problems for Western foreign policy. Just how the Chinese effectively will complicate the political and economic geometry of the late 1970s is contingent on numerous factors, both domestic and international.

Most analyses of contemporary Chinese foreign policy follow one of three major approaches: (1) foreign policy as a function of traditional perspectives, (2) foreign policy as a function of the debate and relative power distribution between the political left and right in the Chinese governmental elite, or (3) foreign policy as a function of China's revolutionary imperatives and degree of progress in economic development. These approaches are not, of course, mutually exclusive; and a fairly accurate appraisal of China's foreign policy decision making necessarily must strike a reasonable balance among the three.

Critics of the tradition-oriented school of thought point out that the most significant factor shaping Chinese attitudes in the 20th century has been "the breakdown of the traditional order in the face of decay from within and the challenge of imperialism."[1] This is undeniably true, since modern Chinese nationalism has been geared to a rejection of many established political traditions and a quest for a radically reformed, totally independent, political order. From Sun Yat-sen's time onward, Chinese politics has been characterized by revolutionaries who sought to create a political state capable of exercising the right of national self-determination--free from the economic exploitation of foreign political control and, after Versailles and the May Fourth Movement, free from what were then viewed as

Table 1.1

Resume of Economic Statistics, China

Area	3,690,550 square miles
Population	estimates range from 700 to 800 million
Population growth rate	0.6 percent[a]
GNP (1970)	$120 billion[b]
Defense expenditures (1970)	U.S. $7.6 to 8.55 billion
Aggregate steel production (1972)	23 million metric tons
Aggregate grain production (1971)	240 million metric tons
GNP growth rate (1971)	10 percent
Value of aggregate trade of China (1970)	U.S. $4.2 billion[c]
Aggregate trade as percentage of GNP (1970)	3.5 percent
Cultivated land area (1958)	107.8 million hectares (266.3 million acres)
Cultivated area as a percentage of total area (1958)	11 percent

[a]International Institute for Strategic Studies, The Military Balance 1972-73 (London: IISS, 1972), p. 45.

[b]Chou En-lai's figure from a 1971 interview with Edgar Snow.

[c]Shinkichi Eto, "Features Characteristic of the Economy of China," in Peace Research in Japan 1971 (Tokyo: Japan Research Group, 1971), p. 25.

Source: Compiled by author.

corrupt, hypocritical, Western philosophies.[2] Nevertheless the foreign policy priorities and goals of all governments are molded by many factors--some of which operate independently of ideology and the distribution of power among political and institutional structures. These include such unalterables as resource endowment, topography, and climate. Mao Tse-tung and Chou En-lai have altered radically the perspectives of Chinese foreign policy thinkers; yet these men too must pay obeisance to the physical geography of their nation, to its resource distribution, and to the cultural universe shared by their people.

SIGNIFICANT HISTORICAL CONCEPTS AND TRENDS

There are several traditional elements in Chinese thinking that we believe have direct significance for the interpretation and comprehension of contemporary Chinese foreign policy. Among these is the emphasis in traditional Chinese culture on the primacy of change. From the age of Lao Tzu and Confucius, Chinese philosophy and ethics have been affected greatly by the paradoxical insight that change is the only constant. Confucius once observed, "Life, death, preservation, loss, failure, success, poverty, riches, worthiness, unworthiness, slander, fame, hunger, thirst, cold, heat--these are the alternations of the world, the workings of fate. Day and night they change place before us and wisdom cannot spy out their source."[3] This perception of change has not been cast aside by latter-day Chinese philosophers. Mao Tse-tung's basic doctrines hinge on the premise that change is basic to existence, because it is continuous change that resolves old contradictions and gives birth to new antagonisms. Struggle in its manifold forms is ceaseless because it is the essence of change. Contradictions are manifest universally in the developmental processes of all phenomenal beings, for without contradictions the universe, in Mao's view (as in Hegel's), would be totally static. In a universe of change, the "dialectical world outlook teaches man chiefly how to observe and analyse skilfully the movement of opposites in various things and, on the basis of such analysis, to find out the methods of solving the contradictions."[4] Thus in both the Confucian and the Maoist systems, a recognition of the universality of change is obligatory.

Although there is a world of difference in the prescriptive recommendations of these two systems because of the Marxist-Leninist injection of will, of "politics in command," of human mastery over the realm of natural necessity and its concomitant change processes, it is important to remember that Mao's teachings are heard by a receptive audience, heirs to a culture with a millennia-long appreciation of change-oriented perspectives. It is not difficult, therefore, to account for popular Chinese acceptance of the idea of a world in permanent flux. This concept of change is also complementary to other fundamental communist theories such as the notion of a continual redistribution of world power from imperialist or socialist revisionist powers to the true representatives of the international proletariat. A 1972 editorial in Jen-min jih-pao [People's Daily] reflects this typically Chinese perception, "The world has been in a state of great upheaval. . . . The basic contradictions in the world have been sharpened. . . . Various political forces are in the process of further division and reorganization. The characteristic feature of the world situation today can be summed up in one word, upheaval or global upheaval."[5]

Such views are, of course, consonant with Mao's thesis that contradiction and struggle "are universal and absolute,"[6] and that the various contradictions, between proletariat and bourgeoisie, between working class and peasant class in socialist society, or between colonies or former colonies and imperialist states, can shift from periods of blatant ("antagonistic") contradiction to periods of less violent "nonantagonistic" contradiction. Without the theoretical rationale of nonantagonistic contradiction and the concept of phased development in international affairs, political detente with the United States or other policies of realpolitik would be exceedingly difficult to justify. Through these concepts, however, radical changes in foreign policy can be explained in a coherent and orderly fashion that is consistent with long run communist goals.

In searching for traditional precedents or historical facts or trends that may bear on present day decision makers in Peking, the student of Chinese foreign policy must bear in mind that recent Chinese history (the last 150 years) is a record of national humiliation and degradation at the hands of foreign "barbarians." Ross Terrill has summed up succinctly the implications of this experience, "The period from the Opium Wars until the present is a seamless stretch of history to Peking. First, because throughout it, China has faced superior material force on its doorstep. Second, because the Chinese mind has felt frustration, and often humiliation, when looking during this period at the West. The West has threatened China; yet the West is more advanced than China. It is a painful mixture for the patriotic Chinese mind. To keep the West at bay and to catch up with the West have both been among China's concerns." Another analyst, John Melby, stated that "the century of humiliation which China experienced is something it will never forget and understandably it will go to any length to prevent its recurrence."[7] I' is perhaps not an undue exaggeration to conclude that the experience of the last century has traumatized the Chinese national psyche and that the fundamental "contradiction" they are attempting to resolve is the gap between their cultural self-image as a preeminently civilized and inherently superior society and their position as an economically underdeveloped nation and, until recently, a marginally significant political power.

Traditionally, the Chinese have seen themselves as the social, political, and economic center of the world. Chinese civilization was "a continental island that had floated in a sea of barbarism not for centuries but for millennia."[8] Until the 19th century, Asia was the whole world and China its center. And indeed the Chinese word for their nation, Chung-kuo, can be translated literally as "middle country." The doctrine of China's superiority arose naturally enough as a result of its cultural isolation. The Chinese knew of no other significant societies. To the south and west the Himalayas cut them off from the Indian subcontinent and its flourishing culture, and to the north they faced the bellicose nomadic tribes of inner Asia. The ruling class of the early Chinese empires thus grew confident of its overall social superiority. Eventually Chinese political mythology reflected this perception. What is curious is not that the Chinese kings claimed superiority but, as John Fairbank notes, "that this claim could have been so thoroughly institutionalized and preserved as the official myth of the state for more than two thousand years."[9]

Unfortunately for the Ch'ing dynasty rulers, the doctrine became increasingly untenable. As the 19th century unfolded, China remained a stagnant society, ensnared by cultural traditions that had become the tools of oppression of the Manchu minority. The doctrine of Chinese superiority was itself one of these tools, though ultimately it was to become an embarrassment to the increasingly beleaguered Manchu rulers. Under the Manchus, China was shoved into the 20th century with a ruling elite that valued orthodoxy, not creativity or ingenuity, that understood only imitation of the "classics" not the importance of erecting a modern culture on the foundations of the old.

This doctrine of superiority—especially social and cultural superiority—constitutes the core of the Middle Kingdom complex, as this component of Chinese psychology is known in Western literature. The sinocentric perspective normally ascribed to contemporary rulers in Peking is in large measure the result of this Chinese perception of their own refinement and sophistication in the face of surrounding barbarism. Traditional perspectives die slowly and, in this case, the belief in cultural superiority has not been rejected but redirected. At least since Liberation in 1949, the Chinese people have seen themselves in the "vanguard" of world political evolution; moreover, since 1963, when the Sino-Soviet rift became a visible ideological break, the Chinese have seen themselves once more in the forefront of the "progressive" forces in the international system. Rather than abandon the doctrine of Chinese superiority, new definitions of value appear to have been substituted for the older Western criteria of material wealth, political influence, and military capability. In this way the ancient doctrine lives on. In Fairbank's words, "The tradition of Chinese superiority has now been hyperactivated, both by a new consciousness of the past century's humiliations and by the peptic euphoria of revolutionary leadership. It will confront us for a long time to come."[10]

If nothing else, the sheer size of China's population will bolster significantly this attitude of superiority and will confirm an implacable self-confidence in the future of the Chinese people and the People's Republic of China. Moreover, Chinese efforts to create an autarkic economic system should promote this self-confidence all the more, provided China's political elite can continue to manage production and development efficiently while providing for a sustained rate of economic growth. In light of these factors, enormous population and officially promoted autarky, it is not improbable that Westerners will once again meet "righteous vituperation" and "arrogant incivility,"[11] should the conditions that gave rise to the Sino-American detente be superseded by circumstances less conducive to cross-bloc harmony.

In addition to an intellectual appreciation of change and the traditional doctrine of superiority, the record of Chinese civilization yields at least two other significant trends: the strategic priority accorded to the inner Asian provinces and the generally apathetic attitude toward the development of sea power.

The importance accorded to inner Asia by the early rulers has been noted by Fairbank, "China's maritime frontier occasionally produced rebels and sea-raiders but no major invasion ever came by sea." In contrast, the nomadic peoples of inner Asia "produced mounted archers raised in the saddle, under tribal leaders who periodically united for invasion."[12] Neither Mao nor Chou nor their chiefs of staff is likely to worry about Mongol invasions directed from Ulan Bator, but each is certainly very much aware of the strategically vulnerable northeastern and far western flanks. In September 1972, some 49 Soviet divisions were holding down an even larger number of Chinese troops, deployed against the contingency of a surprise Russian strike on medium range ballistic missile sites and nuclear armament facilities, or alternatively, the possibility of Soviet intervention in a succession crisis among the members of the Chinese political elite following the death of Mao or Chou.

The recent record in Asia would seem to warrant the view that China is vulnerable to conventional attack and conquest solely from the north. Although it required nearly 15 years, the Japanese thrust from the Pacific through Korea into northern and central China was harassed, halted, and defeated eventually. From a Chinese perspective the failure of U.S. policy in Vietnam demonstrated once more the valuable protection afforded by China's ocean frontier. The Chinese were right in believing the American forces to be overextended.[13]

Historically, China's rulers always have feared a threat from inner Asia. Similarly, in the 20th century, the actions of both the nationalist Chinese under Chiang Kai-shek and the communist Chinese under Mao reflect a common response to the problem of sealing the strategic approaches to the heartland of Chinese power.

In 1924 the Republic of China won an agreement from the USSR whereby the Soviet Union conceded "that Outer Mongolia is an integral part of the Republic of China and [that it would] respect China's sovereignty therein."[14] Evidently under Soviet pressure, Chiang reversed this victory and agreed to Mongolian autonomy provided that the people wanted independence. Naturally the Soviet-supervised plebiscite showed that no less than 100 percent of the Mongolian population desired it. Then in 1950, when securely ensconced in Taipei, the nationalist Chinese reasserted their claim over Mongolia.

As early as 1936, Mao claimed that the People's Republic of China would control the Mongolian sector of east Asia. He relinquished these early claims in the postwar struggle and followed Stalin's line until the latter's death in March 1953. Thereafter, Mao and Chou sought in vain to reopen the question with the Soviet leadership, although they did succeed in raising fears of Chinese irredentism in Moscow, which in turn provoked a massive aid and armaments assistance program to the benefit of the Mongolian leaders in Ulan Bator. By the spring of 1973, there were two or three divisions of Soviet troops in Outer Mongolia as well as an unknown number of ballistic missiles deployed close to Peking and extremely close to Chinese military installations in the Sinkiang-Inner Mongolia-Manchuria arc.[15] In response, Peking mounted a concerted effort to sinicize Inner Mongolia and Sinkiang by relocating farmers. It is estimated that Chinese farmers now outnumber the Mongolian pastoral people six to one in the Inner Mongolian Autonomous Region.

In its 23 years of power, the P.R.C. has not deviated appreciably from this traditional preoccupation with maintaining strategic control over inner Asia. Except for Outer Mongolia, the P.R.C. "has expanded consciously the Han-Chinese nation to fill out . . . the old area of the Ch'ing East Asian empire. Like military colonies of old and criminals banished to the frontier, contingents of young people and refractory intellectuals have been shipped out to populate and develop Inner Asia."[16] It would seem, then, that China's domestic policy of resettlement and control of the inner Asian sphere is directly analogous to the traditional concerns of China's rulers.

The obverse of Chinese preoccupation with control of inner Asia has been the generally low priority assigned to the development of sea power, a trend that is borne out today by the P.R.C.'s insistence on minimizing its dependence on maritime trade. The history of Chinese maritime trade and of Chinese sea power is a record of sporadic interest and truncated growth. Perhaps because of its isolation and the generally low level of economic and cultural development surrounding it, China's rulers, and indeed the Confucian intellectuals, denigrated its maritime interests. At various times in China's history, maritime trade was conducted with peoples as far distant as Persia; yet Chinese naval superiority was never used for aggressive imperialist designs except for the unsuccessful invasion attempts launched against Japan in the 13th century. By the time of the Ming dynasty the Chinese simply lacked motivation to venture abroad. Chinese rulers were content to live within their own nation, a nation they perceived as a culturally superior, land-based civilization possessed of a self-sufficient economic system.

Moreover, the choice of Peking as capital, a city far from the established centers of population and industry in the south, vulnerable to nomadic sorties (being only 40 miles from the passes through the Great Wall by which nomad invaders have at all times swept down into China) caused the Ming rulers continuous problems of defense, problems that were bequeathed to their Manchu successors. These difficulties once and for all established the strategic importance of the land borders, so much so that the Manchus sought to obviate the need for any maritime forces by stifling maritime trade, evacuating the coastal islands, and moving coastal populations inland behind patrolled barriers. British gunboat diplomacy after 1839 led to efforts by the Manchus to rectify their vulnerability to sea attacks; however, they purchased too few ships far too late. Their fleets were destroyed by the French and the Japanese by the turn of the century.

The P.R.C.'s three fleets (nearly 1,250 vessels including 46 submarines) are apparently wholly defensive in their deployment.[17] In terms of capability alone, they certainly cannot mount any expansionist naval thrusts in southeast Asia. And traditional patterns of behavior suggest that the Chinese likely lack the motivation to acquire a diversified naval assault capability. The historical record suggests, on the contrary, that ethnocentrism, a preoccupation with inner Asian security, and the incredibly complex domestic problems inherent in governing three-quarters of a billion people will keep China's strategic thinking focused on continental questions. Costly efforts to expand through aggressive naval-military action are improbable.

In the past, Chinese civilization has been self-contained by choice. In the era of post-Liberation revolutionism it is likely to remain self-contained from domestic necessity. Compared with the rapid extension of American influence into the Pacific region and compared with the record of Russian expansionism under both the tsars and the commissars, the Chinese appear radically isolationist. The farthest west they ever ventured militarily was to the Caspian Sea in A.D. 97. The farthest north any Chinese army marched was in 1372 when General Hsu Ta advanced to the northern side of the Yablonoi Mountains in modern Siberia. In both instances military action was undertaken in an effort to prevent border troubles, to assert cultural hegemony, and to seek tribute. Apparently conquest and colonization never were considered. Similarly, in relations with Korea and Annam, China sought to establish cultural hegemony and a tributary relationship and again showed a reluctance for outright dominance.

Historically, Chinese foreign policy has been negative in its aims and achievements. Positive militarist expansion has played little or no role in Chinese culture. The question is whether this pattern is likely to be perpetuated, if only because of economic and geographic constraints and sinocentric cultural inertia. Although the P.R.C. consistently has preached policies of revolution, it has done so within the framework of a respect for national sovereignty. This is largely the result of its own national experience since 1840. A traditionalist foreign policy approach for China need not involve the goal of creating satellite states--the contemporary equivalent of tributary vassals-- though a wholly traditional approach could involve an attempt to create a zone of semidependent buffer states that would leave the Chinese state free from concerns about territorial integrity. Thus far, the P.R.C.'s foreign policy has not reflected this kind of approach, nor does it seem probable for the future.

Since 1949 the P.R.C. has moved to a policy position that recognizes the completely independent status of those southeast Asian states once tributary to China. It is no longer possible to find the kind of map that appeared in the 1953 publication, Chung-kuo chin-tai chien-shih [Brief History of Modern China], describing Laos, Vietnam, Cambodia, Burma, Malaya, and Korea as "Chinese territories taken by the imperialists in the Old Democratic Revolutionary Era (1840-1919)."[18] Certainly the P.R.C. could attempt to carve out a sphere of influence in the manner of great political powers, but it will probably be done in terms of ideological-cultural leadership and not through imperialist military ventures. For China to adhere to a traditional pattern would mean pursuit of a policy of preoccupation with the continental frontiers and with the strategic approaches from the north and the west to the river-valley heartlands.

What has been termed Middle Kingdom thinking often refers to a desire to reconstruct a system of paternalistic vassalage similar to that of the Sung, Ming, and Ch'ing dynasties. In this sense, Middle Kingdom thinking is virtually dead; but in the sense that Middle Kingdom thinking refers to the maintenance of a secure inner Asia at the expense of maritime interests, it is very much alive. In the sense that it denotes an obsessive, in fact parochial, concern for Chinese culture, it remains a continuing element in Chinese thinking.

NOTES

1. Michael B Yahuda, "Chinese Foreign Policy: A Process of Interaction." Paper presented to the Australian Institute of International Affairs Conference: China and the World Community, June 1972, Melbourne.

2. Concerning the Chinese intellectual revolution following World War I, see John A. Harrison's postscript to developments to Versailles in China since 1800 (New York: Harcourt Brace and World, 1967), pp. 122-25.

3. Chuang Tzu, Basic Writings (New York: Columbia University Press, 1964), p. 70.

4. Mao Tse-tung, "On Contradiction," Selected Works, vol. 2 (London: Lawrence and Wishart, 1954), p. 18.

5. January 1, 1972, cited in William Kintner, China's World View 1972 (Philadelphia: Foreign Policy Research Institute, 1972), p. 1.

6. Mao Tse-tung, "On Contradiction," Quotations from Chairman Mao (Peking: Foreign Language Press, 1972), p. 55.

7. Ross Terrill, "The 800,000,000: China and the World," The Atlantic 229 (January 1972): 62; and John F. Melby, "Great Power Rivalry in East Asia," International Journal 26 (Summer 1971): 461.

8. Harrison E. Salisbury, Orbit of China (New York: Harper & Row, 1967), p. 5.

9. John K. Fairbank, "China's Foreign Policy in Historical Perspective," Foreign Affairs 51 (October 1972): 456.

10. Ibid., p. 461.

11. Ibid.

12. Ibid., p. 452.

13. Chou En-lai recounted in one interview that Chinese leaders generally did not fear American attack since the Americans, in their view, would be prudent enough to avoid a major land war with the most populous nation on earth, on its own territory, while U.S. forces required 7,000-mile lines of support. See Terrill, op. cit., concerning "the political limits of alien military force."

14. Henry S. Bradsher, "The Sovietization of Mongolia," Foreign Affairs 50 (April 1972): 548.

15. Ibid., pp. 552-53.

16. Fairbank, op. cit., p. 453.

17. International Institute for Strategic Studies, The Military Balance 1972-73 (London: IISS, 1972), p. 45.

18. Ross Terrill, "China and Southeast Asia," paper presented to the Australian Institute of International Affairs Conference: China and the World Community, June 1972, Melbourne.

2

THE IDEOLOGICAL FILTER:
MAOIST IDEOLOGY AND
CHINA'S LONG RUN
OBJECTIVES

Once Mao Tse-tung's thought is grasped by the broad
masses it will become an inexhaustible source of
strength and an infinitely powerful spiritual atom bomb.
                                    Lin Piao, December 16, 1966

SALIENT ASPECTS OF MAO TSE-TUNG'S THOUGHT

Maurice Meisner observed of Mao Tse-tung that "few have repeated
so often, and taken so seriously, the old Marxist maxim that Marxism
is a guide to action and not a dogma."[1] Mao's adherence to this view
resulted in his own unique formulation of Marxism-Leninism. The
Maoist synthesis of theory and practice draws heavily on the unique
experience of the Chinese revolution, and ultimately it rejects the
notion of an abstract form of Marxism divorced from concrete historical practice. As a result, Mao's theoretical contribution to
Marxist-Leninist thought is held by the Chinese to be a radically new,
and ideologically pure, formulation of the theory of communist revolutionary action. Mao's theoretical deviations from Marxist-Leninist
orthodoxy--for example, his reliance on the peasant masses rather
than the urban proletariat to direct the thrust of the revolution in
China, his charges of "goulash communism" and "socialist imperialism" against his former Soviet allies, and his celebration of revolutionary struggle and the power of collective will in contrast to Soviet
emphasis on bureaucratic method and the rationality of a hierarchical division of labor--led him to formulate a brand of communism
that is variously described as romantic, utopian, or chiliastic.
    Mao's espousal of visionary utopianism came late in his career as
a professional revolutionary and military tactician, its beginnings co-

inciding roughly with the Great Leap Forward of 1958-60. In general, it was after 1955 that there occurred what Stuart Schram has called "the generalization of the Yenan heritage." In the period of incipient rift with the USSR, Maoist chiliasm was born and elaborated. During the 1960s, this utopianism grew, culminating in the Great Proletarian Cultural Revolution--a phenomenon that has been described aptly as a process of nationwide "intellectual incest" without historical precedent. A detailed review of Mao's variation of Marxism-Leninism is beyond the scope of this work. Nevertheless, it is essential to appreciate some of the major elements in Mao Tse-tung Thought, for they will play a significant role in determining the evolution of the Chinese political system and of the P.R.C.'s relations with the world.

Traditional Confucian values laid great stress on the ethic of subordination, on filial piety, and on a strict observation of the individual's position in the social and political hierarchy. The Maoist revolution has changed Chinese attitudes radically toward the family and respect for authority in general, but there remains a significant residue of authoritarian psychology that has been strengthened by the excessive inculcation of social and psychological conformity as a direct consequence of the practice of "democratic centralism." One of the more paradoxical elements in the Chinese communist movement is that the leadership consistently has sought to root out hierarchical barriers to the upward mobility of the truly loyal party cadres and to extirpate all vestiges of a stratified bourgeois or quasi-bourgeois society by following a program of hypercentralization. All key decisions must be made by reliable communists, and in no instance by crypto-"capitalist roaders." Through bypassing the organs of ministerial power, Mao and his leadership clique hope to achieve direct contact with the masses. The systemic ends of individual ministries thus can be refocused continually on the people's requirements rather than be allowed to evolve in accordance with the logic of rational, structure-oriented, bureaucratic methodology.

Borrowing from Lenin, Mao wrote that "all correct leadership is necessarily from the masses to the masses. This means: take the ideas of the masses (scattered and unsystematic ideas) and concentrate them (through study turn them into concentrated and systematic ideas), then go to the masses and propagate and explain these ideas until the masses embrace them as their own, hold fast to them and translate them into action, and test the correctness of these ideas in such action." And further, that "the harder the struggle, the greater the need for communists to link their leadership closely with the demands of the broad masses, and to combine general calls closely with particular guidance, so as to smash completely subjectivist and bureaucratic methods of leadership. . . . Subjectivists and bureaucrats do not understand the principles of combining the leadership with the masses and the general with the particular; they greatly impede the development of the work of the Party."[2]

The precepts of democratic centralism require, therefore, that the highest echelon of the political elite direct and marshal the forces of the masses and that the "masses" must at all times be as enthusiastically committed to each program as is humanly possible. Voluntary mass participation and skillful elite management constitute the essence of this process. It is a moot point whether democratic centralism can be represented fairly as totalitarianism pure and simple: a truly totalitarian political elite would attempt to break totally from the society's accumulated value system. This the Chinese have not done.

Maoist ideology has, in fact, insisted on utilizing traditional concepts and culture in accordance with the overall view that Mao expressed in 1938.

> Today's China is an outgrowth of historic China. We are Marxist historicists; we must not mutilate history. From Confucius to Sun Yat-sen we must sum it up critically, and we must constitute ourselves the heirs of all that is precious in the past. . . . A communist is a Marxist internationalist, but Marxism must take on a national form before it can be applied. . . . What we call concrete Marxism is Marxism that has taken on a national form, that is, Marxism applied to the concrete struggle in the concrete conditions prevailing in China, and not Marxism abstractly used.[3]

Into his concrete version of Marxism, Mao incorporated not only the lessons drawn from the Chinese communist party's revolutionary experience but also concepts and analogies culled from China's history and literature. In his writings on strategy and tactics he is indebted in no small measure to Sun Tzu, a philosopher-cum-military theorist of the fifth century B.C. In this respect Mao is no totalitarian out to erase traditional culture. He plainly values it and has stressed repeatedly China's rich revolutionary tradition.[4] In short, Mao's rhetoric has presented only a selective critique of Chinese history rather than its total reconstruction so the Chinese nation may feel rooted in its own unique evolutionary process.

Mao Tse-tung's Thought is constructed on the assumptions that man is an educable ethical creature, that rational exhortation and social pressure can lead to qualitative improvements in an individual's conduct, and that leadership through the formulation of right precepts can successfully guide all citizens in all phases of life. It is not difficult, then, to comprehend the logic behind Mao's assertion that "China's 600 million people have two remarkable peculiarities; they are, first of all, poor, and second, blank. That may seem like a bad thing but it is really a good thing. Poor people want change, want to do things, want revolution. A clean sheet of paper has no blotches, and so the newest and most beautiful words can be written on it, the newest and most beautiful pictures can be painted on it."[5] Third World Man as a tabula rasa affords the skillful revolutionary the opportunity of rewriting the human essence in accordance with his own vision of utopian man. And Mao believes that man can be conditioned and modified totally through the "immortalizing vision"[6] of the communists' historical project.

One of the most paradoxical phenomena of the Chinese revolution relates to these values and aspirations that Mao wishes to instill in his fellow countrymen: diligence, frugality, iron self-discipline, honesty, a belief in the moral and spiritual value of work (especially manual labor), and the spirit of self-sacrifice. In one of the great ironies of history, Mao has come full circle to espouse most of the archetypal virtues of the Calvinist bourgeoisie (except for a respect for individual rights). Mao's adoption of these virtues stems in part from his own experiences before and during his stay in Yenan. During this period he acquired a profound appreciation of the psychic benefits of asceticism. Ever after, he has deprecated consistently material incentives as a means of motivating his revolutionary cadres. In Mao's view, true revolutionary ardor is evinced by a thoroughly ascetic selflessness, typified best perhaps by the great Canadian "martyr," Norman Bethune.

Mao's singular emphasis on selfless revolutionary virtue is complemented by two other concepts again derived from his experience in the conflict with Chiang Kai-shek's forces and the war against the Japanese. First, his reliance then on the People's Liberation Army (PLA) as a political instrument was so great that Mao has stressed repeatedly that all of socialist society should be fashioned after the military's paradigm. Courage, heroism, and "rude and savage" physical vigor have ranked high on Mao's personal scale of values. He believes it is only those men who have cultivated physical endurance who can exhibit the dogged decades-long perseverance intense political and military revolutionary activity requires. Mao's selection of the military as the prime symbolic social paradigm stems from his overriding belief in the importance of a strong will and a strong moral character. Stuart Schram is one of many observers who believes that "these attitudes . . . are a projection of the spirit of Yenan and of the Chingkangshan--of the guerrilla period when the ability to mobilize men was more important than technical knowledge, and when only unbending resolve enabled Mao's forces to hold out against a more numerous and far better equipped army."[7] In a truly Platonic fashion, Mao believes that through this tool, the army, he can make good men--a political leader's greatest task and obligation.

Second, Mao believes that it is only through some system of military structure that the masses can be mobilized successfully. Where Stalin relied on the government ministries to balance the power centers within the party, Mao has leaned upon the PLA to rectify any "opportunist" or "adventurist" tendencies of political rivals, to carry on the permanent "war of resistance" against imperialism and social imperialism abroad and against reactionary anticommunist tendencies at home. Following Lenin's precedent, Mao accepts Carl von Clausewitz's well-known dictum on war and applies it in his own unique manner. Of the war against Japan he wrote:

> Victory in this war is inseparable from the overall policy of persistently carrying on our war of resistance and maintaining the united front. It is inseparable from the mobilization of all the people in the nation from political principles such as unity of officers and men, unity of the army and the people, and the disintegration of the enemy forces . . . from cultural mobilization and from efforts to win the support of international forces and of the people of the enemy's country. In a word, war cannot for a single moment be separated from politics.[8]

The mobilization of all the people is accomplished through the dual processes of politicizing the military and militarizing the polity. Only this way can a vigorous, militant, revolutionary consciousness be induced in successive generations of Chinese born in the post-Liberation environment. Only in this way can the death of the revolution be forestalled and the capitalist-roaders defeated. In Maoist ideology, not only political power grows out of gun barrels: "We can also create cadres, create schools, create culture, create mass movements. Everything in Yenan has been created by having guns. All things grow out of the barrel of a gun. According to the Marxist theory of the state, the army is the chief component of state power. Whoever wants to seize and retain state power must have a strong army."[9] Following this doctrine to the letter, the locus of power in the P.R.C. has always been concentrated in, or close to, the organs of the PLA.[10] Mao and Lin Piao, for example, relied greatly on the PLA to retain their institutional power base during the Cultural Revolution.

Mao's millennial quest for his realm of Great Harmony, for what Robert Lifton has termed "revolutionary immortality," has brought him, however, to a significant theoretical impasse. His ideological theory has led him to deprecate complex bureaucratic methods and all forms of social stratification, yet he is confronted with the problems of national defense and strategic security in an epoch of ballistic missiles, computer technology, and satellite surveillance, the development of which has necessitated a highly articulated hierarchical division of labor. In addition Maoism--if not Mao's theory--advocates a thorough-going uniformity of thought for all Chinese citizens and stresses that social, economic, and technical progress in any form is to be credited directly to Mao Tse-tung Thought.

Military observers scoffed at the ritualistic genuflection before Mao Tse-tung Thought when the Chinese completed and tested a hydrogen bomb earlier than expected on June 17, 1967. However, it is worth pondering to what extent Mao Tse-tung has energized the people of China by his exemplary rise to power, by his feat of uniting the country and raising it from a desperate condition to the point where it may assume once more its former greatness. This is not easy to evaluate, yet it is a variable that will have an enormous impact on future Chinese development. For how long will Mao Tse-tung Thought be able to supply adequate motivation? How long can the P.R.C. strive for radical egalitarianism for 99 percent of the population and still segregate much of its scientific and technical manpower in secluded areas of Manchuria and Inner Mongolia in what presumably will evolve into a community with all the trappings of status and organizational power that accrue to members of a technical elite?[11] How long will the 99 percent tolerate such schizoid social development?

If in fact the essence of Maoist ideology is a revolutionism that knows no bounds to its field of action, is it possible that the impetus to scientific and economic development will be weakened significantly by a trend toward moderation and stability on the part of Mao's successors? Will a foreign policy of realpolitik sap both the domestic revolutionary drive and its concomitant human motivation? This of course is dependent entirely on how much of the Chinese identity is defined by the national self-image of radical egalitarianism and to what extent totalitarian controls on the communications media can reinterpret restrained foreign policy postures in terms of such classic Maoist concepts as the "strategic defensive" maneuver.

Since 1965 China's official revolutionary line has adhered to the policy enunciated by Lin Piao in his September 1965 article, "Long Live the Victory of People's War!" wherein he stated:

> Taking the entire globe, if North America and Western Europe can be called "the cities of the world," then Asia, Africa and Latin America constitute "the rural areas of the world." Since World War II, the proletarian revolutionary movement has for various reasons been temporarily held back in the North American and West European capitalist countries, while the people's

revolutionary movement in Asia, Africa and Latin America has been growing vigorously. In a sense, the contemporary world revolution also presents a picture of the <u>encirclement of cities</u> by the rural areas. In the final analysis, the <u>whole</u> cause of world revolution <u>hinges on the revolutionary struggles of the Asian, African and Latin American peoples</u> who make up the overwhelming majority of the world's population. The socialist countries should regard it as their internationalist duty to support the people's revolutionary struggles in Asia, Africa and Latin America. . . . The Chinese revolution has successfully solved the problem of how to link up the national-democratic with the socialist revolution in the colonial and semi-colonial countries.[12]

The metaphorical projection of the Chinese tactics against the Japanese invasion (encircle the cities and pick them off from strong bases in rural areas) to the level of the global confrontation with American imperialism did not originate with Lin but with D. N. Aidit, leader of the Indonesian communist party.[13] Of course, Lin's elaboration of the theme carried much more weight in the world communist movement. As a central tenet of Marxist-Leninist-Maoist ideology, it is a natural development of the Leninist belief that 20th century imperialism effectively had stopped the process of revolutionary fermentation in the industrialized heartlands of Western Europe and North America by placating the demands of the working class with higher wages financed by a percentage of the extortionate profits being drained from the colonial and excolonial countries.[14] For the present, and certainly for the next decade, the revolutionary movement in the "cities of the world" will be viewed by the Chinese and other communists as virtually a waste of time. North America and Western Europe are the "burnt-out hearths" of the international revolutionary movement.[15]

PRACTICAL COROLLARIES

It is not surprising then that the Chinese are following a determined policy of bridge building between the P.R.C. and the nations of the Third World. Since they took over the China seat in the United Nations in the fall of 1971, the P.R.C. has made a systematic bid to appropriate the leadership of the underdeveloped countries. If the present configuration of global forces cannot improve on its past record concerning underdevelopment, poverty, and ecology, if it cannot even define the dimensions of these problems (witness the difficulties of the third United Nations Conference on Trade and Development and the collision of views at the Conference on the Human Environment during 1972), China will have a receptive audience among the world's underprivileged for its claim to hegemony. In this instance there would be no long run problem for Chinese foreign policy decision makers. Issues and negotiations could be cast in terms of "nonantagonistic contradiction," and the P.R.C. could assume a posture of shop foreman in a trade union of the world's have-not nations. There would be no challenge to the fundamental premises of Maoist ideology.

On the other hand, if we make the heroic assumption that there will be substantial progress in these problem areas, we must then consider whether the P.R.C. would be forced to reassess basic ideologic postulates and whether, in turn, the leadership elite could maintain a firm grasp on the social system, should the P.R.C. find its leadership bids consistently rejected by the member nations of the world's "countryside." Certainly lack of progress in solving global problems such as income inequities and the like is by no means a necessary condition for a lack of receptivity to China's leadership bid. It is easy to imagine a total lack of success for the Chinese solely because of communication barriers--because of a simple inability to transplant Chinese cultural norms to foreign sociocultural milieu. It is not improbable that serious challenges to the party elite then would be forthcoming and, further, that in such a situation (say, for example, an attempted military coup) the equilibrium in east Asia could become extremely unstable with the Soviet armed forces waiting along the northern flanks for an opportunity to apply the Brezhnev Doctrine to its former ally. However, this contingency is, on the whole, not very probable.

What does seem probable is that the problems of development, resource scarcity, and ecological deterioration will not be ameliorated appreciably and that the P.R.C. will continue to make substantial headway in its bid for leadership of the developing world, certainly in terms of offsetting Soviet influence in southeast Asia and the Indian Ocean littoral. It will attempt to deny to both the United States and the USSR the opportunity to stabilize the political-military confrontation in the Middle East (with the objective of pinning down many Soviet divisions as far away as possible from the Sino-Soviet frontier). And it will continue to make some marginal gains in the promotion of revolutionary ferment in the Middle East, Africa, and Latin America.

The final element to stress in this brief survey of Maoist ideology is the growing doctrinal irreconcilability between the USSR and the P.R.C. This rift is due in no small measure to the very different historical experiences of the two peoples. Foremost, there is the European cultural heritage of the USSR, so radically different from

Chinese cultural traditions. Second, prerevolutionary Russia was a
successful and powerful nation, a nation that had managed to extend
its influence across Asia to Sakhalin and the Kamchatka Peninsula;
China possessed little more than a record of defeats, concessions,
and humiliations. Third, Lenin's victory in Russia was achieved
quickly, though the process of establishing Soviet rule took a number
of years. The Chinese communist party (CCP) had to come to power
through Mao's strategy of protracted war, which on several occasions
defied the counsel of Stalin's advisers. Fourth, there was a profound
difference in the economic development of the two countries at the
times of their respective revolutions.

In World War I Russia was on the threshold of industrialization,
but in 1949 in China there was scarcely more industrial capacity
than what the Japanese had constructed with their U.S. $2.7-billion
investment in Manchuria (1931-45). Radically different approaches to
economic development were essential, and these subsequently led to
strongly differentiated ideological programs.

These fundamental differences between China and the USSR have
been exacerbated by the unwillingness of the USSR to share its nuclear capability with the Chinese, by the reluctance of the Soviet
Union to accord Mao Tse-tung recognition as a major theoretical in-
novator in the Marxist-Leninist movement, by the total withdrawal of
Soviet aid after 1960, and finally, by the concrete attempts of the
USSR and the P.R.C. since 1962 to undercut each other's political
and strategic influence, culminating in the military confrontation on
the Ussuri River in the spring of 1969 and the P.R.C.'s assertion of
claims to large tracts of the Soviet Far East.

Though these actions have accentuated the ideological separation
of the two communist giants, it is not unreasonable to assume that
they stem from the underlying source of the Sino-Soviet ideological
rivalry: antagonistic claims to global hegemony in the communist
movement and mutually contradictory aspirations for increasing the
national power base on the part of each respective leadership elite.
The summer of 1963 marked the last occasion of an official meeting
of the Soviet and Chinese communist parties. Since then, both sides
have come to realize that they represent two fundamentally different,
and perhaps inevitably antagonistic, approaches to totalitarian socialist government.

The central thrust of Maoist thought will continue to reinforce the
already strong currents of Chinese introspection and to foster an obsessive preoccupation with building their own version of national socialism free from the demands of a geographically adjacent superpower. Nationalist sentiment will continue to play a role in Chinese
society that is virtually equal in importance to the prime social imperative in contemporary China--the rapid construction and perfec-

tion of an egalitarian communist society. Because the sinified version of Marxism-Leninism places such stress on concrete national experience, it seems likely

- that, as the Chinese give increasing priority to national security interests in an increasingly uncertain international environment, the ardor of the P.R.C. for international revolution will be moderated;
- that support by the P.R.C. for wars of national liberation necessarily will become increasingly selective and will be characterized by a progressively greater number of constraints imposed by the Chinese on their would-be insurgent allies; and
- that progress in the domestic implementation of Mao Tse-tung Thought will gain priority over foreign policy victories and that state-to-state diplomacy will become the accepted mode of intercourse for the P.R.C. in its relations with the USSR and the major Western powers, with whom it may be forced to collude in a shifting balance of power. Party-to-party and people-to-people diplomacy will continue to supplement Chinese relations with Africa, Latin America, and other Asian nations.

These are the main elements that will characterize ideological evolution within the P.R.C. as it pertains to foreign policy decision making. In Maoist phraseology, there is inherent in Chinese socialism a basic contradiction between the requirements of building a modern industrial state with a high level of administrative efficiency, scientific research, and economic development and the official doctrinal goal of constructing a social system without bureaucracy and without a system of significant differential economic rewards. As early as 1949 Mao proclaimed, "Not only can the Chinese people live without begging alms from the imperialists, they will live a better life than that of the imperialist countries."[16] Although "better" could be interpreted many ways, it seems likely that the P.R.C.'s leadership elite eventually will give priority to increasing the material standard of living within the nation. Such a policy would be fraught with serious problems, if it becomes the popularly accepted criterion for evaluating governmental performance--especially if the Chinese cannot successfully curb population growth rates, which some demographers recently have claimed to be roughly 2 percent a year in urban areas and 3 to 4 percent in the countryside.

If successive governments cannot institute population controls successfully over the next two decades, Mao's contemporary emphasis on revolutionary asceticism may become a permanent feature of Chinese society. In this respect, we may observe a clearly defined feedback from material growth rates on the shape of ideological programs within China. Similarly, the continued growth of Chinese military capability (for example the possible acquisition of a second-strike capability against the USSR) will have a persistent feedback effect on the ideological system, conferring a wider latitude for action in some spheres of national policy (the ability to affect leadership in adjacent southeast Asian nations), while constraining policy in other areas of decision making (for example, necessitating a strategic detente with the two superpowers).

NOTES

1. Maurice Meisner, "Maoist Utopianism and the Future of Chinese Society," International Journal 26 (Summer 1971): 540.

2. Extracts from a directive of the Central Committee of the Chinese Communist Party, June 1, 1943, contained in S. R. Schram, The Political Thought of Mao Tse-tung (New York: Praeger, 1970), p. 315.

3. From a report to the Sixth Plenum of the Sixth Central Committee in October 1938, in Schram, ibid., p. 172.

4. The rebellion of An Lu-shan (A.D. 755-766) may have resulted in the slaughter of between 20 and 30 millions. See C. P. FitzGerald, China: A Short Cultural History (London: Cresset Press, 1935), pp. 313-14. Some estimates of the loss of life incurred in the T'ai P'ing rebellion (1850-64) range as high as 25 million deaths. See J. J. Gerson, "Rebellions in Pre-Revolutionary Times," in J. M. Gibson and D. M. Johnston, eds., A Century of Struggle (Toronto: Canadian Institute of International Affairs, 1971), p. 19.

5. Mao Tse-tung's comments in the party journal Hung ch'i, June 1958, as quoted by Schram, op. cit., p. 351.

6. R. J. Lifton, Revolutionary Immortality (New York: Random House, 1968), p. 34.

7. Schram, op. cit., p. 103.

8. Mao Tse-tung, "On Protracted War: May 1938," in Six Essays on Military Affairs (Peking: Foreign Language Press, 1971), pp. 266-67.

9. Mao Tse-tung, "Problems of War and Strategy: November 1938," in ibid., pp. 350-51.

10. For a detailed examination of the growth of military influence in China, especially during the Cultural Revolution, see Robert E. Bedelski, "Institutional Legitimacy and External Affairs in Modern China," Orbis 16 (Spring 1972): 237-56; Harvey Nelsen, "Military Forces in the Cultural Revolution," China Quarterly, no. 51 (July 1972); and R. L. Powell, "The Military and the Struggle for Power in China," Current History 63, no. 373 (September 1972).

11. Vice Premier Nieh Jung-chen was attacked (without success) for building "an independent kingdom" through the Commission on Science and Technology and the Party's National Defense, Science, and Technology Committee. For an account of who was victimized in the Cultural Revolution and who was protected, see Parris H. Chang, "China's Scientists in the Cultural Revolution," <u>Bulletin of the Atomic Scientists</u> 25 (May 1969).

12. In K. Fan, ed., <u>Mao Tse-tung and Lin Piao: Post Revolutionary Writings</u> (Garden City, N.Y.: Anchor Books, 1972), pp. 396-97 (emphasis added).

13. Schram, op. cit., p. 123.

14. See, for example, Lenin's argument against Karl Kautsky's "bourgeois reformism" and his denunciation of the parasitic "rentier-state": V. I. Lenin, "Imperialism, the Highest Stage of Capitalism," <u>Selected Works</u> (Moscow: Progress Publishers, 1968), pp. 237-47.

15. According to Schram, Muslim Bolshevik Sultan Galiev, a one-time assistant to Stalin in the Commissariat for Nationalities, regarded Europe as a "burnt-out revolutionary hearth": Schram, op. cit., p. 124.

16. From a report to the Second Plenum of the Seventh Central Committee, March 5, 1949, as translated in Schram, ibid., p. 320.

3

**POPULATION, ECONOMICS,
AND SOCIOPOLITICAL
ORGANIZATION:
THE NEXT DECADE**

Every species of animal naturally multiples in proportion to their means of subsistence, and no species can
ever multiply beyond it.

Adam Smith

DEMOGRAPHY AND THE ECONOMY:
THE POSSIBILITIES

During an interview that he gave to a group of overseas Chinese
visiting Peking, Premier Chou En-lai wryly observed: "Russia is
roughly on the same latitude as Canada. But after fifty years of socialism, she still cannot solve her grain problem, while Canada has
surpluses to sell. What kind of socialism is that?"[1] Chou's ebullient
manner reflected the increasing confidence of the Chinese leadership
in the P.R.C.'s rate of economic progress. If the statistics released
by the New China News Agency in 1972 are reliable, the economy of
the P.R.C. is well on its way to a period of rapid and sustained economic growth. According to these figures, combined production in
the industrial and agricultural sectors rose by 10 percent in 1971.
Iron output was said to have increased by 23 percent, production of
crude oil by 27.2 percent, of coal by 8 percent, of cement by 16.5
percent, of chemical fertilizer by 20.2 percent, of mining equipment
by 24.7 percent, and of metallurgical equipment by 24.7 percent. Aggregate steel production for 1971 amounted to 21 million metric tons
and, perhaps more significantly, total grain production climbed to
246 million metric tons, prompting the claim that the P.R.C. is now
self-sufficient in grain production and that "record reserves of grain
are being held."[2]

Statistics such as these have induced some analysts to project this prodigious growth rate (10 percent a year) indefinitely. But such projections seem unduly optimistic about the potential strength of China's system of political economy. A 10 percent annual growth rate is equivalent to a doubling time of approximately seven years. If such growth were sustained, the P.R.C.'s gross national product (GNP) by the year 2000 would be nearly 16 times its present size, approaching a value of some $1.9 trillion (taking a base figure of $120 billion for 1970). Table 3.1 presents a comparison of the effects of three different rates of growth on two specific estimates of GNP for 1970. An examination of the effects of different growth rates on Chinese population is given in Table 3.2.

The most optimistic assessments of the future of the Chinese economy hinge not only on the assumption that the recently released figures on the economy are accurate but also on the projection that the rate of population growth has dropped precipitously since the late 1950s. The most favorable analyses suggest, therefore, that present per capita GNP is roughly $171 (taking a population figure of 700 million and Chou's GNP statistic of $120 billion for 1970). A small pocket atlas published by the China Cartographic Institute in August 1972 gave an official population figure of 697,270,000 for 1970.[3] Juxtaposition of this figure with that of 582,300,000 for 1953[4] yields an average growth rate of 1.07 percent for the years 1953-70. If the 1970 statistic is compared with official figures for 1958, the average annual increase drops to a mere 0.6 percent.[5] If we assume that these figures are accurate, at least to the extent of reflecting a genuine trend toward a declining population growth rate, and that an extremely optimistic view is warranted regarding the GNP growth rate, then we can combine Table 3.1, column 6, with Table 3.2, case 1, and obtain a projected per capita GNP of $4,310 for the year 2000--a 25-fold increase over the optimist's figure for 1970.

However, there are many pessimistic estimates and projections of population and GNP growth. If we take a figure of 800 million for the Chinese population for 1970 and $80 billion for the 1970 GNP and make the least favorable assumptions regarding growth trends (Table 3.2, case 8, and Table 3.1, column 1), then we obtain a projected per capita GNP of $154 for the year 2000, which represents an absolute increase of only 54 percent over 30 years from the pessimist's level of per capita GNP in 1970--$100.

For the reasons given below we reject these extreme views and consider either a low population growth and low GNP growth scenario, or a low population growth and medium GNP growth scenario to be more realistic.

The leadership of the P.R.C. thoroughly understands the implications of a high rate of population growth and therefore the average an-

TABLE 3.1

Comparison of the Effect of Low, Medium, and High Growth Rates
on the GNP of the P.R.C.

	Low[a]	Medium[b]	High[c]	Low[a]	Medium[b]	High[c]
1970	80	80	80	120	120	120
1980	118	173	249	178	259	373
1990	175	373	772	263	559	1,158
2000	259	805	2,397	389	1,207	3,596

Assume GNP for 1970 is U.S.$80 billion, one of the lower estimates	Assume GNP in 1970 is U.S.$120 billion--Chou En-lai's official figure for 1970 (as told to Edgar Snow)

[a]4 percent.
[b]8 percent.
[c]12 percent.

Source: Compiled by author.

nual increase in the population probably will be forced down to 0.6
percent in the near future--if this has not already been accomplished.
Certainly it will be forced well below 2.0 percent a year. Many Western journalists[6] have observed that Chinese families are now limited
to two children (no food ration cards are issued for additional off-
spring), that men do not marry until ages 28-30 and women until
26-28, and that more and more urban couples remain childless. It
is reasonable to assume therefore that the birthrate has been reduced
dramatically. If totalitarian social controls such as thought reform
possess any virtue at all, it must surely lie in their ability to shat-
ter traditional patterns of fertility and traditional expectations concerning the role of the family, so the birthrate can be brought more
easily into line with the precipitate declines in mortality rates that
accompany modernization and industrialization. For these reasons
a projection of low population growth seems in order (Table 3.2,
either case 1 or case 5).

TABLE 3.2

Effect of Different Annual Average Growth Rates on Population
in the P.R.C.

	1970	1980	1990	2000
Case 1 (0.6 percent)	700	742	787	834
Case 2 (1.5 percent)	700	812	942	1,092
Case 3 (2.0 percent)	700	853	1,040	1,268
Case 4 (2.5 percent)	700	896	1,147	1,468
Case 5 (0.6 percent)	800	848	899	953
Case 6 (1.5 percent)	800	928	1,076	1,248
Case 7 (2.0 percent)	800	975	1,189	1,449
Case 8 (2.5 percent)	800	1,024	1,311	1,678

Note: The percentages for cases 1-4 are on a base of 700 million; for cases 5-8 they are on a base of 800 million.

Source: Compiled by author.

Official Chinese estimates frequently overstate actual productivity; but we tend to accept the official figures regarding the 1970 GNP, if only because they emanate from the only men with direct access to aggregate data concerning the P.R.C.'s economic trends. A low rate of real growth in GNP (say 4 percent--Table 3.3, column 4) would result, therefore, in a GNP of $178 billion by 1980, $263 billion by 1990, and $389 billion by 2000. Coupled with a low population estimate and a low population growth projection (Table 3.2, case 1), the resulting per capita GNP for the year 2000 of $466 would represent an absolute increase of 170 percent over the present most optimistic estimate of $171 for 1970.

The past economic record of the Chinese government is impressive considering the abysmal conditions prevailing throughout China in 1949. Since then, China's economy certainly has grown steadily, if erratically. (The main recession occurred from 1960-63 following the calamitous measures enforced in the Great Leap Forward 1958-59.) Total industrial output has risen at an annual average rate of only slightly less than 15 percent, though the rate drops to about 10 percent if the years of economic recovery, 1949-52, are excluded.[7] Although this growth rate does not match the phenomenal pace of Japan's economic growth, it is a generally enviable record of economic expansion when compared with that of other developed or developing countries. Canada, for example, averaged but 6 percent in its rate of industrial growth in the years 1948-65.

With an industrial capacity the equal of the Netherlands or Belgium, the P.R.C. does not yet have the potential for global economic impact. It is many decades away from attaining the degree of economic influence wielded by the Japanese. However, the Chinese political and military elite has proved its capacity for harnessing and focusing the collective efforts of the people. In addition they have shown, thus far, an ability to adapt quickly in the realm of economic affairs. As T. G. Rawski observed,[8] the wide range of new, technologically sophisticated products being produced in mainland China suggests that the Chinese economy already may have acquired an immanent capacity for rapid, self-sustaining economic growth. If so, the P.R.C.'s industrial sector may be able to follow in the footsteps of the German and Japanese economic "miracles." In this event a low population growth and a medium (to high) GNP growth projection would not be impossible.

The great imponderable in these calculations is the extent to which political policies, summed up by the slogan "politics takes command," will be reflected in future five-year plans. If priority is given to the political-psychological conditions required to produce "revolutionary consciousness," the whole process of development could be jeopardized gravely and economic stagnation or severe depression could result. In China, as nowhere else in the world, the realm of the economic is utterly contingent on the realm of the political. The P.R.C. is truly a system of political economy.

THE ECONOMICS OF AUTARKY

The slogan "politics takes command" originated, naturally enough, in the years of the Great Leap. As a summary of the economic policies of the leftist leadership, it warrants close scrutiny. Essentially this slogan is but one manifestation of the P.R.C.'s determination to achieve a state of autarky. It exemplifies the typically Chinese approach to economics--production by exhortation. The clearest statement of this belief in the virtue of, and the necessity for, autarkical "self-reliance" is to be found in the writings of Lin Piao:

> In order to make a revolution and to fight a people's war and be victorious, it is imperative to adhere to the policy of self-reliance, rely on the strength of the masses in one's country and prepare to carry on the

fight independently even when all material aid from outside is cut off. If one does not operate by one's own efforts, does not independently ponder and solve the problems of the revolution in one's own country and does not rely on the strength of the masses, but leans wholly on foreign aid--even though this be aid from socialist countries which persist in revolution--no victory can be won, or be consolidated even if it is won.[9]

In contrast with the more pragmatic spirit of a Chou En-lai, the leftist "hawk" will espouse the virtue of self-reliance in accordance with his belief that dependence on others destroys not only one's self-respect but also weakens the revolutionary fiber of the people. The radical stratum of the Chinese elite views domestic economic policy from a warfighting perspective. The policy of self-reliance is consequently a strategic necessity that must never be compromised.

The effects of this approach on policy making have been far from marginal. In the early 1950s one of the priorities was the achievement of self-sufficiency in the production of capital goods. By 1957 producer goods accounted for more than two-thirds of the P.R.C.'s industrial output. By 1957 the manufacture of textiles and food processing constituted a mere 31 percent of aggregate industrial production, whereas well over 60 percent of India's industrial output, a nation at a similar stage of economic development, fell into these two categories.[10] The effect of China's drive to self-sufficiency is reflected most graphically in Table 3.3. According to T. G. Rawski's estimates, the value share of imported goods in China's total machinery supply fell from about 50 percent in 1955 to less than 10 percent in 1965.[11]

Self-reliance typifies the P.R.C.'s approach to trade and the financing of investment expenditures as well. Officials of the P.R.C.'s Ministry of Foreign Affairs reiterate incessantly that China is absolutely free of both internal and external debt.[12] Although China did receive substantial economic assistance from the USSR, the total volume of Soviet credits was relatively small; and it did not take long for the P.R.C. to achieve the status of a net lender rather than a borrower in the field of international capital flows. That China has been able to achieve a substantial export surplus since 1958, to the point where all Soviet debts were repaid in full by 1965, provides clear evidence that the Peking regime was very much in command as far as foreign trade and the overall management of the balance of payments is concerned.

As a result of its record of prompt settlement of outstanding bills, the P.R.C. has an extremely high international credit rating. China's foreign obligations hit a peak of U.S.$1.6 billion at the end

TABLE 3.3

Coefficient of Import Dependence for Machine Tools, 1953-57
(in percent)

	China	Japan	India	USSR	United States
1953	36	42	86	--	--
1954	41	52	89	--	--
1955	29	57	89	--	2.2
1956	24	27	88	2.5	--
1957	4	45	--	2.6	3.8

Note: Coefficient of import dependence is defined as $M/(Q + M - X)$, where M, Q, and X refer to imports, domestic production, and exports.

Source: T. G. Rawski, "Foreign Contacts and Industrialization," International Journal 26 (Summer 1971): 525.

of 1955; since then China has been a net exporter of capital every year.[13] Because of this proven ability to repay debts, it has been estimated that the P.R.C. probably could acquire up to $3 billion in long term loans from Japanese, American, and west European financial institutions.[14] Such additional lines of credit could be used to import the latest, most sophisticated technological processes from the advanced industrial nations and thereby boost the P.R.C.'s growth rate by a sizable percentage.

If the Sino-American detente became a stable component of the Chinese weltanschaung, the existence of this potential source of additional investment funds could prove too tempting to resist in subsequent years. If the spirit of detente persists, this attitude of "self-reliance," this persistent desire to achieve a condition of complete autarky, could be overthrown or, at the least, confined to such fields as the production of "strategic commodities." However, the newly achieved accord with the P.R.C. is still too recent to warrant a prediction concerning the direction China will lean in the 1970s and 1980s.

AGRICULTURE: A PERENNIAL MILLSTONE

The chief constraint on a GNP growth rate of 10 to 12 percent for China is the agricultural sector's perpetually low growth rate, usually about 4 to 5 percent in good years. Evidently the new seed hybrids have yet to be adapted to the P.R.C.'s agricultural environment. Such a technological breakthrough is an absolute prerequisite for sustaining a growth rate of 4 to 5 percent in this sector. If and when such adaptation is achieved, the P.R.C. may be able to cease the food imports that have incurred annual expenditures of $260 million to $300 million in recent years.[15] Should China become a perennial net exporter of wheat, rice, and soybeans, the enlarged inflow of foreign exchange would enhance further the prospects for a rapid development of both heavy and light industry, since an ever growing influx of machinery and Western industrial methods could be purchased with this currency.

In its economic programs since 1957, the People's Republic has not followed the approach to economic development that emphasizes heavy industry at the expense of both agriculture and light industry. Following Mao's line of "walking on two legs" (that is, balanced economic development), the last two five-year plans have stressed considerable expenditure on agricultural development. Exhibiting considerably more acumen than Soviet economic planners of the 1920s and 1930s, Mao declared in 1957:

> As China is a large agricultural country, with over 80 percent of her population in the rural areas, industry must develop with agriculture, for only thus can industry secure raw materials and a market, and only thus is it possible to accumulate fairly large funds for building a powerful heavy industry. . . . Without agriculture there can be no light industry. But it is not yet so clearly understood that agriculture provides heavy industry with an important market. This fact, however, will be more readily appreciated as gradual progress in the technical improvement and modernization of agriculture calls for more and more machinery, fertilizer, water conservancy and electric power projects and transport facilities for the farms, as well as fuel and building materials for the rural consumers.[16]

The P.R.C.'s remarkable economic achievements since the 1950s are in large measure the result of this highly sensible policy.

Although all problems in the agricultural sector have not been solved, China is not in danger of the severe famines it suffered in the early 1950s and in the drought years, 1960-61. Recent economic assessments of the P.R.C. generally concede that the battle against hunger is almost won. But to realize fully the potential of the new seed technology, a new agricultural calendar must be accepted by the peasantry, insect control measures must be applied widely, many more agricultural implements must be made available to permit widespread multiple cropping, and new storage facilities will have to be constructed. One recent analysis estimated that this will require 15 to 20 years of effort by the P.R.C.'s agronomists and peasants. This same analyst believes that the agricultural sector will grow only moderately and that its share of GNP in 1980 will amount to some 21 to 22 percent compared with the 30 percent of recent years.[17] Thus agriculture likely will remain the principal drag on the overall growth rate of China for the next two decades. But it probably will not require massive capital outlays to forestall incipient crises in the food supply (barring natural disasters).

INDUSTRIALIZATION: ALTERNATIVE PATHS TO THE WORLD OF GREAT HARMONY

Today there are two Chinas--a rural China of peasantry, large communes, and regional markets and an urban China of tenements, factories, and salaried laborers. The second China has grown rapidly. In 1949 the P.R.C.'s urban population was approximately 50 million; by 1970 it was in the order of 140 to 160 million, constituting 20 percent of the total population.[18] However, it is doubtful whether this trend will continue, since the economic planners have been following a policy of decentralization of industry since 1969, ostensibly so the country can possess a greater capacity for withstanding attack from either the USSR or the United States.

The years 1949-52 saw the P.R.C.'s governmental elite consolidate their control over industry and trade through a combination of balanced budgets (to reduce inflation) and price and wage controls. In the period following (1953-57), the P.R.C. carried out its first five-year plan with a significant amount of Soviet assistance. Fashioning this first plan after the Soviet plan of 1928-32, there was overwhelming emphasis on steel, machine building, chemicals, electric power, and other essential components of a heavy industry sector (see Table 3.4). Light industry was not neglected totally, but there was little of the balanced allocation of investment that has characterized the years since 1958.

TABLE 3.4

Investment in Heavy and Light Industry, 1953-57

Year	Light Industry (percent)	Heavy Industry (percent)	Ratio of Light to Heavy Industry
1953	17.6	82.4	1:4.7
1954	17.6	82.4	1:4.7
1955	12.3	87.7	1:7.1
1956	13.8	86.2	1:6.2
1957	15.2	84.8	1:5.6
1953-57 average	15.0	85.0	1:5.7

Source: Ten Great Years (Peking), p. 61, as cited in Jan S. Prybyla, The Political Economy of Communist China (Scranton, Pa.: International Textbook Publishers, 1970), p. 137.

Under detailed Soviet supervision and with Soviet credit, major projects were constructed, such as the iron-steel complex at Paotow, machinery and textile plants at Sian, and a totally new industrial city near Loyang, which produces tractors, mining machinery, and ball bearings.[19] By 1963 the USSR had set up 198 industrial plants in all and had begun 88 others. In addition, the Soviet Union provided extensive technical assistance for Chinese engineering personnel. Some 21,000 sets of scientific-technical documentation were given to the Chinese, and an additional 1,400 blueprints of large plants. To raise the quality of the Chinese industrial-scientific establishment, 14,000 Chinese students received their higher education in the USSR before 1962, there were 38,000 apprentices trained in Soviet factories, and 11,000 Soviet experts and nearly 1,500 east European technicians aided in the construction and preliminary operation of new plants. Finally, to provide China with a core of highly trained specialists in nuclear technology, 950 students either graduated from or received substantial training at the Dubna Institute of Nuclear Research.[20]

It was soon seen that the mammoth projects of 1953-57 were both a strategic and an economic liability. Subsequent to the disastrous attempt to foster backyard industrialization during the Great Leap Forward, government policy began to favor small and medium sized enterprises. Since the Cultural Revolution, the emphasis on construction of smaller light industry in rural regions has been even more pronounced. A Canadian official reported in November 1971 that "small factories and enterprises of all kinds are being built throughout the countryside, primarily industries supporting agriculture, because more than 80 percent of the 750 million Chinese are directly involved in farming." Journalist Tillman Durdin confirmed this report with his observation that "the idea of big, centralized industrial complexes, which was initially borrowed from the Russians and translated during the 1950's into large installations in Wuhan, Paotow, Taiyuan, Shenyang and elsewhere, has not been dropped."[21] This new emphasis on decentralized industrial development is partly a result of the new powers given to regional governments in an attempt to simplify the administrative functions of the central government; however, as noted, the primary reason appears to be the desire to disperse the urban population and the scientific and industrial resources of the nation so fewer concentrated target areas will be presented to any potential aggressor.

It is especially significant that the Chinese planners still are thinking in terms of warfighting capability, rather than of their nascent capacity to deter conventional incursions. In any event, the trend toward industrial dispersion probably will continue because of the inherent economic logic of locating light industry near its market and the desire on the part of economic planners to slow China's rate of urbanization and thus spread out over many years the large investment in infrastructure necessitated by rural-urban migration. (The hsia-fang campaigns of the late 1950s and early 1960s were essentially an attempt to send people to the countryside in an effort to postpone needed investments in urban housing, transportation, public utilities, and the transportation of foodstuffs.) As well, there is a belief that urban environments are hot-beds of ideological deviance and that cities corrupt the honest working man and tempt many with "bourgeois thought."[22]

The P.R.C.'s transition to a full-fledged industrial power with a high per capita income is decades away, even if the most optimistic growth rate assumptions are made. One final qualification must be put forth, again concerning the detrimental effects of a high birthrate. Some economists have proposed that population growth is, in fact, a stimulus to rapid economic growth. There is, of course, good evidence to support their case. The industrial revolution in Western Europe was preceded by an unprecedented population boom from 1750-1850. Many Keynesian analysts argue that rapid population growth ensures a continuing increase in aggregate demand, which will guarantee in turn that high rates of public saving will be channeled into a rapidly expanding spectrum of investment opportunities. Although periodic excesses of saving relative to investment opportunities may have been a source of difficulty in the economic history of Western Europe, the problem in underdeveloped countries such as China is, instead, one of scarcity of investment capital, of social overhead investment (in roads, communications, and so on), and, latterly, of a sophisticated technological infrastructure. In China's case, rapid population growth must be totally detrimental to its long term interests.

Evidence indicates that the population growth rate either is falling or has fallen drastically. The evidence is far from definitive, however; and should it prove incorrect, the P.R.C. could face severe domestic problems. The public hygiene measures instituted after 1949 slashed the mortality rate. It remained to cut the fertility rate to a similar or even greater degree. By 1960 this still had not been accomplished, largely because of the ideological blinkers of the Marxist-Leninist perspective, which absolutely deny the possibility of overpopulation in a socialist state.

In the 1960s the hard facts of agricultural economics impressed many members of the elite, and extensive remedial action was undertaken. If these measures (limited issuance of ration cards, widespread use of various birth control measures, low cost or free abortion services, official support for late marriage[23]) have not succeeded in rural China, then the dependency load of Chinese society (the percentage of the population under 15 or over 75 who contribute to production, if at all, at a very low rate) will grow rapidly, and once more population will press on the productive capacity of the economic system. At best, it would mean a severe cut in the GNP's growth rate; at worst, it could mean extensive famine and a grave threat to the political stability of the government.

China does not have extensive "virgin lands" that can be brought into production with marginal investment in irrigation systems or concentrated use of fertilizers. On the question of potentially reclaimable land, Pi-chao Chen observed,

> According to the official estimate, China possesses about 100 million hectares of potentially reclaimable wasteland, approximately the amount of land presently under cultivation. Of these potentially reclaimable areas, 5.3 million hectares had been surveyed by 1957, about 3 million of which were found suitable for cultivation. Even if China does possess such a vast amount of potentially reclaimable wasteland (which is quite possible despite contradicting previous estimates), reclamation still does not provide a satisfactory solution to the high man/land ratio. Assuming that each settler were allotted 2 hectares (4.94 acres) of wasteland, the total of 3 million hectares could absorb only 1.4 million potential settlers.[24]

In a nation with a rural population of over 500 million, such incremental expansion would do little to improve the annual per capita food supply. And if the attempts to reclaim this land were made out of desperation caused by an impossibly high population growth rate (even 2 percent is too high), then the land reclaimed would not even begin to cope with the problems posed by adding 16 million persons to ration lists each year.

The current problems of chronic unemployment, underemployment, and seasonal employment fluctuations in rural areas, and of effecting a smooth transfer of workers from the agricultural to the more productive industrial sector, would appear miniscule in relation to the range of problems that a decade of population increases at an annual rate of 2 percent would create. Without a continuing and successful birth control program, the primary sector would not be able to produce increased quantities of grain to feed a growing urban-industrial sector, provide raw materials to expand light industry, or provide agricultural surplus for export in exchange for capital goods.[25] Without population control, China's economic development would be retarded severely, perhaps even reversed.

TRADE POLICY

It has been a tradition of most Westerners who attempt to assess the potential of China as a market for their goods to see only a vast population of potential buyers. The Chinese themselves rarely, if ever, have reciprocated with optimistic assessments of the value of trade with the West. The P.R.C. holds to the traditional view that production for export is a necessary evil, a practice in which it must engage to pay for imports of sophisticated capital goods and, in lean years, foodstuffs.

Hong Kong is far and away China's most important trading partner. It supplies the P.R.C. with a perpetually large balance of foreign currency (see Table 3.5), net earnings from the Hong Kong trade amounting to more than U.S.$400 million annually. Over the last two decades, the Hong Kong trade has more than financed all necessary food imports, a fact that probably will guarantee Hong Kong's security indefinitely. Roughly 23 percent of P.R.C. exports to Hong Kong have been reexported to other markets including Indonesia, Singapore, Japan, Switzerland, Malaysia, and Canada.[26]

In accordance with the policy of self-sufficiency, foreign trade has always been of marginal significance in the P.R.C. economy, rarely amounting to more than 9 percent of gross domestic production. All products imported by the P.R.C. are directed basically toward supplementing local production. In recent years, for example, Can-

TABLE 3.5

China's Aggregate External Trade, 1952-71, and the Hong Kong
Trade Surplus, 1952-70
(millions of U.S. dollars)

Year	Total External Trade	P.R.C. Exports to Hong Kong	P.R.C. Imports from Hong Kong	Gross Trade Balance with Hong Kong
1952	1,906	145.3	91.0	54.3
1953	2,235	150.0	94.6	55.4
1954	2,504	121.1	68.4	52.7
1955	2,741	157.1	31.8	125.3
1956	3,133	181.7	23.8	157.9
1957	3,095	179.9	21.6	176.3
1958	3,762	244.5	27.3	217.2
1959	4,274	181.0	20.0	161.0
1960	3,970	207.5	21.0	186.5
1961	2,938	180.0	17.3	162.7
1962	2,647	212.3	14.9	197.4
1963	2,760	260.2	12.3	247.9
1964	3,178	344.8	10.4	334.4
1965	3,759	406.3	12.5	393.8
1966	4,077	484.6	12.1	472.5
1967	3,859	397.2	8.4	388.8
1968	3,709	400.2	7.4	393.5
1969	3,884	445.5	6.2	439.3
1970	4,225	467.0	10.5	466.5
1971	4,208	553.2	n.a.	n.a.
Total				5,383.4

Sources: For the years 1952-66, Claude E. Forget,
China's External Trade: A Canadian Perspective (Montreal,
1971). For 1967-71, figures were obtained from Australia, Department of Trade and Industry, "Australia's Trade with the People's
Republic of China," paper presented to the Australian Institute of International Affairs Conference: China and the World Community,
June 1972, Melbourne, p. 11. For the figures 1967-71, a conversion
rate of $1 Australian = U.S.$1.12 was used.

ada has exported considerable amounts of wheat to the P.R.C., but little else: representing 97.7 percent of Canadian exports to China in 1969, 86 percent in 1970. Even the prospects for continued high wheat sales are not good according to a recent study by P. S. Ho and Ralph W. Huenemann,[27] largely because of the Chinese government's successful policies with regard to agriculture and population. Barring a major expansion in its foreign aid program of rice exports (a policy that would force a parallel increase in wheat imports), the P.R.C.'s potential as a market for Canadian wheat is likely to decline--unless China decides it is to its diplomatic advantage to try to acquire leverage with the Canadian government or unless P.R.C. planners decide that China can obtain more grain indirectly (through increased foreign purchases financed by concentration on the production and sale in world markets of cotton textiles, for example) than by growing wheat itself. Although considerations of diplomatic leverage may dominate present and future trade policies in the P.R.C., the comparative advantage argument is unlikely to carry any weight whatsoever.

The Ho-Huenemann study concluded that although Canada could obtain significant access to Chinese markets in some commodities, such as phosphate and potassium fertilizers (potash), the overall prospects for Sino-Canadian trade are not especially bright.[28]

Though the possibility for an increased economic interdependence between China and the West does exist, there is a very low probability that the Chinese ever will be able to use trade concessions to try to "penetrate" the Western alliance system. It is possible that the P.R.C. could try to use its trade policy to canvass Japanese, Australian, Canadian, and American support at the United Nations in future confrontations with the USSR. The recent expansion in trade and the prospect of American development of Chinese offshore oil resources is ample illustration of the potential for interdependent, mutually beneficial economic relations with the United States and its allies. In spite of these optimistic developments, trade relations with China must be kept in perspective. For all of China's Western trading partners, Canada, Australia, and Japan included, trade with the P.R.C. is certain to be negligible in proportion to the aggregate trade of each nation. Increased interdependence seems certain, but the acquisition of political influence through the threat of trade diversion is improbable. By way of illustration let us consider Japan.

Table 3.6 recounts the history of Sino-Japanese trade relations, 1954-71. The most disturbing aspect of the China trade for the Japanese is its extreme volatility. In 1959 and 1960, Japanese exports to the P.R.C. plummeted to less than 8 percent of the 1958 figure, reflecting the Chinese policy of politics in command. On this occasion, Peking was attempting to demonstrate its disapproval of the terms of

TABLE 3.6

Sino-Japanese Trade, 1954-71

Year	Japanese Exports (X) to China (millions of U.S. dollars)	Japanese Imports (Y) from China	X + Y	Aggregate Japanese Trade (billions of U.S. dollars)	Aggregate Trade of the P.R.C.
1954	19	40	59	4.0	2.3
1955	29	80	109	4.5	3.0
1956	67	83	150	5.7	3.1
1957	60	80	140	7.1	3.0
1958	51	54	105	5.9	3.7
1959	4	19	23	7.0	4.3
1960	3	20	23	8.5	4.0
1961	17	31	47	10.0	3.0
1962	38	46	84	10.5	2.7
1963	62	75	137	12.1	2.8
1964	153	158	311	14.6	3.2
1965	245	225	470	16.6	4.2
1966	315	306	621	19.3	4.6
1967	288	269	558	22.1	3.9
1968	325	224	550	26.0	3.6
1969	390	235	625	31.0	3.8
1970	569	254	823	38.2	4.2
1971	598	324	922	n.a.	4.2

Sources: Shinkichi Eto, "Features Characteristic of the Economy of China," in Peace Research in Japan 1971 (Tokyo: Japan Peace Research Group, 1971), pp. 22-25; and Australia, Department of Trade and Industry, "Australia's Trade with the People's Republic of China," paper presented to Australian Institute of International Affairs Conference: China and the World Community, June 1972, Melbourne.

the Fourth Non-Governmental Trade Agreement between Japan and China. Only after the completion of a more acceptable pact (the Liao Cheng-shih-Takasaki Tatsunosuke trade negotiations), did Japanese exports rise above the 1958 level. In 1967 and 1968, trade again declined severely; however, this apparently was due to the turmoil generated by the Cultural Revolution, rather than to Chinese dissatisfaction with the policies of the Sato government. Indeed, all China's trade declined in the years after 1967 and still has not regained the value it achieved in the peak year of 1966.

It is extremely important for future economic development in China that these gross and unpredictable oscillations in the flow of foreign trade be dampened as much as possible. Without a sustained flow of capital imports, the investment allocation process will become disjointed and less efficient. Many economists concur that Chinese aggregate trade necessarily will increase as the base of industrialization in the P.R.C. widens over the next two decades and that China's GNP growth rate will be characterized by a moderate but steady pace. Shinkichi Eto, unlike some Japanese economists who envision a phenomenal multiplication in the Sino-Japanese trade flow, agrees with this prognosis. "China's foreseeable economic prospects seem neither to be particularly rosy nor particularly bleak--rather, moderate growth seems to be in store. Japan's trade with China, therefore, will be about the same as its trade with South Korea, Taiwan and the Soviet Union for the time being."[29]

To date, the economic achievements of the Chinese government have been notable. By their own criteria, they have attained most of their goals. They have constructed a matrix of organizational and institutional structures upon which they can build a strategically potent and socialistically prosperous economy. The evidence suggests that they have made substantial progress in lowering the birthrate and, further, that the political leadership has the requisite will to force it still lower. They have succeeded in transforming the social structure of China and the educational component of the socialization process. The net effect of these measures may be the establishment of the groundwork for an extensive psychological revolution in the P.R.C. that will be less obvious in its external manifestations than the Cultural Revolution but may be much more significant in its long range impact on economic growth rates.

China is not now a consumer-oriented society, and it is highly doubtful that it will ever become so. In a high-saving, production-oriented society, the industrial establishment can have a great effect on defense procurement capability. In a society that has no steel-devouring automotive industry, that uses no steel in building, and that does not use large amounts of steel in highway construction, the output of steel and iron can be used to manufacture an immeasurably larger flow of armaments than a similar steel production capacity in a Western European or North American nation. The P.R.C. now engages in the mass production of all its major weapons systems and is thus pursuing self-reliance in this area with considerable success.

The P.R.C. managerial elite may have succeeded in devising a means for effecting a rapid dispersion of new technology into the rural areas. The new policy of encouraging light industry in these areas has created numerous "growing points" or "change agents" in these otherwise conservative, tradition-oriented regions.

Finally, the thorough-going application of behavioral conditioning in accordance with the dictates of Mao Tse-tung Thought may have prepared the way for the creation of a social megamachine capable of phenomenally focused, purposive, collective action. Contrary to Herman Kahn and Anthony Wiener, who seemed to imply that the so-called "blue ant" myth of the P.R.C. was merely paranoid delusion,[30] the potential for a highly focused collective effort could provide a greater impetus to a high economic growth rate than any other single factor thus far discussed.[31] The reawakened collective self-consciousness of the Chinese people is vitally significant. It is going to have a sizable impact in the future on all indexes of material progress. The Chinese will is strong--and focused. Significant economic achievements are therefore highly probable. Barring politically motivated slowdowns, the growth rate of GNP will probably be high--approaching 8 to 10 percent a year over the next decade.

NOTES

1. Sanford Lee, "Chou Is Cool on McGovern," Toronto Star, October 25, 1972, p. 47.

2. Ronald Anderson, "The Vast Economic Expansion of China," Toronto Globe and Mail, July 25, 1972.

3. Cited in Current History 63, no. 374 (October 1972), p. 188.

4. Official communique released November 1, 1954; cited in Pi-Chao Chen, "The Political Economics of Population Growth," World Politics 23 (January 1971): 248-50.

5. See International Institute for Strategic Studies, The Military Balance 1972-73 (London: IISS, 1972), note on population, p. 45.

6. For example, Tillman Durdin in "The New Face of Maoist China," Problems of Communism 20 (September-October 1971): 11-12.

7. Thomas G. Rawski, "Trade, Industry and Urban Development," in J. M. Gibson and D. M. Johnston, eds., A Century of Struggle (Toronto: Canadian Institute of International Affairs, 1971), p. 99.

8. Ibid., pp. 99-100.

9. Lin Piao, "Long Live the Victory of People's War!" in K. Fan, ed., Mao Tse-Tung and Lin Piao: Post-Revolutionary Writings (Garden City, N.Y.: Anchor Books, 1972), p. 390.

10. T. G. Rawski, "Foreign Contacts and Industrialization," International Journal 26 (Summer 1971): 524.

11. Ibid., p. 525.

12. R. G. Godson, "China Trade Winds Are Blowing," Canada Commerce 135 (November 1971): 12.

13. Rawski, "Foreign Contacts," presents a concise graphical presentation of China's position, first as recipient then as donor of international economic aid.

14. Kuan-I Chen, "The Outlook for China's Economy," Current History 61, no. 361 (September 1971): 107.

15. Ibid.

16. "On the Correct Handling of Contradictions among the People: China's Path to Industrialization," in Fan, Mao Tse-Tung and Lin Piao: Post-Revolutionary Writings, pp. 193-94.

17. Chen, op. cit., p. 134.

18. For 1949: Rawski, "Trade, Industry, and Urban Development," p. 94; for 1970: based on Pi-Chao Chen's figures for 1960 in "The Political Economics of Population Growth," World Politics 23 (January 1971): 262-63.

19. Rawski, "Trade, Industry, and Urban Development," p. 96.

20. K. Subrahmanyam, "Defense Preparations in India and China," Bulletin of the Atomic Scientist 24 (May 1968): 29.

21. Godson, op. cit., p. 11; Durdin, op. cit., p. 10.

22. See Shinkichi Eto, "Features Characteristic of the Economy of China," in Peace Research in Japan 1971 (Tokyo: Japan Research Group, 1971), pp. 21-22.

23. Robert W. Barnett, "China and Taiwan: The Economic Issues," Foreign Affairs 50 (April 1972): 449.

24. Pi-Chao Chen, op. cit., p. 255.

25. See ibid., pp. 264-70, for a development of these points. At the time Chen wrote this article the only evidence available pointed to a population growth rate of between 2.0 and 2.5 percent. As late as 1963, Chou En-lai reported that the birthrate was 30 per thousand, though many Western demographic specialists estimated that it was as high as 40 per thousand. See Harrison Salisbury's high estimates in Orbit of China (New York: Harper & Row, 1967), pp. 168-70. In the same speech, Chou stressed that the rate must cut back to seven per thousand.

26. Australia, Department of Trade and Industry, "Australia's Trade with the People's Republic of China," paper presented at Australian Institute of International Affairs Conference: China and the

World Community, June 1972, Melbourne, p. 4.

27. Samuel P. S. Ho and Ralph W. Huenemann, Canada's Trade with China: Patterns and Prospects (Montreal: Canadian Economic Policy Committee, 1972), p. 36.

28. Ibid., p. 47.

29. Eto, op. cit., p. 28.

30. Herman Kahn and Anthony J. Wiener, The Year 2000: A Framework for Speculation on the Next Thirty-Three Years (New York: Macmillan, 1967), p. 230.

31. Robert Lifton's superb analysis of the potential for human motivation latent in the thought and personal example of Mao deserves especially close scrutiny for those students of the psycho-adaptive capability of Chinese culture. See Revolutionary Immortality (New York: Random House, 1968); and Thought Reform and the Psychology of Totalism (New York: W. W. Norton, 1961).

4

THE MILITARY ESTABLISHMENT: CAPABILITY, STRATEGIC GOALS, AND THE PARTY-GUN DILEMMA

> We have always held that the atom-bomb is a paper
> tiger. We felt about it that way when we did not have
> nuclear weapons. And that is the way we feel about
> it now that we have them.
>
> Jen-min Jih-pao, December 31, 1964

The People's Republic of China is the only nation in the world to have been threatened with attack from both the United States and the USSR. In 1954 and 1958 during the offshore islands crises, the P.R.C.'s leaders had to adjust their strategic thinking and foreign policy decision making to accommodate the Dulles Doctrine of massive retaliation. In 1969 the Chinese military elite had to prepare for a possible Soviet nuclear attack on military installations in northern China. Thus the phrase "nuclear blackmail" acquired a concrete meaning for the men in Peking.

THREATS TO CHINESE SECURITY AND THE DOCTRINAL-STRATEGIC RESPONSE

Orthodox strategists in the P.R.C. have adhered strictly to the military doctrines enunciated by Mao during his long years in the field against Chiang Kai-shek and the Japanese.[1] The foremost of these is the principle that men, not weapons, decide military conflicts, that superior will and morale always will achieve victory over reactionary, counterrevolutionary forces, who by definition are divorced from a basis of popular support--the key element in all Mao's recipes for final victory in wars of national liberation. The equally important principle that nuclear weapons and the two thermonuclear superpowers are in reality "paper tigers" is a corollary to the principle of "men over weapons." In Chinese scenarios, final victory is ultimately contingent on winning approval and active support from the people. Even after hydrogen bombs are dropped, the aggressors must come to occupy "conquered" territory; then the traditional formula of "millet and rifles" and flexible tactics will carry the day for the people's army. As Lin Piao was fond of observing, the Chinese infantry units are among the best fighting men in the world--at a distance of 200 meters or less.[2] Since Liberation, the People's Liberation Army (PLA) has been trained to fight and kill at the closest possible range. Hand-to-hand combat has been its strength.

Until 1967, of the two and one-half million men in the PLA, 95 percent were deployed east of Tibet and east of Sinkiang to shore up border defenses in the northeast against the triple threat of Soviet incursions from Siberia, South Korean-American operations launched from south of the 38th parallel, and nationalist Chinese attacks on the mainland. Until fighting broke out in March 1969 over Chen-pao Island in the Ussuri River, and flared up later in the Ili River region between Alma Ata and T'a-ch'eng (April to August 1969), PLA troop deployments had not yet begun to reflect the prime threat to Chinese sovereignty. Only after these incidents did frontier security in the far west and the northeast become a priority for the Chinese military establishment.[3]

At least until 1971 the Chinese forces had to concede to their Soviet opponents an overwhelming superiority in tactical and strategic air support, firepower, and overall mobility. The PLA's sole statistical advantage was in manpower available for large scale fighting. Even that advantage has been somewhat eroded by recent Soviet troop reinforcements: from the 15 regular divisions stationed near the 4,150-mile frontier with China in 1968, the USSR's strength steadily increased to 49 heavily equipped divisions in the fall of 1972.[4]

Facing this alarming growth in Soviet military power, the Chinese leadership has sought to strengthen its forces by turning to a policy and strategy that involves an increased reliance on weapons (especially nuclear weapons). The more traditional reliance on hordes of infantry instilled with a "discipline that conquers the natural fear of death"[5] has been supplemented, perhaps even superseded, by an altogether avant-garde dependence on the gross destructive potential of modern weapons.

Defense spending in the P.R.C. since 1965 has been estimated to have been in the order of U.S.$8 billion a year,[6] and these funds have been channeled into such measures as the acquisition of a first-generation deterrent capability against the USSR through the construction and deployment of a Chinese version of the USSR's medium range bomber, the twin-jet Tu-16 Badger (operational radium about 1,600 miles); the creation of a more credible mixed deterrent force by the addition of several scores of medium and intermediate range ballistic missle (MRBM and IRBM) emplacements close to soft, countervalue targets in the Soviet Far East and Kazakhstan; the upgrading of conventional air defense capabilities along the Sino–Soviet border by embarking on extensive mass production and deployment of the wholly Chinese-designed F-9 fighter (Mach-2 capability); continued production of MiG-19 and MiG-21 aircraft; and the deployment of redesigned air defense radars and surface-to-air (SAM) equipment. By the end of 1971, the People's Liberation Army Air Force (PLAAF) had more than 3,600 combat aircraft, making it the third largest air force in the world.[7]

Coeval with these improvements in delivery systems, the Chinese nuclear research program has advanced rapidly and has succeeded in reducing the weight-to-yield ratio of its fission warheads by about 90 percent.[8] A strategy of defense that entails significant utilization of tactical nuclear weapons is now a practical reality.[9]

There is little doubt that the P.R.C. decided to exercise the nuclear option as a purely defensive measure. However, following a pattern reminiscent of NATO doctrines of an earlier era, the P.R.C. probably will seek to build a nuclear "shield" capability to free the use of a conventional "sword." Thus, what began as a defensive response eventually will augment the P.R.C.'s offensive strategic capability. Certainly Moscow has much to fear from an emerging nuclear stalemate with China. Once the USSR's nuclear advantage is nullified, a continued upgrading of China's conventional forces would heighten immeasurably the prospects for Chinese irredentist thrusts against Outer Mongolia and the region of the Soviet Far East south of the Stanovoy Mountains.

With over 100 TU-16 bombers and more than 300 F-9 tactical support aircraft (capable of carrying nuclear warheads), with 15 to 30 MRBMs and 5 to 15 IRBMs already operational,[10] and with a current stockpile of at least 300 warheads,[11] the Chinese have achieved (or, at worst, will achieve by late 1973) a credible threat of retaliation against all major cities and principal troop concentrations in the Soviet Far East. Second, the PLAAF is capable of annihilating any concentrated forces that manage to breach Chinese ground defenses. In light of this recently acquired strategic and tactical capability, it seems probable that the P.R.C. will continue to seek the following five strategic objectives:

1. At a minimum, the preservation of the territorial integrity of mainland China;

2. At a maximum, the acquisition of military and political control over Outer Mongolia and the Soviet Far East, either through negotiated settlement or through the use of force;

3. Even greater isolation of the nationalist regime in Taipei and the eventual integration of Taiwan into the P.R.C.'s system of political control, following either a negotiated renunciation of sovereignty by Chiang's successors, or subversion of the nationalist regime through guerrilla insurrection, or, most improbably, nuclear blackmail by the P.R.C. if and when the United States withdraws its present security guarantee to the nationalists;

4. Maintenance and improvement of coastal defenses to provide military support to the P.R.C. claims over contested islands such as the Senkakus and Quemoy and Matsu;

5. The widening of the economic–industrial basis of the P.R.C.'s strategic capabilities through higher levels of expenditure on nuclear armaments, intercontinental ballistic missle (ICBM) delivery systems (including the necessary electronics software), satellite reconnaissance, and advanced conventional armaments of Chinese manufacture. The object will be the attainment of mutual deterrence in relation to the USSR and the United States. If the current limitations on antiballistic missile systems under the terms of the Strategic Arms Limitation Agreement of May 22-29, 1972 are fully respected by both the Russians and the Americans, then Peking's prospects for achieving a fully credible first-strike deterrent posture by 1975-78 are very favorable. Creation of a genuine second-strike capability is a much longer term goal; its attainment will be contingent on Chinese progress in building a viable submarine-launched ballistic missile (SLBM) force.

These constitute the main strategic goals of the P.R.C. over the next decade. To achieve even minimal success, the Chinese will have to upgrade this already formidable strategic capability. At present the most obvious deficiency in the P.R.C.'s forces is a conspicuous lack of amphibious assault capability. Some U.S. military analysts tend to discount this notable fact by pointing out that the P.R.C.'s naval arm has the third largest submarine fleet and the third largest corps of naval personnel in the world. One observer has noted that the Chinese possess a fleet of fast missile, gun, and torpedo boats that is growing at a rate that soon may enable the Chinese to deploy the most formidable coastal defense network in the world, and that China's growing corps of trained naval personnel points to a potential for extensive regional control in the area of the China Seas, the Indonesian-Malaysian archipelago, and perhaps the Indian Ocean.[12]

Certainly the potential exists for creating a substantial power of naval interdiction in south and southeast Asian waters; yet it is doubtful that this potential will become reality before 1980--if ever. According to some estimates, the P.R.C. still is developing its first nuclear powered attack submarine, with up to three submarines in various stages of construction.[13] They will carry conventional torpedoes, and it is not known whether they will be capable of carrying SLBMs. The P.R.C. navy currently has one Soviet C-class submarine (diesel-powered), which is equipped with missile tubes but which lacks rockets. Although it is not unlikely that the Chinese will proceed with development and deployment of a seaborne strategic deterrent arm, it does seem unlikely that they will build a sizable amphibious assault adjunct to an already imposing array of surface ships and submarines. As noted earlier, the P.R.C. is likely to remain preoccupied with the land based conventional threat. Now that the American presence on the Asian mainland has diminished appreciably, the sole long term threat from the sea is Japan. This threat (analyzed in Part II) is nonexistent in terms of present military deployment and will remain a factor in Chinese strategic calculations only in terms of Japan's potential for becoming a major military power in the Pacific-Asian region.

While the Chinese strive to allay Japanese fears over China's growing nuclear capability, they also will be instituting measures designed to enhance their own deterrent status in relation to the USSR. These measures, as embodied in both the material force deployments and the theoretical concepts under which they will be employed, necessarily will provoke serious anxiety among the more radically militant elements of the Japanese political elite. The options open to the Japanese government are limited by certain domestic and international factors, but the Chinese certainly must make allowances for the possibility of driving Japan to nuclear armament. The Japanese are no doubt fully aware that Chinese missiles aimed at Japanese cities would be an inevitable factor in any future crises in the Sino-American relationship.

Given the present trends in the evolving Asian balance of power, the Chinese appear to be headed for a minor crisis in the management of their foreign policy. In large measure this is due to the contradictory goals of providing no support for the views of militarist elements in both Japan and India, while maintaining sufficient latitude in other areas to be able to press claims against the Taipei regime, against the Himalayan border states, and against the Soviet Union. If the Chinese elect to follow a hard line on Taiwan (or possibly concerning the Himalayan states of Nepal, Bhutan, and Sikkim), the net effect on the continuing debate within both India and Japan could be to shift public opinion toward support of the more hawkish elements in the governments of these two neighbors. Certainly one of China's major foreign policy goals must remain the prevention of the nuclearization of either Japan or India through fear of China. If China's foreign policy fails in this regard, the damage to her security position and her international prestige as the only nonwhite, nuclear equipped nation would be considerable.*

Historically, the communist Chinese polity has conformed to foreign policy principles that give predominance to the maintenance of China's territorial integrity, to the extension of Chinese control over what have been regarded as traditionally Chinese domains (Taiwan, Tibet, Outer Mongolia), and to the establishment of political, strategic, and economic autonomy. The means by which these ends have been sought have varied, ranging from the sophisticated application of diplomatic pressures (as at Geneva 1954 and throughout the first period of united front-detente tactics, 1954–57) to the outright use of force to secure or attempt to secure limited territorial goals (the conquest of Tibet, the Indian border disputes, and the Soviet border disputes).

Within this framework of broad, systemic ends, the Chinese military establishment has had to cope with the intractable problem of the P.R.C.'s military vulnerability and the concomitant inability of the government to allocate sufficient resources for acquiring the necessary weaponry for creating a modern armed forces establishment. Furthermore, as often has been noted by Western military observers, the Chinese army simply could not function at distances greater than 100 miles from their borders for lack of sufficient logistic capability. Substantial military aggression against China's major neighbors thus seems entirely out of the question.

In addition to these physical constraints on China's purportedly aggressive designs, the People's Republic also is limited by serious deficiencies in its strategic doctrines. Military theory in China is virtually synonymous with the thought of Mao Tse-tung, but that aspect of his writing germane to operational tactics and methodology in the conduct of war does not deal in any way with the techniques of invasion and conquest. Mao's theory is designed to counsel the guerrilla leader in his native country, not the massively armed general about to invade an adjacent state.

Even a cursory glance at the historical record should serve to bear out the thesis that the Chinese are not by nature either imperialist or irrationally aggressive. Since 1949 they have engaged in the Korean conflict, but reluctantly and only as a result of a very substantial American threat to their own territory. Even then, the Chinese practiced a pragmatic policy of conflict limitation, refraining from bombing American staging areas in Japan in return for nonuse of atomic weapons by the U.S. and UN forces.[14] On two oc-

---

*See Postscript for comments on the implications for China of India's first atomic test.

casions (1954-55 and 1958), the Chinese pressed the Taiwanese government to relinquish the offshore islands but then relaxed this pressure in the face of invincible American opposition and a decided lack of enthusiasm for the P.R.C.'s cause on the part of the Soviet Union. Tibet was brought forcibly under indirect Chinese rule in 1951 and direct rule by 1964. Considering the manner of its execution, this takeover is unquestionably the most notable instance of what some choose to call Chinese imperialism, but from a historical perspective the Chinese case for suzerainty over Tibet is not without justification. Finally, in the Sino-Indian border dispute, the Chinese campaign evidently was conceived and executed in a near flawless plan to acquire control of territory that was strategically vital for the Chinese: the Aksai Chin plateau in the Ladakh region of Kashmir. The sporadic border conflicts with India from 1959 through 1962 were in large measure the result of China's policy of taking more territory in the east, in the region of the poorly defined, weakly justifiable McMahon Line, which then could be given back to India in return for clear title to the Aksai Chin sector where one of the P.R.C.'s principal access routes to western Tibet was situated. In short, the Chinese leadership had no broadly aggressive designs on Indian territory.

Except for the outstanding claims against Taiwan and the Soviet Union, the Chinese quest to reclaim those areas they define as terra irredenta largely has been satisfied. Their strategic doctrines and military theory in no way recommend military expansionism. Maoist philosophy is, above all, a theory of national revolution and a theory of nationalist self-determination within the broader evolutionary flow of international communism.

Chinese military debates have been preoccupied with the problems of defense, not attack. Defense of the revolutionary homeland always has been and will remain the primary task of the People's Liberation Army. From 1949-53, the Chinese did little but approve of overall political-military strategy enunciated by Stalin. The outbursts of militant tirade and vituperation and the policy of military bombardment of the offshore islands should be viewed more as an attempt to test the limits of Soviet support than as limited actions against Chiang's regime. It is important to note that the two campaigns against the offshore islands and China's generally more militant posture on many issues did have the very salutary effect, for the Chinese, of Soviet attempts at appeasement of their revolutionary comrades first through the joint declarations of October 12, 1954, which instituted a massive scientific and technical aid program, and, second, through the New Technology for National Defense Agreement of October 15, 1957, which, according to Peking, provided for Soviet aid to China's nuclear weapons program in the form of a specimen atomic bomb and

data pertinent to its manufacture. The Russians definitely were trying to bribe the Chinese to support a less provocative posture for the
communist countries as a whole, to conform to the overall line of
peaceful coexistence announced at the 20th Congress of the Communist
Party of the Soviet Union (CPSU).

For China, detente and peaceful coexistence could have been tol-
erable had the Soviet leaders made an exception for what the Chinese
viewed as legitimate irredentist claims. The USSR did not, and the
Chinese therefore redoubled their efforts to construct a nuclear
shield to cover their conventional thrusts aimed at rectifying their
borders. Ironically enough, while the Chinese redoubled their effort
and investment in their nuclear weapons program, official strategy
continued to adhere to the general themes of "man over weapons" and
the impossibility of vanquishing a nation of 600 million people (at
least 200 million would survive American nuclear attack it was ar-
gued).[15] The strategic debate of the mid-1950s resulted in tacit but
reluctant collusion in Soviet aims and a policy that sought defense
and deterrence through China's protracted war capability, a low level
of short term investment in needed air defense equipment to counter
the American threat, and a general reliance on postattack mobilization in the event of a nuclear strike by the United States. In addition,
the Chinese leadership approved a continued emphasis on the political
role of the PLA and a priority policy of furthering "socialist economic
construction" and "national defense construction," which would, in
the long term, remedy the P.R.C.'s dependence on the goodwill of the
Soviet leadership.

The inability to elicit Soviet support for the P.R.C.'s foreign
policy objectives with respect to Taiwan and the Himalayan border
area surely must be counted as one of the principal factors in the
growth of the Sino-Soviet rift. The Chinese wanted desperately to
exploit the Soviet technical advances of the mid-1950s (the USSR
tested its first hydrogen bomb in August 1953 and had constructed its
first ICBMs by late 1956) but were frustrated continually by Soviet
reluctance to risk serious conflict with the United States over issues
and territory of no direct importance to the Soviet Union.

The paradox of the Chinese asserting with voluble sincerity that
human will has more to do with the resolution of conflicts than nuclear
capability, while frantically pursuing a nuclear weapons development
program, can be explained in part by China's need for an interim
strategy that did not paralyze its foreign policy and negate its revolutionary experience and doctrines. The propaganda theme of man over
weapons and its corresponding reliance on strategic-defensive guerrilla warfare served exceedingly well to insulate those who gave priority to economic development from charges that they were leaving
the country defenseless to nuclear attack. Similarly it has provided

a theoretical rationale and support for following an independent and antagonistic foreign policy in relation to the USSR since 1963.

PARTY-ARMY RELATIONS

The strategic debate following the Soviet technological advances of the mid-1950s and the fact of China's unalterable condition of strategic vulnerability during the 1960s gave the basic shape to all subsequent foreign policy and defense policy strategy. However, as of 1972, China entered a new era in its political and diplomatic history. It is thus rather appropriate that Lin Piao, the archetypal mass-line leftist, a man often more Maoist than Mao Tse-tung, was "purged" in September 1971 following an attempted military coup in Peking.[16] An ensuing purge of all military men loyal to Lin (conducted by Chou En-lai) effectively prepared the way for new initiatives in Chinese foreign policy. This does not mean, however, that the armed forces have been relegated to a secondary role in Chinese politics, with the party wholly "in command of the gun." Mao's view with respect to the use of the army in molding a new and truly revolutionary society will not be laid aside. And the next generation of PLA commanders will continue to have considerable power over the direction of future policies, both domestic and foreign, in the P.R.C.

With the P.R.C. entering the 1970s still adhering to the extreme doctrine of people's war, in addition to the more recently acquired (and tacitly employed) doctrine of nuclear deterrence, it still will be necessary for the armed forces to deploy "hordes" of infantry (there were in 1970 some 150 PLA army divisions, more than the previous year), even though they will be acquiring an ever more formidable nuclear capability. A buoyant economy should be able to sustain continued improvement in the armaments available to all three divisions of the armed services. Defense expenditures are at least in the range of $8 to $10 billion,[17] with some British estimates as high as $16 billion.

When one considers that the PLA is obliged to set an example for society at large in terms of implementing the egalitarian ethos of Chinese ideology, it appears probable that financial outlays for salaries will be negligible per soldier, though with total manpower over three million, the aggregate outlay will be significant. It is also doubtful that the PLA has suffered from the phenomenon of grade creep that has plagued Western military establishments by undermining the capital expenditure/operational costs ratio. If the political-ethical emphasis remains high, if the PLA remains true to its traditions that sought to foster a "closely knit military-religious order,"[18] then operational costs per man will remain at a relatively low level.

If, on the other hand, a new type of professionalism asserts itself within the PLA's upper echelons and a new generation of experts develops who clamor for more hierarchy, a more technically efficient methodology, more centralized decision making (that is, less party control), and appropriate pay incentives, then the PLA's wage bill could rise quickly. In view of the current distribution of power, few such demands would be met. The Cultural Revolution is still too recent an experience to permit a renewed growth of counterrevolutionary bureaucratic professionalism.

In keeping with orthodox Maoist doctrine, the Chinese political elite has sought to maintain party supremacy in military matters. The party must direct the gun. Yet in recent years it has become increasingly difficult to maintain this centralized control on the armed forces. Lin Piao's attempted coup during the autumn of 1971 is yet another example of the "Bonapartist" threat that always has lurked just below the surface of this militaristic society.[19]

The chief instrument for governing and directing the armed forces remains the Military Affairs Commission.[20] Through it, the political elite periodically has conducted political indoctrination programs to consolidate the party's hold on the command-and-control structure and to ensure the maintenance of an effective internal security network.[21] In spite of the widespread efficacy of mutual criticism measures, the PLA's professionals periodically defy Peking's strategic direction of the economic development effort. Subsequent investigations concerning the causes of Lin Piao's attempted coup may reveal that unrequited service appetities may have generated substantial support for the attempted takeover among prominent PLA officers. It was Lin Piao who acted to assuage partially the army professionals in October of 1960 by instituting new training programs for the conduct of chemical and nuclear warfare. It is possible that he decided during 1971 that the time had come to grant the army's additional requests for newer, more advanced equipment. It may be that with such promises he won the support of key military leaders such as the PLA's chief of staff, Huang Yung-sheng, the PLAAF commander, Wu Fa-hsien, and others--men who wanted a greater share of the P.R.C.'s resources to go to immediate national defense needs and who were as upset as Lin at the prospect of Sino-American rapprochement.

The struggle between the army and the party in the P.R.C. has been endemic since Liberation. It is likely to remain so. From 1955-60, army-party tensions hinged on three questions: professionalism versus multilevel political controls, the optimum strategy for national defense, and the relative priority of economic development. In the years 1960-65, these questions temporarily were resolved by the adoption of an interim strategy of defensive war (in the case of attack), reliance on close combat, and a civilian militia trained in the art of guerrilla warfare. The years 1965-69 were dominated by the political power struggle, yet the Cultural Revolution afforded the PLA elite the opportunity to bargain with leading political contenders. Since 1969 the key issue has been whether to continue to rely on a strategy of defensive war or, until a substantial nuclear deterrent force has been deployed, to devote more resources to the modernization of conventional border defenses. In essence Mao's purge from below prevented the articulation of the desires for conventional modernization by the PLA's key leaders, but it did not eliminate these goals. The coup attempt showed the heightened dissatisfaction with the Mao-Chou faction's foreign and defense policy.

The postponement of the appointment of a new defense minister to succeed Lin may indicate that the political leaders, especially Mao and Chou, are extremely loath to give anyone from the highest army echelon the substantial political influence that has accrued to this position. Yeh Chien-ying, the 72-year-old former PLA marshal is currently "China's foremost military figure," according to press reports that indicate he has been appointed vice chairman of the Military Affairs Commission;[22] however, he has not yet been named minister of defense. It is probable that the political elite is seeking to undercut systematically the political influence of PLA leaders in response to the widespread growth of army power following the Ninth Party Congress in April 1969. In the autumn of 1969, at the height of Lin's political influence, party-soldiers (men who hold both party and army offices) constituted 45 percent of the new Central Committee, while the new 21-man ruling Politburo included four marshals, six generals, and Lin's wife.[23] Events since September 12, 1971 have "rectified" this abnormal army representation among the highest "ruling circles" to some degree, but the internal distribution of power in the P.R.C. still leaves PLA interests as a primary determinant of the outcome of policy disputes.

It is perhaps too soon to be able to ascertain whether the influence of the army inevitably will lead to a substantial redefinition of foreign policy goals. In part, the difficulty of prediction stems from trying to define one set of coherent group interests for the PLA when in fact the armed forces are composed of different subelites in the three services and at the various levels of regional and district administration. Then, too, there is the problem of determining what deviations, if any, will result from the change in composition of the military elite as the Long March veterans gradually die off or retire from active political life. In theory, the long range strategic goals delineated above should not be altered seriously by either intra-PLA interest conflict or the generational devolution of power. In theory, the long term strategic goals of the P.R.C. are determined almost independently of the view of any one definable interest group; but theory does not always correspond to human reality. It is conceivable that a strong professionalist faction could regain control of the Military Affairs Commission and even the Central Committee of the CCP itself. In that event, it is possible that rapprochement with the USSR could be entertained as a means for improving the P.R.C.'s security position as a least-cost policy. It is possible, but highly improbable. In many respects the PLA has more to gain by following a policy of ideological and strategic independence, because the potential threat of Soviet mechanized divisions would seem to compel an equivalent force deployment from the Chinese if they are not going to be left with the sole alternative of rapid escalation to the level of tactical nuclear warfare should they be confronted by a Soviet attack.

At present the nature of the Sino-Soviet rift seems so wide and so profound that it precludes totally any such rapprochement in the foreseeable future. Even should the party lose control of the gun, it seems reasonable that the armed forces would continue to define their goals within the broad framework of continued Sino-Soviet antagonism.

NOTES

1. See Mao Tse-tung's Six Essays on Military Affairs (Peking: Foreign Language Press, 1971) for a concise but complete collection of all of Mao's thoughts pertinent to strategy and tactics of revolutionary warfare.

2. Harrison Salisbury, Orbit of China (New York: Harper & Row, 1967), pp. 160-61.

3. International Institute for Strategic Studies, Strategic Survey 1969 (London: IISS, 1970), pp. 70-71.

4. International Institute for Strategic Studies, Strategic Survey 1971 (London: IISS, 1972), p. 56; and the Toronto Globe and Mail, September 11, 1972.

5. Cited in A. L. George, The Chinese Communist Army in Action (New York: Columbia University Press, 1967), p. 226.

6. IISS, Strategic Survey 1971, p. 57.

7. International Institute for Strategic Studies, The Military Balance, 1972-73 (London: IISS, 1972), p. 45.

8. Charles Murphy, "China's Nuclear Deterrent," Air Force Magazine (April 1972): 23.

9. William Beecher, Toronto Globe and Mail, July 27, 1972.

10. Ibid.

11. Murphy, op. cit., p. 23.

12. John R. Dewenter, "China Afloat," Foreign Affairs 50 (July 1972).

13. Ibid., p. 746.

14. Richard M. Bueschel in Communist Chinese Air Power (New York: Praeger, 1968), p. 23, has claimed that, through a process of tacit negotiation, the United States achieved a diplomatic victory of sorts by threatening to bomb Chinese cities with atomic weapons if the P.R.C. initiated bombing in South Korea or China. The Chinese apparently threatened to bomb Japan and South Korea if the Americans struck at targets in Mahchuria. Thus a "contract" was reached, and conflict escalation to the level of strategic bombing was prevented.

15. P'eng Teh-huai, Minister of Defense, in Akio Doi, Sashimukai no Mo Taku-To, as cited by Alice Langley Hsieh, Communist China's Strategy in the Nuclear Era (Englewood Cliffs, N.J.: Prentice-Hall, 1962), p. 52.

16. As of November 1972, Yeh Chien-ying, a 72-year-old former Red Army marshal had taken over Lin's duties as minister of defense, apparently on an interim basis. Official statements of July 1972 assert Lin Piao was killed in the aftermath of an unsuccessful assassination attempt. The official account does contain, however, several inconsistencies. What has been established firmly is that Lin Piao and the former chief of staff of the PLA, Huang Yung-sheng, as well as Wu Fa-hsien, commander of the PLAAF, and Li Tso-peng, first political commissar of the navy, another deputy of chief of staff, and Lin Piao's son and wife were all killed as a result of the attempt --possibly in a plane crash. Toronto Globe and Mail, July 29, 1972.

17. IISS, The Military Balance, 1972-73, pp. 43-45.

18. George, op. cit., p. 27.

19. In 1960 parts of China erupted in full scale rebellion, and many PLA units responded sluggishly to central directives aimed at restoring order. Again in 1965-67, the question of PLA control was revived as some units openly defied directives from the Military Affairs Commission.

20. For a detailed look at the operational role of the commission, see John Gittings, "Military Control and Leadership, 1954-64," China Quarterly, no. 26 (April-June 1966); and Harvey Nelsen, "Military Forces in the Cultural Revolution," China Quarterly, no. 51 (July-September 1972).

21. See Nelsen, ibid.; and Morton H. Halperin and J. W. Lewis, "New Tensions in Army--Party Relations in China 1965-66," China Quarterly, no. 26 (April-June 1966): 59-62.

22. Toronto Globe and Mail, November 8, 1972.

23. Ralph L. Powell, "The Military and the Struggle for Power in China," Current History 63, no. 373 (September 1972): 99.

5

FOREIGN POLICY AND
THE IDEOLOGICAL
COMMITMENT TO
REVOLUTION

Know the enemy and know yourself; in a hundred battles
you will never be in peril.

Sun Tzu, The Art of War

The foreign policy of any state is the result of the complex inter-
weaving of internal political and environmental-interactional processes.
These phenomena can be classified in four categories: (1) traditional
influences (that is, basic perceptions, behavioral norms, values, and
motivations inherent in the society in general); (2) structural parame-
ters--economic and political-institutional--that govern the modalities
of collective response and initiative; (3) fundamental security requirements without which the sovereignty of the polity would be called into
question and which are common to all states; and (4) international systemic constraints--the exogenously determined opportunities for, and
barriers to, a willful, conscious, and rational restructuring of the
global political milieu. Influences from the latter two categories have
dominated the choice of the P.R.C.'s tactical and, somewhat less
frequently, strategic options in its policy toward adjacent nations.
However they are much less significant in China's policy toward the
Third World in general.

The Chinese believe that the doctrine of people's war is still valid
for Asia, especially against the large "imperialist" nations, specifically the United States, wherein public opinion will not condone participation in protracted wars. In the Chinese view, the Americans are
on the retreat and henceforth will be extremely reluctant to become
involved again in Asia. The Nixon Doctrine can be taken at face value.
American policy is dedicated to the proposition that "Asians should
fight Asians"--since from the American point of view it is the only way
in which a "people's war" can be combated effectively. The Chinese

thus are not overly concerned with the residual American presence, large though it is, knowing as they do that the current U.S. administration does not seek renewed involvement and thus will undertake little in the way of aggressive, counterinsurgency measures in other nations in southeast Asia. China's security interests with respect to its southern borders therefore are more than satisfied. In consequence it would not be unreasonable to expect a growing emphasis on the incitement of revolution in some of these adjacent states.

Nevertheless, the Chinese commitment to revolution in southeast Asia must always be tempered with a prudent respect for the policies and aims of the two superpowers. The Chinese are not going to undertake any operations that will cause either renewed American involvement or the involvement of the USSR in southeast Asia. The P.R.C.'s foreign policy is in fact in the midst of a period of soft diplomatic negotiations. The Chinese leadership probably see themselves in the process of executing a strategic-defensive maneuver. The primary aim of Chinese foreign policy in this period must remain focused on preventing an integration or coordination of policy by the United States and the USSR. Yet this, the broadest goal of Chinese foreign policy, does not encompass the whole thrust of China's policies toward its external environment. China's commitment to revolution consistently has found material expression in its relations with the "global countryside."

RELATIONS WITH THE LESS DEVELOPED COUNTRIES

With respect to the underdeveloped countries of Africa, the Middle East, and Latin America, the Chinese leadership is no doubt increasingly aware of the opportunities for supporting subversion and guerrilla infiltration. The growing awareness in Third World countries concerning the stark gap in incomes that separates the industrialized from the underdeveloped nations is a major source of politically exploitable discontent. The current wave of anticolonialist or rather antineocolonialist sentiments finds expression in continuing disputes between these two groups of nations. The initial successes of the Organization of Petroleum Exporting Countries (OPEC) cartel and the clashes at the Stockholm Conference on the Human Environment and at recent UNCTAD meetings typify what could become a common practice in trade and environmental negotiations between the rich and poor countries. The Chinese surely must be monitoring these developments closely. It is probable that China's future foreign policy will be conducted to maintain and strengthen the Sino-American linkage, since in the short to medium term there are fewer material and strategic "contradictions" between the United States and China. Simultaneously, however, the P.R.C. will attempt to promote, directly or indirectly, all national liberation movements that show either a substantial prospect for victory in any specific country or provide a politically exploitable, popular symbol of superpower imperialism.

The problems China will pose for foreign policy and defense policy planning in the Western nations are thus most crucial with regard to relations with resource-rich less developed countries (LDCs). Certainly it is toward this sector of the states system that the P.R.C. will direct most of its diplomatic, political, and military efforts over the next two decades, though not necessarily by following any overt predatory strategic design against Western economies. China will be adhering to previously established goals. As all great powers must, it will follow a policy of calculated opportunism. But the primary long range goal of Chinese foreign policy is the incitement of revolution in, not direct political control of, the global countryside. In a sense the Chinese are at a stage of sociocultural development analogous to the epoch of religiously inspired colonialism in Western Europe. There is, however, one radical difference to the Chinese approach toward "colonization" and "empire." To date the Chinese have demonstrated a complete indifference toward the acquisition of direct control over the recipients of their aid program. Rather, they are seeking political allies in their two-front struggle against what they perceive to be the American and Soviet _imperia_. They desire to "win friends and influence people" through the projection of their model of "revolutionary praxis" into the African, Latin American, Middle Eastern, and South Asian regions. China's major forays into the Third World, and in fact most of its significant political and diplomatic victories (and setbacks), have occurred in Africa, with the Middle East and Asia in second place.

As early as 1956, the Chinese were making offers of active support to African and Middle Eastern leaders. In that year the P.R.C. offered to send 300,000 troops to aid Nasser's forces. Diplomatic contacts were initiated with Syria, Lebanon, and Ghana. By 1958 the Chinese were anxious to promote ties with both Yemen and Iraq, signing friendship treaties and offering loans to these governments. In 1960 relations were established with Guinea, Tanganyika, and Congo-Brazzaville; and members of at least one African national liberation army (from Cameroon) were given training in sabotage and guerrilla warfare techniques. From 1963-66 the P.R.C. tried to follow a much more aggressive policy in its support for subversion and national liberation movements. However measures such as Chinese support for Watusi attacks on Rwanda eventually led to a severe reversal in China's fortunes that saw its embassies in Burundi, Dahomey, Upper Volta, and the Central African Republic forcibly closed. No doubt influenced by the turbulence and disorder mounting within the P.R.C., Chinese activities in Africa and the Middle East from 1966-70 succeeded only in alienating many of their former allies. By 1967 the situation had become so grave that the Chinese actually were expelled from the Afro-Asian Peoples Solidarity Organization Conference in Nicosia. By 1970 except for the new links resulting from the commencement of Chinese work on the Lusaka-Dar-es-Salaam railway, China's policies had produced few positive results. The anticipated wave of revolutionary discontent did not materialize.

In Asia, meanwhile, China's ideological commitments were being overriden by the exigencies imposed by the Vietnam war and a desire to undercut Soviet influence in the region. The Chinese apparently reached agreement with Hanoi over spheres of ideological-revolutionary influence in April 1970.[1] At this meeting of Chinese and North Vietnamese leaders it was agreed that Hanoi would concentrate its efforts on South Vietnam, Laos, and Cambodia, while the Chinese would support materially and advise the "national liberation struggles" in Malaysia, Burma, and Thailand. With respect to Indochina, the Chinese are apparently willing to undertake an ideological division of labor, not so much because they wish to see North Vietnam become a firmly entrenched force in this area but because they do not want to risk giving offense to Hanoi, causing it to look to the USSR for still greater support. Furthermore, the P.R.C. would rather concentrate its material resources and propaganda expertise on both Burma and Thailand. The Burmese government of Ne Win is relatively weak, plagued with enormous economic problems, and split by dissident minority groups. Burma will continue to exist only by placating the Chinese, that is by remaining neutral and making sure that no foreign troops hostile to China ever use Burmese soil either to launch or threaten an attack on China.

The primary goal of both the ideological and security components of Chinese foreign policy in southeast Asia remains the overthrow of the present Thai government. At a minimum, Peking would settle for neutralization of Thailand provided this meant the complete withdrawal of the American air force from its seven Thai bases and the withdrawal of Thailand from the Southeast Asian Treaty Organization (SEATO). In November of 1971, just prior to the coup in Thailand, the Chinese were said to have approached the then Thai foreign minister, Thanat Kohman, "regarding the possibility of terminating Chinese support to the insurgents in Thailand in exchange for the removal of American air bases from Thai soil."[2] Had this diplomatic move not been nullified by the coup, it is probable that China's ideological commitment to revolution would have been sacrificed willingly to its short run security interests. Again this illustrates the inevitable tension and duality in Chinese foreign policy as the object under consideration moves closer to the Chinese border. Nevertheless, it would be incorrect to deduce that its ideological commitment to revolution is ephemeral ritualistic dogma and not a substantial part of Chinese foreign policy. The Chinese commitment to socialist revolution is genuine. It should not be viewed as an increasingly vestigial component of its domestic political culture. That the Chinese can temper their doctrinaire program with large doses of pragmatism with respect to one area of the globe is no justification for concluding that their doctrine is becoming irrelevant.

It is true that, as far as Asia is concerned, Chinese foreign policy is dominated normally by pragmatic assessments of threats to national security and of the most efficient political and diplomatic postures to neutralize these threats. Ideological considerations have indeed been relegated to an entirely secondary role. However, it would be patently absurd to claim that Chinese decision making is characterized by a totalitarian administration, which adheres solely to Machiavellian concepts and calculations and which frames a Chinese security strategy based on the "national interest" alone. It seems to be an implicit premise of many "realist" analysts that the quest for power and the irrational enjoyment of enslaving large populations is the fundamental trait of the mind of the communist autocrat. However, if any vaguely appropriate parallels to the Chinese mentality are to be found in the history of Western civilization, it would be perhaps in the idealistic, formative years following the American revolution. More than any other contemporary world leadership the men in Peking are devoted to their principles, to the values for which they fought so long and sacrificed so much. Irrespective of a subjective assessment of the merit of these values, it will be many years, at least another generation, before China's leaders exhibit a willingness to compromise fundamental principles in the manner that has typified Soviet leadership since the death of Stalin.

In the arcane science of international relations it is a generally accepted truism that political leaders who are men of principle and conviction are often the most dangerous sources of instability in the regular intercourse of nations. It is for this reason that a moderate Chinese foreign policy and a moderate Chinese mentality have been welcomed universally. However, this "moderation" may be suspect.

We proposed earlier that the P.R.C. ought to be considered sui generis rather than viewed as a fraternal twin or even a close cousin of the Soviet system. However, insofar as Chinese foreign policy decision making is dominated by fundamental security considerations and the environmental constraints imposed by the regional power balances of the international system, the character of Chinese decisions necessarily will resemble that of Soviet operations. Thus, it is not altogether inappropriate to speak of the collision of the Russian and Han "empires" in northeastern Asia and of their partly blind and ordinarily intransigent demands of unilateral concessions. In this sphere of conflict there exists a classic confrontation of global powers and radically contradictory perceptions of reality and of each other's roles therein. Thus, it is to be expected that a genuine modus vivendi will be achieved on the battlefield rather than in the council chamber, that brute force, not a confrontation of intellects, will decide contending claims.

Depending on one's philosophical-theoretical propensities, one could attribute the Sino-Soviet conflict to geography. In what is becoming a fashionable neogeopolitical "explanation" of reality, one could portray this conflict in general, and China's policies in Asia specifically, as determined by factors of geography, demography, and economics. We do not espouse wholly this doctrine, but it does provide a useful, if overly simplistic, description of the primary contradiction in Asia: the struggle of two vast and complex social systems for territory, resources, and status.

The reassessment of the international environment that Mao Tse-tung evidently instigated and promulgated in the years 1968-71, resulting in Chinese receptivity toward the idea of detente with the United States, was also a product of security-environmental considerations, as was Chinese policy toward Pakistan in the Indo-Pakistani war of December 1971. Important as these events are in the historical record of Peking's foreign relations, this type of decision does not reflect the full scope of motivations that apparently move a large majority of the Chinese elite. The record of the past four years is not overwhelmingly conducive to the view that the P.R.C. has abandoned its revolutionary ardor.

The P.R.C. is an extremely nationalistic state that champions the cause of all small nations in every major statement of foreign policy. In the Sino-American communique of February 27, 1972, the Chinese side declared, "All nations big or small should be equal; big nations should not bully the small and strong nations should not bully the weak." It follows this diplomatic line not only because of Chinese hypersensitivity to infringements on national sovereignty, not only because the logical corollary to an absolute respect for sovereignty is a "withdrawal of all troops to their respective countries," thereby helping to force the United States out of Indochina completely, but also because conciliatory diplomacy is a mandatory activity in periods of "strategic-defensive" operations.

It is a central tenet of Mao Tse-tung Thought that one should never engage in conflict unless victory is certain. A truly effective (and victorious) revolutionary diplomacy is designed to postpone the final confrontation of the Chinese and Western systems (since at present the West holds every material strategic advantage) until the Chinese are in a position of preponderant strength. Progress is inevitable, either through the creation of a diffuse united front of socialist, quasi-socialist, and even more "reactionary" governments, or through a long term erosion of the opponent's will to resist localized wars (for example, supporting revolutionary groups in the enemy's own society and exploiting "revolutionary contradictions" between the opposition government and its population--many of whom will desert the cause during the course of a protracted war). Whether following the strategy of diplomatic isolation of the opponent through united front tactics or relying simply on patience and endurance, the practitioners of Mao Tse-tung Thought are confident that they can guarantee an inevitable progression of local victories--a few minor setbacks and defeats notwithstanding.

As long as there is a "base area," there is room for maneuvering, for infiltration, and for concentration of superior forces in each separate locality, all of which will permit a continuing series of local victories. These are the tactics and strategems of successful revolutionary foreign policy. In sum, "Fight no battle unprepared, fight no battle you are not sure of winning; make every effort to be well prepared for each battle, make every effort to ensure victory in the given set of conditions as between the enemy and ourselves."[3]

Here is the motto of the dedicated ideologue, of the radical voluntarist able to endure ages of conflict in the service of the collective good out of loyalty and filial obedience to the leader, the nation, and the international proletariat. Here is the essential tactic of the self-sacrificing, long suffering, but profoundly confident party cadre. (Here too is the root of the Western dilemma in east Asia and, more particularly, Indochina.)

Either by shrewd insight or good fortune, or perhaps a combination of both, Mao Tse-tung and Chou En-lai have placed P.R.C. foreign policy in a superb strategic position where they may be able to exploit the maturing forces of nationalism in Africa and the revolutionary potential of anti-American, anticolonial sentiment in the Middle East, Latin America, and southeast Asia. In the latest phase of their foreign involvements, since the denouement of the Cultural Revolution and the resumption and expansion of diplomatic linkages, the P.R.C. consistently has sought to foment insurrection, to supply training, materiel, and, where needed, Chinese personnel to build a number of nucleuses or focuses for the spread of truly revolutionary (that is, pro-Chinese) insurrections in the LDCs.

Since 1967 Chinese efforts have focused on the creation of a base area for the spread of revolutionary insurrection in Africa south of the equator through the acquisition of two allies in Nyerere's Tanzania and Kaunda's Zambia. In this instance the Chinese hope that black revolutionaries with their support can attempt to penetrate north-west into "reactionary" Zaire, or west and south into Portuguese controlled Angola and Mozambique. The subversion of Mozambique and Angola would precede a two-pronged attack (involving domestic insurrection and perhaps outright conventional intervention by the black African nations to the north) on Ian Smith's regime in Rhodesia. Eventually Chinese supported black Africans would be encouraged to mount an attack on the bastion of apartheid itself, South Africa, and to drive every white south of the Zambezi out of Africa. In the long run, this may well occur without Chinese support; but only China is in a position to exploit black resentment of the white colonialists. The Russians, like the North Americans and Western Europeans, are barred from meaningful involvement in the black revolutionary move-ment south of the Sahara.

In a not dissimilar pattern, the P.R.C. has sought to increase its influence in the Somali Democratic Republic. From this base, subversion and guerrilla warfare, supported by moderate infusions of Chinese weaponry, could be directed at Ethiopia and the Sudan. In the recent past the Somali government (a Supreme Revolutionary Coun-cil) has leaned consistently toward the USSR--accepting Soviet arma-ments and military advisers. However, should that government even-tually side with the Chinese, the P.R.C. would have the basis for a stronghold on the Gulf of Aden, since the government of South Yemen has expressed even greater interest in Chinese aid and Chinese so-cialism.

Chinese activity in the Middle East similarly is aimed at toppling reactionary governments or pro-Soviet factions in existing communist parties. From 1956-59 the P.R.C. directed considerable efforts to-ward North Africa and the Middle East, hoping to instill "revolutionary consciousness" in the Arab peoples. During the Suez crisis of 1956 it even went as far as to threaten the intervention of 300,000 Chinese soldiers. This was an extreme declaration for the Chinese and was primarily a propaganda gesture. Yet is it not an isolated example of Chinese interest in the area? Communist revolution in the Arab world long has been a Chinese goal since the Chinese view Israel's position in this region as somewhat analogous to Taiwan's in east Asia. Both nations are a prime source of "revolutionary contradic-tions." Both nations have helped to polarize local populations and augment antiimperialist and anti-American sentiments among the local inhabitants, thereby helping to generate two important "storm centers" in the global intermediate zone. In recent years the P.R.C.'s chief activities in the Arab world have centered on aiding the many liberation organizations attempting to harass Israel. Al Fatah has had a permanent representative in Peking since 1965. And the Chi-nese have been active in Syrian politics, supporting at least one important faction in the ruling Ba'thist regime at all times. However, China's efforts to acquire political and economic influence in North Africa were weakened severely when the deposition of Ben Bella of Algeria on June 19, 1965 led to the cancellation of the P.R.C. plan to hold a conference in Algiers later that month to reaffirm the solidarity of Bandung.

Apart from its support for various political movements, the P.R.C. has promoted trade and aid where possible in Africa and the Middle East, although given China's comparatively small trade/GNP ratio, the effects of this policy are negligible when spread over such a large area. Furthermore the Chinese rarely are able to provide a market for these countries, although they do attempt to buy North African cotton, Tanzanian cloves, and the like. Nor is the P.R.C. in a position to offer alternative markets to Arab oil producers--save at extreme cost to the Chinese economy. The P.R.C.'s industrial sector is still relatively small, and China is virtually self-sufficient in oil relative to its foreseeable requirements over the next 30 years. The whole question of "petroleum politics," important as it is to energy-short Western Europe, Japan, and the continental United States, is secondary, indeed almost incidental, to Peking's larger purpose in Africa and the Middle East.

The April 25, 1961 issue of the work bulletin of the PLA's General Political Department gave a succinct summation of the Chinese view of Africa:

> In Africa there are many rightists, not many leftists
> in power. . . . We must explain the Chinese revolution
> from the time of the Taiping revolt through the Boxer re-
> bellion and Sun Yat-sen to the present Communist revo-
> lution. They [the Africans] must act for themselves,
> foreign assistance being secondary only . . . [but] if
> there were one or two among the independent countries
> that would effect a real nationalist revolution their in-
> fluence would be great and a revolutionary wave would
> roll up the African continent. [4]

For a variety of reasons, Chinese influence in Latin America has been negligible. One difficulty is that the Latin American nations have firmly entrenched social and political institutions. As well, the numerous rightist military juntas have denied the P.R.C. ambassadorial representation and trade and/or cultural exchanges. The different terrain and the modern American and European armaments these regimes possess give them the capability to annihilate guerrilla movements whenever they try to impose their rule on outlying villages. Helicopter-lifted forces and a paratroop capability frequently are cited by the Cubans as evidence that Chinese methods will not succeed in Latin America, that small guerrilla groups can be wiped out easily no matter how well entrenched their base area.[5]

Chinese influence is still quite insignificant compared to the fluctuating power exercised by both Moscow (in Chile and Venezuela) and Havana (in Colombia, Venezuela, Guatemala, Uruguay, Argentina, and Peru).[6] The existing Latin American communist parties identify with either the Soviet revolutionary model or the Cuban model. The P.R.C.'s primary efforts remain at the level of exporting translations of Maoist literature and regular broadcasts in Spanish and Portuguese to these countries. And indeed the Chinese seem to be having some difficulty (because of the culture gap) in translating their "revolutionary experience" in China into comprehensible, meaningful suggestions for concrete action for the Latin Americans. In short, China has yet to obtain a sound foothold in the Western Hemisphere.

REVOLUTION OR REALPOLITIK?

Despite these difficulties in Latin America, the promotion of revolution remains a prime goal of Chinese foreign policy, especially as it pertains to the LDCs. Nevertheless, some argue that the exploitation of tactical advantages and of diplomatic-strategic opportunities ultimately could compromise China's wholehearted pursuit of world revolution. Dealing with kings, tribal chieftains, and Latin American dictators, negotiating and abiding by agreements with the two superpowers, supporting established governments (as in the case of Ceylon in 1971) rather than automatically siding with a revolutionary cause--actions such as these seem to suggest that raisons d'etat are playing an ever increasing role in Chinese foreign policy in contradistinction to the original revolutionary mania of the early 1950s and mid-1960s. Barring a radical reformulation and revision of Mao Tse-tung Thought, the authors do not believe this to be the case. The revolutionism of P.R.C. foreign policy in the 1970s merely will be more sophisticated. The acquisition of a nuclear deterrent inevitably brings with it a greater degree of circumspection, of prudence, of calculation and restraint. Hence the Chinese will exhibit a certain sophistication in the orchestration of their political and diplomatic initiatives. Beneath the gloss of raison d'etat, however, the active instigation of revolutions must remain the first goal of China's foreign policy planning because it is the very substance of China's own raison d'etre.

Another proposition, often advanced in support of a less revolutionary Chinese foreign policy, is that China's policy is increasingly dominated by security considerations, as the locations of conflict approach Chinese territory. This is at best a half-truth. Certainly the Chinese wish to maintain the territorial integrity of their nation, and in some instances (Tibet, Ladakh-Kashmir, Burma, and the Trans-Siberian region of the USSR) may even wish to press irredentist claims--if the opportunity presents itself. To some extent they will be willing to trade off the attainment of revolutionary goals in the short run--to sacrifice a present-day revolution in South Vietnam, Laos, or Cambodia to guarantee the security of their homeland--by effecting a withdrawal of U.S. troops and aircraft from the approaches to China's heartland. Yet, in their view, this is merely a necessary and prudent postponement of an ultimately certain victory for Chinese-style socialism in Indochina. The Chinese never will betray their revolutionary allies. The trauma of guilt would be too great. What they will undertake, however, is a "strategically defensive" operation in the face of a greater opposing force.

Some Western analysts would argue that it is mere rationalization for the Chinese to protect the "socialist motherland" in the name of protecting socialism in one country. It is equally arguable, and this is the view of the authors, that the defense of Chinese territory and of the Chinese socioeconomic system against the "revolutionist Kautskyites" to the north, against the Russian "collaborators," is a matter of common sense. If one believes one's country has the sole access to revealed truth, it will be an easy matter to justify to one's allies a concerned defense of the homeland even at the cost of supporting local revolutions in adjacent states. China is, after all, the base area of the global "countryside."

Moreover, it is an integral part of Mao Tse-tung Thought that each revolutionary movement must practice self-reliance. And, of course, the necessity for self-reliance minimizes the importance of the withdrawal of Chinese support for a revolution. Some analysts are disposed to view this policy as yet another rationalization of China's economic weakness, of the P.R.C.'s inability to buy revolutionary parties abroad in the Russian style. It is often said that if the P.R.C. had the resources, self-reliance would cease to be emphasized in Chinese propaganda. These are questionable propositions.

It is precisely because the Chinese wish to harness the power of nationalist sentiment to the revolutionary cause that they do not seek to create dependent allies. Instead they usually have attempted to foster "revolutionary self-reliance" in all the movements they have supported abroad. Genuine nationalism is by definition self-reliant. From their own revolutionary experience, the Chinese intuitively understand that for any prospect of eventual success a revolutionary movement must be based on profound, passionate emotions. Hence

China supported men such as Nasser, Ben Bella, Ho Chi Minh, and Nkrumah, men who they thought could inspire a diffuse popular will for national liberation. Although the Chinese believe in the capacity of the human will to overturn the most powerful and menacing opponents (the paper tiger theme), that will cannot be supplied by Chinese tanks and rifles. The determination to resist, to revolt, and also to conquer must come from the revolutionaries themselves. A successful revolutionary movement must be rooted in local tradition, local nationalism, and a local identity.

As their forebears, the most significant export of the Chinese today is culture, not commodities. Evidently firm believers in the demonstration effect, the Chinese see themselves as the purest and therefore most exemplary incarnation of the revolutionary spirit. The Chinese role in the world is to maintain the purity of the faith, to maintain and promote revolutionary consciousness.

Conflict in the Chinese view is not decided on the battlefield. It is decided long before the troops meet. It is decided in the minds of the men concerned. Wars are decided by "revolutionary political work," by creating and maintaining, through the widespread use of mutual- and self-criticism techniques, an army that fears neither suffering nor death. In some respects this ubiquitous emphasis on psychological purity, on inculcating a selfless devotion to a higher cause (liberation of one's people) is similar to fundamentalist or messianic religious movements. If the members only will believe, they are told, if they will only root out every last vestige of "sin," of selfish individualism, they will be saved.

China's totalistic uniformity does impose clearly defined obligations and constraints on the P.R.C.'s leadership. They cannot compromise the basic values for which they stand and expect to see their quasi-Orwellian system of thought control remain effective domestically. For this reason alone, it seems unlikely that the P.R.C.'s foreign policy emphasis on international revolution will degenerate into mere ritualism that invokes the symbol of revolution but avoids concrete revolutionary "praxis."

To sum up, the P.R.C.'s goals in the Third World are focused on the attainment of the revolutionary imperatives inherent in Marxist-Leninist-Maoist ideology. World revolution is still the dominant foreign policy target of China. It would be utterly naive to believe that this goal will be appreciably altered in the decades to come, although it is conceivable that its pursuit can be deflected in the short run.

The contemporary emphasis on revolutionary diplomacy, on building links with all the nations of the "intermediate" zone, on bridge-building with the arch-imperialists, the Americans, must be seen both as an attempt to increase the political costs of Soviet attack on the P.R.C. (diplomacy as a deterrence enhancer) and as an integral component of a "united front" or "strategic-defensive" period of Chinese foreign policy.

P.R.C.-supported revolutionary wars of national liberation thus will continue to be a significant source of instability in the states system in the years ahead--especially in southeast Asia, Africa, and the Middle East. Pragmatic moderation will figure in the formulation of the immediate tactics but not the long range strategy of Chinese foreign policy. In fact, it could be more useful to consider Chinese desires to conquer Taiwan and their other terra irredenta and their desire to effect a complete rollback of American forces from Indochina as a subset to the overall commitment to revolution. These security goals are means to the large end of global revolution. China's continued interest in inciting national revolution in Africa and the Middle East, its desire to prevent the spread of Soviet heresy to Pyongyang and Hanoi, exemplifies the fact that this larger purpose is the bedrock of Chinese foreign policy.

NOTES

1. Franz Michael, "Is China Expansionist: A Design for Aggression," Problems of Communism 20 (January-April 1971).

2. F. C. Darling, "Thailand and the Early Post-Vietnam Era," Current History 63 (December 1972): 265.

3. Mao Tse-tung, "The Present Situation and Our Tasks," in Six Essays on Military Affairs (Peking: Foreign Language Press, 1971), p. 388.

4. Cited in John K. Cooley, East Wind over Africa: Red China's African Offensive (New York: Walker, 1966), p. 236.

5. See Cecil Johnson's Communist China and Latin America 1959-67 (New York: Columbia University Press, 1970), for a detailed analysis of the obstacles to penetration in Latin America.

6. Brian Crozier, "The Strategic Uses of Revolutionary War," in Alastair Buchan, Problems of Modern Strategy (London: Chatto and Windus, 1970), pp. 213-14.

6

RELATIONS AMONG THE
ASIAN NUCLEAR POWERS

Soviet communism has bloomed a Soviet flower and
Chinese communism a Chinese one. Both are equally
communism but their flowers are of different hues.

Ch'en Yi, January 1963

SINO-SOVIET RELATIONS

Peking's principal preoccupation, as we have stressed, is the
threat to its sovereignty from the Soviet Union. What began as little
more than disputation between friends evolved, through "frank criticism" and heated ideological attack, to a military confrontation. As
the alientation between China and Russia grew, a corresponding interest arose in both Peking and Washington in reaching some accommodation that, from the American perspective, would permit a graceful departure from Vietnam and, from the Chinese perspective, would eliminate the distasteful and costly necessity of defending two military
fronts.

It required, however, the outbreak of actual armed conflict on
the Sino-Soviet frontier to justify such an acute reformulation of Chinese political and military thinking. When it became obvious that the
Soviet Union was absolutely unwilling to renegotiate its frontiers with
China and when it also became clear that the Russians were preparing
actively to exploit any opportunities for direct military intervention
in China, Mao's recommendation for a policy of detente with the
United States became progressively more acceptable to a majority of
the political elite. By 1969 the "twists and turns" on the path of
revolutionary diplomacy had become hairpin corners. The historical
dialectic had imposed on the P.R.C. the obligation of forming a united
front with the archimperialists themselves, "the U.S. aggressors and

all their running dogs." Even though it led to the violent deaths of key members of the Chinese politburo, the volte-face in Chinese thinking was achieved remarkably smoothly considering the magnitude of the psychological reorientation.

With the purge of Lin Piao and those who favored a rapprochement with Moscow rather than Washington, it became a central tenet of Chinese foreign policy that "to settle accounts with American imperialism it is necessary to settle accounts with Soviet revisionism."[1] This thesis was advanced by Mao during the August 1966 plenum of the Chinese Communist Party, and perhaps it was not entirely coincidental that during this same gathering of the faithful Mao nearly was ousted from office.[2]

The growth of the Sino-Soviet rift is one of the most significant developments in world politics in the postwar era, not because of any immediate political and strategic advantages that have accrued to the West, but rather because the split confirmed Chinese autonomy and, more important, established a rival center of communist orthodoxy. In the long run it would be naive to assume that the Sino-Soviet rift automatically will enhance the position of Western representative democracies. In the first place, the establishment of China as an autonomous source of communist-totalitarian political initiative may prepare the way for an ideological and strategic "division of labor" among a loose, polycentric communist alliance.[3] The possibility that the present discord in Sino-Soviet relations may be merely a prelude to a more effective regrouping of the communist forces should not be dismissed too quickly.

Second, Chinese unwillingness to acknowledge Soviet political and doctrinal hegemony has enabled the P.R.C. to experiment in alternative modes of totalitarian government. The Chinese innovations in the practice of "democratic centralism," that is to say their creation of institutionalized processes of thought control (the mutual-criticism and self-criticism techniques), have strengthened immeasurably the revolutionary prospects of the communist movement throughout the less developed countries. From the Chinese perspective, socialist revolution cannot be exported by means of takeovers, coups, or simple military aggression on their part. No doubt they consider the East European "revolutionary model" a farce. In the Chinese view, successful and genuine revolution must arise by definition from the native people, and from their transformed revolutionary consciousness. The Chinese leaders, especially Mao and his close supporters, thus have undertaken a much more ambitious revolutionary program than their Russian predecessors. They seek to accelerate the attainment of socialism by an immediate and total transformation of the psychology of people. Herein lies the secret of their success in China and, ultimately, the essence of the Chinese threat to the West.

Soviet military might is highly visible to Western electorates, and therefore it is not likely to remain undeterred. Soviet propaganda, although it received much attention in the West during the 1950s, was relatively ineffectual. Chinese behavioral modification methods are, however, qualitatively different. They are suited specifically to the psychological warfare that will develop in the less developed countries during the remaining years of this century. Mao's assessment of the Chinese people in April 1958 certainly applies to the contemporary populations of the underdeveloped nations. As the Chinese people, they are poor and "poor people want change, want to do things, want revolution." As the Chinese, many of these people are largely or totally illiterate. In Mao's conception they are all "blank pages of paper" on which "the newest and most beautiful words can be written."[4]

Thus Mao's periodic optimistic assessments of the global revolutionary situation are not merely propagandistic ritual. They reflect his sincere belief in the revolutionary potential of these nations.

Although the Sino-Soviet rift did not give the primary thrust to Chinese innovations in revolutionary practice, the split did create a situation in which the Chinese felt impelled to spread their version of Marxist-Leninist thought to the nations of the world. The rift conferred on the P.R.C. the "historical obligation" to send out missionaries to the unenlightened to combat not only "American imperialist exploitation," but also the Soviet revisionist, "social-imperialist," "social-fascist" heresy. In sum, the severe rift with Khrushchev and his successors has given the P.R.C. additional ideological-evangelical impetus.

In addition there is, for the Chinese, the question of sheer survival. The Soviet invasion of Czechoslovakia in August 1968 and the enunciation of the Brezhnev Doctrine left a grave impression on the Chinese leaders. Undoubtedly their reaction to the first electronic intelligence concerning Soviet troop buildup north of the Amur and Ussuri was graver still. As Allen Whiting observed, "The doubling of Soviet divisions, the movement of nuclear missiles into the arc surrounding Northeast China, and the appearance of new Soviet airfields in the Mongolian People's Republic posed a formidable threat which the Czech invasion put into alarming perspective."[5]

As a result, Chou En-lai explicitly raised the possibility of a Soviet invasion during his National Day address of October 1, 1968, declaring that the Chinese were prepared to "smash any invasion launched by U.S. imperialism, Soviet revisionism and their lackeys, whether individually or collectively."[6]

THE SINO-AMERICAN RAPPROCHEMENT

The Chinese postponed talks with the United States scheduled for February 1969 in Warsaw. But President Richard Nixon's occasional conciliatory comments directed at the Chinese must have found a receptive audience, especially the statements regarding the revision of American Asian policy in his Guam speech of July 25, 1969 when he outlined the so-called Nixon Doctrine.[7] Scheduled Warsaw talks were postponed again in 1970 because the American and South Vietnamese forces had begun their operations against North Vietnamese and Vietcong "sanctuaries" in Cambodia (May 1970). In spite of the tense situation on the northern border, the Chinese leaders were not going to rush into any strategic accommodation with the United States. No doubt there were several factions in the P.R.C.'s leadership elite, possibly aligned according to service interests,[8] who were extremely reluctant to initiate moves toward the United States.

By early 1971, however, the policy debate must have been largely resolved since Peking accorded Nixon's adviser, Henry Kissinger, a cordial welcome during his secret trip to China in July. In spite of the Nixon administration's desperate diplomatic moves to save the China seat in the United Nations for the Republic of China, Peking retained a profound interest in President Nixon's forthcoming visit to China, February 21-27, 1972. The product of Nixon's highly publicized, politically exploitable tour was a vague joint communique, which resolved none of the substantive obstacles between the two countries (Taiwan and their mutually exclusive policies for Indochina and southeast Asia) but which at least opened the way for greater contact between the two governments. According to the communique, future relations between the two governments would be based on

- the five principles of peaceful coexistence,
- a mutual renunciation of hegemony "in the Asia-Pacific region,"
- a mutual commitment to refrain from collusion with other "major countries," and
- a mutual commitment to refrain from policies that seek "to divide the world up into spheres of interest."

Whether there is sufficient political and economic basis for the indefinite perpetuation of the spirit of this agreement is questionable. Recent developments suggest that there is. As of September 1972, Premier Chou En-lai was reported to have affirmed to Prime Minister Tanaka that the government of the P.R.C. was "enormously worried about Soviet intentions regarding China" and that the Chinese are therefore exceedingly interested in promoting relations with "nations that might be helpful in deterring potential Soviet military action against China."[9] Whether this situation, in which the Chinese feel compelled to adopt a diffuse, united-front policy, will persist is the most critical single factor in the Asian-Pacific balance of power. The authors' analysis of the factors that lie behind the Sino-Soviet rift indicates that the hostility between the two communist giants is likely to persist.

Since the initial violence on the frontier, the Sino-Soviet dispute has become suffused thoroughly with nationalist sentiment. When the potent forces of nationalism and racism are added to the history of mutual ideological criticism and denunciation, the obstacles to a new entente become formidable indeed. Only the mutual perception of a serious common threat to both countries is likely to drive the P.R.C. and the USSR back together. Neither Japan, the United States, nor Western Europe, separately or in conjunction, is likely to generate such a threat.

At present Taiwan is a relatively modest barrier to further improvement in the Sino-American relationship. Soviet territory acquired under the "unequal treaties" of the 19th century constitutes a much more serious obstacle to significant amelioration of Soviet relations with the P.R.C.—primarily because the Chinese can expect so much more resistance from the USSR. The Chinese leaders, no matter who succeeds Mao and Chou, are not likely to abandon these territorial claims. Neither is the "Soviet revisionist, renegade clique" likely to compromise its claims to territory in the Far East. Continuing border incidents are therefore likely to become a routine topic in Sino-Soviet negotiations.[10]

Chinese territorial claims against the USSR amount to more than 1.5 million square kilometers. The value of the resources in this land, the heavy investment that the USSR has made to develop these territories, and the strategic importance of the Far Eastern ports for the rapidly growing Soviet navy are sufficient incentives to preclude any serious consideration of a negotiated return of these territories. There is, moreover, the question of the Soviet-controlled territory that has been added to the Soviet Union's western regions since World War II. Any concessions to China in the east could create problematic and embarrassing demands in the west from Finland, the former Baltic states, Poland, Czechoslovakia, and Romania.

SUMMATION

In the two and a half decades since Liberation in 1949, the most problematic task in managing the P.R.C.'s external relations has been to define the legitimate demands of national security. In contrast, the goals of Chinese ideology have always been clear-cut.

During the early postrevolutionary phase and the years of Bandung diplomacy and peaceful coexistence, economic reconstruction and the construction of socialism were the prime domestic targets of the revolution. The years of militant antiimperialism (roughly 1957-65) saw a corresponding radicalization of domestic economic policy with the Great Leap Forward. During all these phases the Chinese decision makers appear to have held a fairly constant perception of what constituted the P.R.C.'s legitimate national security claims against its smaller Asian neighbors: the reacquisition of Taiwan and other Chinese territories and the enforcement of the Chinese claim that adjacent states should not participate in the American defense network and thereby endanger China's frontiers. The acquisition of a nuclear capability became established policy during the Bandung phase--apparently in reaction to the policies of detente and peaceful coexistence formulated by Nikita Khrushchev, which, so the Chinese believed, jeopardized the prospects for the reacquisition of Taiwan.

During the years from 1950-64, the P.R.C. was always ready to listen to suggestions of enforced neutralization for Indochina and southeast Asia. By 1955 China was ringed with American air bases and national security policy was therefore focused on the prime goal of reducing the American presence in the western Pacific. The Chinese thus adopted a low profile at the Geneva Conference of 1954, even persuading the North Vietnamese to drop important demands concerning their Pathet Lao and Khmer Rouge allies.[11] Between 1954 and the rightist coup of 1964, the Chinese apparently were willing to agree to a demilitarized Laos. It was only after the coup led to the eviction of leftist forces from Vientiane and only after "covert" American military aid and advisers began pouring into Laos (in violation of the 1962 agreement) that the Chinese decided to abandon this policy. Thus there is some justification for believing that the P.R.C. might agree to neutralization proposals in the short run; though from a long term ideological perspective, it no doubt will try to press toward the communization of southeast Asia. How, and how rapidly, this policy will be implemented is exceedingly difficult to estimate because of the probable emergence of several other security goals in Chinese foreign policy.

In the years since the Cultural Revolution, China's leaders have come to appreciate the gravity of the Soviet threat. The implications for foreign policy are considerable. The Chinese see clearly that the United States is scaling down its commitments to southeast Asian security, and they also see that this policy has ramifications for the credibility of the American security guarantee to its Asian allies-- most important for Japan, Taiwan, and South Korea. From the Chinese point of view it most certainly would be preferable to have a lingering American presence to guarantee that the Soviet Union will not move in to fill a military-strategic vacuum created by the Americans' departure. The P.R.C. is in no position, economically or doctrinally, to take advantage of an American retreat to a fortress America.

In this situation the Chinese must tread cautiously, being careful not to alienate Japan to such an extent that the Japanese would be driven toward nuclear armament. The P.R.C. also must avoid creating threats to Indian security in the hope that a peaceful accommodation can forestall the proliferation of nuclear weapons to India. (See Postscript for comment.) Thus in the years since the enunciation of the Nixon Doctrine and the border conflicts between the P.R.C. and the USSR, a fundamental rethinking of Chinese foreign policy has been required. In light of the Chinese reassessment of the constellation of forces in Asia, the Chinese apparently suggested to the Japanese that it is conceivable that Peking could even join forces with Washington in defending Japan, and that an increase in Japanese defense capabilities would be welcomed by the Chinese "as a potential counterweight to the Soviet Union's aggressive designs in Asia."[12]

That such a proposal could be made by the Chinese is certainly remarkable. Although such offers contain more diplomatic gesture than strategic substance, the desire of the Chinese leadership to publicly signal a willingness to entertain radically new political-strategic perspectives surely must betoken a high degree of consensus in the P.R.C.'s decision-making elite concerning the fundamental necessity for maximizing its foreign policy options and, where possible, creating the basis for what in the future could constitute a Chinese alliance system for Asia. Obviously China's policies toward the other Asian nuclear powers inevitably will attempt to minimize the degree of Soviet-American cooperation and simultaneously to promote a rate of American withdrawal from Asia that is consistent with the prevention of any corresponding augmentation in Soviet influence. With respect to their competition with the Soviet Union for influence in east Asia, the Chinese surely must feel they are playing a zero-sum game. If the USSR gains, the P.R.C. automatically loses.

In years to come, the problem for China will be to try to maintain and to increase its influence over Indochina and the western Pacific rimlands, once these areas come largely or fully under the control of locally autonomous, authoritarian political systems (communist or nominally "Western"), who will in all probability attempt to maximize economic and political concessions from the P.R.C. by threatening to lean to the Soviet side. It is also probable that the Chinese increasingly will be concerned with yet another rival--albeit a reluctant one--who by its very nature will be acting to challenge the ideological validity of Chinese communism. It is to Japan that our attention now turns.

NOTES

1. Christian Science Monitor, November 11, 1970.
2. Ibid., March 11, 1967.
3. For a detailed statement of this theme see Franz Michael, "Is China Expansionist? A Design for Aggression," Problems of Communism 20 (January-April 1971).
4. Mao Tse-tung, "Introducing a Farm Co-op" in K. Fan, ed., Mao Tse-tung and Lin Piao: Post-Revolutionary Writings (Garden City, N.Y.: Anchor Books, 1972).
5. Allen S. Whiting, "The Sino-American Detente: Genesis and Prospect," paper presented to the Australian Institute for International Affairs Conference: China and the World Community, June 1972, Melbourne, p. 2.
6. Peking Review October 4, 1968, quoted in ibid., pp. 4-5 (emphasis added).
7. See ibid.
8. Whiting, for one, considers this a plausible interpretation (see ibid., pp. 8-9).
9. William Beecher, "Chou Is Said to Have Given Japan Military Assurances," New York Times, December 14, 1972.
10. Serious incidents occurred as recently as November 1972. See Toronto Globe and Mail, December 11, 1972.
11. Ross Terrill, "China and Southeast Asia," paper presented to the Australian Institute for International Affairs Conference: China and the World Community, June 1972, Melbourne, p. 7.
12. Beecher, op. cit.

PART

II

JAPAN

There are only two alternatives for noble men; either to be at the head of all, or to fade away into the forest.

Hindu proverb

7

A TIME OF
REASSESSMENT

Stick to one thing and all will come; aim at everything
and all will go.

Hindu proverb

THE ECONOMIC MIRACLE

For the past quarter-century Japan has focused its national ener-
gies on a single all-consuming objective; the maximization of economic growth. The unprecedented magnitude of the Japanese accomplishment led George Ball to write that "compared with this island
nation's progress the German economic miracle appears as appren-
tice magic."[1] The statistical record bears witness to the extraordinary development of Japanese economic might. Japan's gross national product (GNP) has grown from a mere U.S.$14 billion in 1951
to U.S.$255 billion in 1971 and is now surpassed only by those of the
United States and the Soviet Union. The annual volume growth of
Japan's GNP at constant (1963) prices averaged 12.1 percent during
the 1965-70 period (see Table 7.1). Even in 1971, at the height of
its longest postwar recession, Japan's economy still was able to
generate a real GNP growth of 6 percent.[2]

Japan has not gained merely membership in the elite group of
advanced industrial nations; it has become an economic superpower
with global interests. Japan leads the world in such areas as shipbuilding, transistorized television sets, and commercial motor vehicles. In the production of such items as computers, rayon, aluminum,
copper, steel, cement, and plastics Japan ranks second. From 1965-
70, Japan expanded its share of the world's exports from 4.8 to 6.9
percent.[3] Japan's trade was 10 times greater in 1970 than in 1955.

TABLE 7.1

GNP Annual Volume Growth at Constant (1963) Prices for
Selected Countries, 1965-70
(in percent)

Japan	12.1
Italy	6.0
France	5.8
West Germany	4.5
Canada	4.5
Sweden	3.9
United States	3.3
United Kingdom	2.1

Source: Organization for Economic Cooperation and Development, Economic Surveys: Japan 1972 (Paris: OECD, 1972), abstracted from data in chart following p. 72.

Yet the ratios of exports and imports to GNP have not changed significantly since 1955, and they are smaller than in any industrial country except the United States (see Tables 7.2 and 7.3).

There is little disagreement about the key elements that cumulatively have generated Japan's postwar economic dynamism. Only the relative weighting of the various components is open to speculation.

Foremost among the sociopolitical factors is the singular degree of racial, cultural, and linguistic homogeneity in Japanese society that provides the foundation for national unity. This homogeneity is largely the product of Japan's geographical isolation, an isolation that has meant an historical absence of both large scale migration into the Japanese islands and, until 1945, a successful foreign invasion. This society, perhaps because of its homogeneity, also appears to possess an extraordinary propensity for what Herman Kahn has called "purposive communal action." That is to say, Japan has exhibited a unique capacity to define long range national goals that could command virtually total support and dedication. In the postwar era, the national objective has been "catching up with the West" through the maximization of economic growth. And this goal has been achieved, it is said, largely because the Japanese people, individually and collectively, are highly motivated, well educated (particularly in mathematics and the sciences), achievement- and work-oriented, energetic, self-disciplined, and loyal (to family, to firm,

TABLE 7.2

Exports and Imports as Percentage of GNP for Selected Countries
at 1969 Prices

	Exports	Imports
Canada	24.8	25.3
France	15.1	15.7
Germany	23.6	21.0
Italy	20.5	18.2
Netherlands	48.3	48.0
Sweden	23.1	23.8
United Kingdom	24.4	22.7
Japan	11.4	10.0
United States	5.9	5.6

Source: Organization for Economic Cooperation and Development, Economic Surveys: Japan 1972 (Paris: OECD, 1972), abstracted from data in chart following p. 78.

TABLE 7.3

Exports and Imports as Percentage of Japan's GNP, Current Prices

	Exports	Imports
1955	11.4	10.5
1969	11.4	10.0
1971	12.6	9.9

Sources: The 1955 figures are taken from the GATT study, Japan's Economic Expansion and Foreign Trade 1955-1970 (Geneva: GATT, 1971); the 1969 and 1971 figures are from Organization for Economic Cooperation and Development, Economic Surveys: Japan 1972 (Paris: OECD, 1972).

and to country). In addition, postwar Japan has enjoyed a lengthy period of relative sociopolitical stability in which to pursue its economic growth. The American occupation (1945-52) preempted an internal division of the Japanese state along cold war East-West lines and introduced a constitutional framework that provided a workable and stable government system essential to rebuilding the national polity from the rubble and chaos of defeat. After 1949, the American policy to "contain" the People's Republic of China implied that a militarily secure, politically stable, and economically sound Japan was a matter of vital interest to the United States.

Among the inland economic changes contributing to Japan's growth (see Table 7.4) was the postwar movement of large numbers of people from the primary agricultural sector to the developing urban industrial centers, thus providing the Japanese economy with an unlimited and cheap supply of labor until the mid-1960s. During the same period, rapid increases in personal income made possible growing domestic consumption and, therefore, an expanding domestic market. In addition, an exceptionally high propensity for personal savings (around 20 percent of a constantly rising personal income) yielded an expanding pool of capital, which Japanese banks made available for large scale investment. Wartime destruction together with an extremely high investment ratio (the ratio of gross investment to GNP for the period 1955-64 was a remarkable 33 percent, about twice the U.S. figure[4]) made it possible to create modern and efficient plants and equipment on a massive scale. Many of these new industrial complexes were constructed on the coast of Japan, which has permitted the delivery of raw materials as well as the movement of finished products by inexpensive maritime transport. A large prewar technological lag made possible a rapid introduction (usually through licensing arrangements with foreign companies-- mostly American and West German--thereby allowing independence in ownership and management) and adaptation of new methods at a rate faster than the rate of technological progress in countries that were already at or near the frontiers of known technology.

The institution of an official policy of economic protectionism-- in the form of stringent exchange controls and restrictions on imports and foreign investment--provided the prophylactic necessary in the early stages of postwar Japanese economic expansion. The continued existence of buoyant world markets in which Japan initially had a small or even negligible share, together with a systematically undervalued currency, made possible a rapid growth in Japanese exports without excessive disruption of other national economies. The expansion of Japanese exports in turn generated further investment, usually in increasingly sophisticated and technologically intensive products, thereby reinforcing whatever competitive advantage Japanese exports already enjoyed.

TABLE 7.4

Basic Statistics of Japan

Area:	370,000 sq. km.*
Population (1971 estimate):	104,890,000
Net average annual population increase (1960-70):	1.06 percent
Persons per sq. km. (1971):	283
Production:	
1970 GNP:	U.S.$195 billion
1971 estimated GNP:	U.S.$255 billion
Annual volume growth of GNP at 1963 constant prices (1970):	10.9 percent
Gross saving as percent of GNP (1965-69 average):	37.9 percent
Foreign trade 1971:	
Commodity exports, FOB:	U.S.$23,650 million
Commodity imports, FOB:	U.S.$15,750 million
Current balance:	U.S.$5,898 million
Basic balance:	U.S.$4,737 million
Export of goods and services as percent of GNP:	12.6
Imports of goods and services as percent of GNP:	9.9

(July 1971: U.S.$1 = 360 yen; July 1972: U.S.$1 = 308 yen)

Net flow of resources to developing countries as percent of GNP (1970):	0.93 percent
Defense budget:	
1971-72:	$1.864 billion
1972-73:	$2.600 billion
Defense expenditures as percent of GNP:	0.80 percent

*Or 143,663 sq. miles.

Source: Compiled by author.

The American military effort during the Korean and, to a lesser degree, the Vietnam wars involved the extensive use of Japanese territory as a major forward base for operations on and around the Asian mainland. The additional economic stimulus that the American presence generated is difficult to quantify but should not be underestimated.

Finally, although defense expenditures have increased from U.S.$86 million in 1951 to U.S.$1.86 billion in 1971, postwar Japanese military spending consistently has been under 1 percent of GNP, less than most industrialized nations.[5] This has freed large amounts of capital, manpower, and talent for use elsewhere in the economy.

CHANGING DOMESTIC PRIORITIES

Japan's spectacular and rapid postwar recovery, achieved through the single-minded pursuit of economic growth, has left in its wake pressing social and economic problems whose solution will influence profoundly the structure of Japan's economy over the next decade. In the words of an official Japanese document, "the time has come when the growth of the Japanese economy must be geared primarily to the development of a high welfare society."[6]

Massive capital expenditure on social development is called for in several fields. Social and health care are woefully inadequate by Western standards. Transport related services were unable to keep pace with rapid increases in demand, averaging 18.5 percent a year during the 1960s, despite rising government expenditures. Only 15 percent of Japan's roads were paved in 1969, but the number of passenger automobiles increased more than threefold.[7] The scale of postwar industrialization and its heavy concentration in the Tokyo-Osaka belt renders further and more extensive government measures in the field of environmental pollution indispensable during the 1970s if Japan is not to "choke on its GNP."[8] The need for housing is both astonishingly large and increasingly rapid. According to the Ministry of Construction, 3 million households out of a total of 29 million were in urgent need of new housing in 1969.[9] A further complication of the housing problem has been the rapid increase in construction costs due to labor shortages and the price of urban land, which rose an average of 17.5 percent a year from 1960-70.[10] These soaring prices substantially eroded funds allocated not only to housing but also to public works in general.

The transition to a high-welfare economy involves the difficult task of altering an established and highly successful (in terms of maximizing growth) economic structure. The Japanese government is not unaware of the immensity and urgency of the task and of the necessity to involve the public sector increasingly in the creation of social goods and social capital. The New Economic and Social Development Plan for 1970-75 called for the share of government investment in real GNP to increase from 8.6 percent in fiscal year 1969 to 10.1 percent in fiscal year 1975. These figures would indicate an annual growth rate of 13.5 percent at constant prices. The Japanese Economic Research Center predicted an annual rise of 21.5 percent in public investment for the same period. Recent data released by the Ministry of Construction project a 14 percent share for government fixed investment in GNP (at 1965 prices) for the 1970-80 period.[11] The high level of government expenditure in fiscal year 1972 on such items as road building, housing, health services, and social welfare is intended to mark a permanent shift in the pattern of national priorities, objectives, and expenditures, as well as to serve the immediate purpose of combating Japan's most severe postwar recession.

Although its precise magnitude is still in doubt, the shift in resource utilization required by expanding public intervention in the creation of a high-welfare economy clearly will need to be sizable. It will necessitate a diminishing emphasis on private capital investment (a key element in Japan's record of economic dynamism) and a concomitant rise in public investment, income transfers, and tax revenue in relation to GNP. Improving social and health care and growing public consumption will tend to alter savings and investment ratios and will affect traditional employment and production patterns. The allocation of a higher proportion of resources to national welfare undoubtedly will result in a somewhat slower growth of real GNP during the next decade than the 12 percent achieved over the 1965-70 period. The size of the slowdown is difficult to estimate. The New Economic and Social Development Plan projected a 10.6 percent average annual growth rate in real GNP for fiscal years 1970-75. This plan, however, was drawn up in the late 1960s and presently is being revised by the government.

It is the peculiar dilemma of advanced industrial nations that the problems generated by rapid economic growth can be solved only by continued growth. This is strikingly true in the case of Japan. On the one hand, continuing economic prosperity is essential if the rising expectations created over the past 25 years are to be met and social and political stability maintained. On the other hand, a massive shift in national priorities and in the allocation of national resources--changes that will almost certainly result in some slowdown in growth--is urgently required if the negative byproducts of earlier expansion are to be dealt with. Japan's present and potential wealth, its historical success in creating and adapting to economic structural transformations, and its national capacities for flexibility and discipline provide grounds for optimism as Japan moves from rapid economic expansion to maturity as an economic superpower.

THE NIXON DOCTRINE

The reassessment of Japan's domestic economic strategy has been paralleled by the necessity to reexamine the assumptions on which Japan has based its postwar external relations and the international environment in which it must operate in the 1970s. This has come about as the result of an apparently fundamental shift in the foreign policy of the United States, Japan's chief ally and the guarantor of its strategic security. In his inaugural address in 1961 President John Kennedy enunciated U.S. foreign policy to America's allies and adversaries: "Let every nation know, whether it wishes us well or ill, that we shall pay any price, bear any burden, meet any hardship, support any friend, oppose any foe to assure the survival and success of liberty. This much we pledge--and more." In the aftermath of the Indochina war, this unequivocal posture has given way to a more cautious foreign policy for the 1970s: "We shall do our share in defending peace and freedom in the world, but we shall expect others to do their share. The time has passed when America will make every other nation's conflict our own, or make every other nation's future our responsibility, or presume to tell other nations how to manage their own affairs."[12]

The principal elements of this posture--the Nixon Doctrine--had been outlined by President Nixon on November 3, 1969. Briefly, these were three in number.

- "The United States will keep all its treaty commitments."
- "We shall provide a shield if a nuclear power threatens the freedom of a nation allied with us, or of a nation whose survival we consider vital to our security and the security of the region [Asia] as a whole."
- "In cases involving other types of aggression we shall furnish military and economic assistance when requested and as appropriate. But we shall look to the nation directly threatened to assume the primary responsibility of providing the manpower for its defense."[13]

The Nixon Doctrine grew from the president's now well-known perception of an emerging world order characterized by a multipolar configuration that includes the United States, the Soviet Union, the People's Republic of China, the expanded European community, and Japan. In addition, the doctrine reflects the president's emphasis in the conduct of foreign and strategic policy on greater self-restraint through the minimization of overseas manpower deployments and defense expenditures incurred as a result of relations with allies, and greater flexibility through an expansion of the dialogue--from a position of strength and leadership--with traditional enemies.

In sum, Nixon appears to envision a world order in which the conventional defense of American allies will be repatriated progressively with the help of U.S. military assistance and under the continued protection of the U.S. nuclear umbrella, thereby facilitating the evolution of a series of regional equilibriums to replace the post-war bipolar system.

Japan's response to the Nixon Doctrine is best described as ambivalent. The principles of the doctrine and the growing atmosphere of detente that the doctrine, in part, has helped to bring about facilitate (indeed, necessitate) the exercise of greater autonomy by Japan in its diplomatic strategy, particularly toward China. As such, it is welcomed. Nevertheless, it is difficult for many Japanese to see how the United States can be committed to honoring its treaty responsibilities while simultaneously hoping to lighten its defense burden with respect to its allies. The credibility of the American security umbrella is thought to be placed in some doubt by what is perceived as a weakening of the American will to maintain international order (the threat of neoisolationism). The Nixon Doctrine, it is feared, eventually will result in the large scale reduction of American military power in Asia.

President Nixon stated that Japan is crucial to the successful implementation of the Nixon Doctrine in Asia.[14] The four-power configuration, which he sees evolving in Asia, suggests that the president expects Japan to become a military (possibly nuclear) and diplomatic power, as well as an economic and political one.[15] Japan does not appear anxious to take on such a role. Indeed, barring dramatic changes in the domestic and international environment, it is most unlikely that Japan will become a military/diplomatic power on a scale comparable with the United States, the USSR, or even China during the 1970s.

Uncertainty--and therefore anxiety--as to how stability and peace in Asia are to be obtained under the Nixon Doctrine, and what form Japan's contribution is to take, thus has been created. This situation was no doubt aggravated by Nixon's unilateral initiatives toward China (despite repeated presidential statements on the need for a U.S.-Japan partnership) and a growing tendency on the part of the United States-- vividly exemplified by the economic shock tactics in August 1971--to treat Japan as a competitor/adversary as well as an ally.

The Nixon Doctrine has forced Japan to define for itself an active foreign policy and a role in Asia and the world concomitant with its international economic and political stature. Although this will not be an easy task, the necessity of undertaking it is clearly understood in Tokyo. Japan's posture toward the Soviet Union and the People's Republic of China--long determined by the precepts of cold war power politics--has begun to change both rapidly and profoundly. But perhaps most important, Japan inevitably will endeavor to move its relationship with the United States in the direction of greater equality.

NOTES

1. George W. Ball, The Discipline of Power (Boston: Little, Brown, and Co., 1968), p. 184.

2. Organization for Economic Cooperation and Development, Economic Surveys: Japan 1972 (Paris: OECD, 1972), chart following p. 5 and p. 78.

3. John K. Emmerson, Arms, Yen and Power (New York: Dunellen, 1971), p. 12.

4. B. Higgins, Economic Development: Problems, Principles and Policies (New York: W. W. Norton, 1968), p. 630.

5. International Institute for Strategic Studies, Military Balance 1972-3 (London: IISS, 1972), p. 73.

6. Japan, Economic Planning Agency, Economic Survey of Japan, 1969-70 (Tokyo: Japan Times, 1970), p. 149.

7. See Economic Planning Agency, Economic Survey of Japan, 1968-69 (Tokyo: Japan Times, 1969), pp. 187-88.

8. See Japan Institute of International Affairs, "The Human Environment in Japan," in White Papers of Japan 1970-71 (Tokyo: J.I.I.A., 1972), pp. 246-47.

9. OECD, op. cit., p. 49.

10. Ibid., p. 16.

11. Ibid., p. 52.

12. Richard M. Nixon, Second Inaugural Address, 1973.

13. U.S. Foreign Policy for the 1970's: A New Strategy for Peace, A Report to the Congress by Richard Nixon, February 18, 1970 (Washington, D.C.: U.S. Government Printing Office, 1970), pp. 55-56.

14. Ibid., p. 58.

15. Nixon has said, however, that "we shall not ask Japan to assume responsibilities inconsistent with the deeply felt concerns of its people." Ibid., p. 61.

8

THE RELATIONSHIP
WITH THE UNITED STATES

It is easy to dodge the arrow of an enemy, but difficult
to avoid the spear of a friend.

Epigram from Ming Dynasty

Relations with the United States have for the two decades, since
the recovery of national independence in 1952, been the principal consideration of Japan's foreign and security policy calculations. That
the preservation of stable and amiable relations with the United States
was the fundamental prerequisite for Japan's economic recovery and
sense of national security has been a view widely held within the Japanese political/bureaucratic/business elite, which has ruled the country virtually without interruption for the past 20 years. The primacy
of the Japan-U.S. relationship and the concomitant belief that Japan's
basic interests coincided with America's allowed Japan to adopt a
"low" external political posture and the position that economic and
political matters were separable in international affairs.

The original pattern of Japan's security policy was forged largely
by the harsh realities of an emerging cold war bipolarity during the
immediate postwar period. The international environment of those
years produced a variety of political and military developments that
profoundly affected the options available to Japanese policy makers.

After an initial demobilization of forces in the aftermath of World
War II, an action not duplicated by the Soviet Union, the president of
the United States enunciated the Truman Doctrine to the Congress on
March 12, 1947. The path of appeasement was not to be taken again.
During the 1947 May Day parade in Moscow, the Russians displayed
for the first time their new four-engine jet bomber and a new two-
engine jet fighter. In February 1948, Czechoslovakia fell to a communist coup; and in June a massive allied airlift was required to relieve

Soviet pressure on West Berlin, that vulnerable outpost just inside the iron curtain. The USSR exploded its first atomic device in September 1949, a brief five months after the formation of the North Atlantic Treaty Organization (NATO) alliance and two years earlier than even the most pessimistic of Western predictions. As 1949 came to a close, Mao Tse-tung's armies completed the "liberation" of the Chinese mainland and Mao traveled to Moscow to sign the Treaty of Friendship, Alliance, and Mutual Assistance. By mid-1950, communist armies were again on the march, this time on the Korean peninsula. Communism appeared to assume truly global dimensions.

Within this international environment, Japan sought to ensure its economic and political recovery and its national security. Two specific threats were believed to menace Japan: the Soviet Union's military force stationed in east Asia and the possibility of a Soviet-inspired and Soviet-assisted insurrection.

When the USSR, in violation of its neutrality pact with Japan, entered the war in the Pacific in August 1945, Soviet forces captured and occupied four small Japanese islands immediately off the northern coast of Hokkaido-Etorofu and Kunashiri, commonly referred to as the southern Kuriles, and Shikotan and Habomai. With an area of some 2,000 square miles, these islands are large enough for military operations. Habomai is a mere five miles from Hokkaido, and Kunashiri about 20 miles. The island of Sakhalin, where Soviet forces were stationed, is 50 miles from Hokkaido. Although the deployment of these Soviet forces within easy range of Japanese population and industrial centers was not taken to signal imminent invasion, their existence hardly could be ignored by a demilitarized Japan with neither the means nor the will to defend the nation.

The internal threat to Japan's security seemed equally compelling during the immediate postwar period. Japanese prisoners held in Manchuria by Soviet forces began to be repatriated during 1947. These men had received a thorough communist indoctrination[1] and had been told to support the Japanese communist party.[2] After months of economic disruption by Japanese labor unions (some of which had received organizational assistance from a massive 400-man Soviet mission in Tokyo[3]), a nationwide general strike was called for February 1, 1947 by a coalition of left-wing socialists and communists. The strike, which no doubt would have crippled the struggling Japanese economy, was prohibited successfully by order of General Douglas MacArthur, backed by American occupation forces. Although abortive, the strike provided undeniable evidence of a powerful threat to Japan's internal stability and security.

In response to these two fundamental dangers, successive Japanese governments have sought, first, an American security guarantee against attack by a foreign power, and, second, to create indigenous forces that, at a minimum, could maintain internal peace and stability. In the bipolar cold war world, a world in which U.S. strategy involved the containment of Soviet and Chinese power through the global deployment of massive strategic and conventional military power, there could be no realistic alternative to a Japan-U.S. security relationship.

The 1951 and 1960 security treaties have been the core of this relationship. The 1951 treaty was signed in San Francisco on September 8.[4] The treaty placed no limitations on the use of American military installations and forces in Japan and in this way provided a de facto guarantee of Japanese security. "The United States assumes no treaty obligation to maintain land, air and sea forces in and about Japan or to guarantee the security and independence of Japan, although this will be a practical result of the exercise by the United States of its right to station its forces in Japan."[5] Although the treaty avoided stating any direct commitment to extensive Japanese rearmament, it did express the hope that Japan would take steps, subject to the limitations imposed by the availability of resources and the Japanese constitution,[6] to create forces capable of taking increasing responsibility for Japan's external and internal security.

The Treaty of Mutual Cooperation and Security,[7] signed on January 19, 1960, was, from Japan's point of view, a more favorable arrangement than the 1951 treaty, even though widespread and violent demonstrations accompanying its ratification by the Japanese Diet in June 1960 forced cancellation of President Dwight Eisenhower's trip to Japan and brought down the government of Prime Minister Nobusuke Kishi. Article V of that treaty clearly committed the United States to the defense of Japan but limited Japan's defense responsibilities to Japanese territory. "Each Party recognizes that an armed attack against either Party in the territories under the administration of Japan would be dangerous to its own peace and safety and declares that it would act to meet the common danger in accordance with its constitutional provisions and processes."

Article VI of the treaty allowed U.S. forces continued access to military installations in Japan, "for the purpose of contributing to the security of Japan and the maintenance of international peace and security in the Far East." However, the continued existence of the treaty was not related to article VI. It expressed Japan's willingness to place facilities at the disposal of U.S. military forces; it in no way committed the United States to make use of these facilities. At the insistence of the Japanese government, a formal exchange of notes accompanied the 1960 treaty. Designed to provide Japan with some control over U.S. facilities and forces in Japan, it stated, "Major changes in the deployment into Japan of United States armed forces, major changes in their equipment, and the use of facilities and areas in Japan as bases for military combat operations to be undertaken from Japan other than those conducted under Article V of the said Treaty, shall be the subjects of prior consultation with the Government of Japan." Needless to say, the strategically vital U.S. facilities on Okinawa were unaffected by this provision since Okinawa was not (until May 1972) under the jurisdiction of the Japanese government.

Finally, by avoiding all references to internal security, the 1960 treaty, unlike its predecessor, removed the possibility that U.S. forces stationed in Japan could be used to maintain domestic stability. Internal security became the sole responsibility of the Japanese government.

As the 1960s came to an end, Japan, now an economic power with growing national confidence and pride, seemed willing to move a step farther and acknowledge security interests beyond the commitment to defend the Japanese homeland. The Sato-Nixon joint communique of November 21, 1969, [8] for example, stated that "the security of the Republic of Korea was essential to Japan's own security" and that "the maintenance of peace and security in the Taiwan area was also a most important factor for the security of Japan." The communique seemed to announce Japanese acceptance of the Nixon Doctrine, whose enunciation had appeared to signal the beginning of the end of cold war bipolarity and the emergence of political and economic, if not military, multipolarity. A generally lowered American profile, particularly in Asia, and the need for increasing responsibility on the part of the U.S. allies for their own defense, clearly were indicated. "The United States will participate in the defense and development of allies and friends, but . . . America cannot--and will not--conceive all the plans, design all the programs, execute all the decisions and undertake all the defense of the free nations of the world. We will help where it makes a real difference and is considered in our interest."[9]

Despite Nixon's repeated assurances that the United States would not abandon "old friends," the implementation of the Nixon Doctrine generated unavoidable and understandable concern in Japan regarding the precise ramifications of the doctrine for U.S. commitments and force deployment in Asia, particularly in the event of an American withdrawal from Indochina. These anxieties escalated appreciably during 1971. On July 15 came Nixon's startling announcement that Kissinger had conducted secret talks with Chou En-lai and that the president himself would visit China early in 1972, thus signaling the end of the policy of "containment." One month later, on August 15, the president delivered a second blow, aimed largely at Japan, in the form of his new economic policies. These measures included the imposition of a 10 percent surcharge on U.S. imports, the suspension of dollar convertibility to gold, and the imposition of textile quotas, all of which led directly to an upward revaluation of the Japanese yen in December 1971.

The China "shock" resulted more from the form than from the content of the announcement. For years the United States had stressed the necessity for coordination and consultation with respect to China policy, a matter of great importance to both countries. Yet Nixon's decision to seek an improvement in U.S.-China relations was taken without consulting its closest and oldest ally in Asia. This new China policy had a number of repercussions in Tokyo. The general trust and good faith with which the Sato government had conducted its relations with the United States seemed seriously discredited. A more independent style would be required in the future, and a change in leadership became inevitable.

The threat to Japan's security posed by a China armed with nuclear weapons, already marginal in Japanese eyes, seemed further diminished. But the unilateral American efforts to generate detente with China made it necessary to reexamine Japan's own policy toward Peking.

The Shanghai communique,[10] signed by Nixon and Chou En-lai at the end of the president's trip to China, contained a Chinese denunciation of "the revival and outward expansion of Japanese militarism" that was alleviated only nominally by the affirmation that the United States continued to place the "highest value on friendly relations with Japan." From Tokyo's perspective, the credibility of the U.S. security guarantee to Japan seemed to be in some doubt.

Many Japanese, most notably the opposition parties, already had come to believe that the original assumptions underlying the Japan-United States Security Treaty (which was extended automatically by the Sato government in 1970) were no longer valid (see Table 8.1). The international environment at the time the treaty was negotiated was characterized by cold war bipolarity between the United States and the USSR, and the principal objective of American foreign policy in Asia was the containment of China. Critics of the 1960 treaty now maintain that with the recent thaw in Sino-American hostility, the gradual lessening of tension between the United States and the USSR, and the continuing Sino-Soviet rift, the treaty has lost its fundamental raison d'etre. They therefore demand its abrogation.

Such an analysis, however, is overly simplistic. Although the international climate clearly is improving, Japan's defense planners (who must be concerned with the medium and long term as well as the short term) are not likely to ignore the potential threats that Chinese and, more important, Soviet military power continue to pose for Japanese strategic security. The termination of the treaty would create intense pressure for a rapid expansion of Japan's mili-

TABLE 8.1

Changing Japanese Public Opinion on the Security Treaty
(in percent)

Year	Support	Oppose	Do Not Know
1947	40.1	28.2	31
1958	21	28	51
1969	31.7	24.1	44.2

Source: Yomiuri Shimbun poll, Yomiuri Shimbun, 16, December 1969, p. 21, cited in K. H. Pringsheim, "Japan's Position in East Asia," paper presented at a conference on Japan and Superpowers--Friend, Partner, Rival, February 18-19, Saskatoon.

tary capability, probably including the acquisition of nuclear weapons. Such a policy would entail heavy domestic and external political and economic costs for Tokyo. The continued existence and credibility of the treaty also can be seen to be in the interests of the Soviet Union and of China insofar as the treaty tends to contain the development of an expanded, autonomous Japanese military capability by curbing a Japanese conventional and (more important) nuclear buildup.

There seems to be no viable alternative to maintenance of the Japanese-U.S. security relationship in the near to medium term. The United States will continue to provide Japan with its largest market (taking over 30 percent of Japan's exports) and the ultimate protection of its nuclear deterrent. However, the realities of Japanese strength and the changing international system necessarily will transform the relationship in the direction of greater equality and reciprocity.

The Fourth Defense Build-Up Plan announced that Japan would seek to provide conventional defense for the home islands as American forces are reduced. An American security guarantee without the stationing of U.S. forces on Japanese soil may be the eventual outcome.

Emerging multipolarity implies "looser ties between associates as well as a modest rapprochement between opponents."[11] The increasing political mobility that the new international environment confers on Japan will provide Tokyo with added leverage in its dealings with Washington. The recent improvement in Sino-Japanese relations and a possible warming of Soviet-Japanese relations will tend to increase the American interest in maintaining friendly and equitable relations with Japan.

NOTES

1. For a more detailed discussion of this matter see R. Swearingen and P. F. Langer, Red Flag in Japan (Cambridge, Mass.: Harvard University Press, 1952), pp. 232-34; W. J. Sebald, With MacArthur in Japan (New York: W. W. Norton, 1965), pp. 136-48; and C. A. Willoughby and J. Chamberlain, MacArthur: 1941-1945 (New York: McGraw-Hill, 1954), pp. 320-21.

2. The Japanese party became a legal political party in October 1945 as part of the attempt by the occupation authority to democratize Japan by guaranteeing freedom of political expression.

3. Sebald, op. cit., p. 134; Willoughby and Chamberlain, op. cit., p. 325.

4. The text of the treaty may be found in U.S. Department of State, Bulletin 25 (September 10, 1951); 464-65. For an analysis of the negotiations leading to its signature, see Martin E. Weinstein, Japan's Postwar Defense Policy (New York: Columbia University Press, 1971), pp. 43-63.

5. John Foster Dulles, "Security in the Pacific," Foreign Affairs 30 (January 1952): 179.

6. The so-called "no-war" article, article IX in the Japanese constitution, renounces war and the use of armed forces as a "means of settling international disputes."

7. The text of the treaty and accompanying documents may be found in U.S. Department of State, Bulletin 42 (February 8, 1960): 179-200. For an analysis of the negotiations leading to its signature, see Weinstein, op. cit., pp. 87-103.

8. Text may be found in U.S. Department of State, Bulletin 61 (December 15, 1969): 555-58.

9. U.S. Foreign Policy for the 1970's: A New Strategy for Peace, A Report to the Congress by Richard Nixon, February 18, 1970 (Washington, D.C.: U.S. Government Printing Office, 1970), p. 6.

10. Text may be found in U.S. Department of State, Bulletin 66 (March 20, 1972): 435.

11. International Institute for Strategic Studies, Strategic Survey 1971 (London: IISS, 1972), p. 5.

Even a sheep bites a man without a stick.

Hindu proverb

SECURITY THREATS

Japan is not menaced by any <u>immediate</u> external threat to its
national security. However, both Japanese and foreign strategic analysts identify two <u>potential</u> military threats to Japan: the People's
Republic of China and the Soviet Union.

The P.R.C.'s limited but growing nuclear capability has been
monitored closely by Tokyo. However, because of the protection offered by the American nuclear umbrella, the fundamentally defensive
orientation of Chinese military posture, and the Sino-Soviet rift (cli-
maxing in armed clashes in 1969 and rumors of a possible Soviet
"surgical" strike against Chinese nuclear installations), the Chinese
nuclear arsenal has generated little visible concern within the Japanese government. In addition, the P.R.C. lacks the capability to
launch a conventional naval and/or air strike against the Japanese
islands. Finally, the thaw in Sino-American relations and, more important, the normalization of Sino-Japanese relations on September
29, 1972 (less than three months after Tanaka was sworn in as Premier Eisaku Sato's successor) can serve only to reinforce the (justifiable) perception in Tokyo that the potential military threat posed by
the P.R.C. is marginal.

The Soviet Union, on the other hand, continues to be perceived
by Tokyo as posing <u>the</u> potential external military threat for Japanese
security. The Soviet attack on Japan during the last days of World
War II despite a Soviet-Japanese neutrality pact, the brutal treatment

received by some 600,000 Japanese prisoners of war in Soviet-occupied Manchuria, the seizure (and continuing occupation) of four small Japanese islands just off the north shore of Hokkaido, the harassment of Japanese fishermen--these events have not been forgotten by the Japanese public and government. The USSR is a superpower possessing an advanced industrial economy, the total output of which is surpassed at present only by that of the United States. The Soviet nuclear force, which, unlike the Chinese arsenal, includes an invulnerable second-strike capability, has achieved a rough parity with the American deterrent. Also, the USSR possesses an expanding conventional capability (particularly in naval forces) with a growing potential for global intervention, hitherto a monopoly enjoyed by the United States. This development is particularly important for Japan in light of its virtually total dependence on the import of raw materials by maritime transport, often over long distances. To mention but one obvious example, over 95 percent of Japan's oil requirements are at present shipped by tanker from the Middle East (an area where Soviet influence is not unimportant) and pass through the vulnerable Malacca Straits. The future strategic implications of the large scale withdrawal of British forces from Asia and the simultaneous expansion of the activities of the Soviet Pacific fleet, particularly in the Indian Ocean,[1] have not been lost on Japanese defense planners.

At least over the short to medium term, Japan's ultimate security seems destined to remain dependent on the American nuclear guarantee. However, from Tokyo's perspective, the future credibility of the U.S. strategic umbrella may be in some doubt, since America's relative power and the will to exercise it against the Soviet Union commonly is perceived to be declining and since the posture of U.S. forces in the Far East is being lowered progressively in line with the Nixon Doctrine. The ultimate extent of the American presence in Asia after the cessation of armed conflict in Vietnam is therefore a source of considerable concern to the Asian allies of the United States. This concern persists despite the fact that American military power in Asia--although less visible than in the past and with an altered configuration and purpose--seems likely to remain substantial. Security commitments that do not have direct and tangible ramifications for fundamental U.S. national interests will be avoided. Nevertheless, the United States likely will maintain a highly mobile and flexible offshore presence supported by an extensive logistics and deployment capability (for example, the C-5A and the projected Fast Deployment Logistics Ships), which will make possible a rapid interposition of U.S. forces without a massive, forward-based presence on the Asian mainland.

CONSTRAINTS ON JAPAN'S SECURITY POLICY

Japan's 1970 defense white paper, The Defense of Japan, predicts that "the 1970's will be the time when Japan's national power will have an unprecedented weight and influence in world affairs." However, the paper goes on to specify, "Japan will become a big power in terms of economy, but never will it be so in terms of military strength."[2] These statements, proclaiming a continuing low defense posture, reflect four principal limitations that operate on Japan's security policy.

First, although Japanese pride and nationalism clearly are increasing (particularly among those born after World War II), a strong element of pacifism (the reaction to the excesses of imperial Japan) persists in Japanese public opinion, especially within the influential mass media. Second, nervousness over a possible revival of Japanese militarism remains an important element in Japan's relations with its Asian neighbors. The probable political and economic costs associated with any sudden, overt, and massive Japanese rearmament exercise a powerful constraining influence on Japan's security policy options.

Third, article IX of Japan's constitution is a key restraint on defense policy. That article reads as follows:

> Aspiring sincerely to an international peace based on justice and order the Japanese people forever renounce war as a sovereign right of the nation and the threat of force as means of settling international disputes.
>
> In order to accomplish the aim of the preceding paragraph, land, sea, and air forces, as well as other war potential, will never be maintained. The right of belligerency of the State will not be recognized.[3]

Article IX, however, has not been interpreted as a prohibition of the creation and, if necessary, the use of armed forces to defend Japan against external attack. The Supreme Court of Japan, in the Sunakawa judgment of 1958, ruled, "There is nothing in it which would deny the right of self-defense inherent in our nation as a sovereign power. The pacifism advanced in our Constitution was never intended to mean defenselessness or non resistance. . . . That our country can take measures for self-defense necessary to maintain its peace and security and to ensure its survival must be said to be a matter of course, as the exercise of the functions inherent to a state."[4] The Japanese constitution thus limits Japan's military power "strictly and exclusively to defensive means."[5] Consequently, "all such questions as the size and the quality of defense power, the kind of weapons with which the Self-Defense Forces will be equipped, and the form of reaction which should be taken in the case of dealing with aggression will be limited to the scope of self-defense." Thus, weapons conferring a capability for offensive warfare, such as "long-range bombers like B-52's, attack aircraft carriers, and ICBMs" are presently prohibited. In line with this defensive posture, the 1970 white paper declares, "so-called overseas dispatch of forces will not be carried out."[6]

Fourth, on the question of nuclear weapons (to which Chapter 10 is devoted), the Japanese government continues to adhere to the three-point nuclear principle: Japan will not manufacture or possess nuclear weapons and will not allow such weapons to be introduced into territory under its jurisdiction by any foreign power. It is important to note, however, that the Japanese government has moved to keep its options open on the nuclear question. The 1970 defense white paper states that "even though it would be possible to say that in [a] legal and theoretical sense [the] possession of small nuclear weapons, falling within the minimum requirements for [the] capacity necessary for self-defense and not posing a threat of aggression to other countries, would be permissible, the government, as its policy, adopts the principle of not attempting nuclear armament which might be possible under the Constitution."[7]

These four factors--a generally antimilitary domestic public opinion, foreign sensitivity to large scale conventional or nuclear rearmament, the Japanese constitution, and Japan's antinuclear principles--although not insurmountable or unchangeable, clearly affect Japan's present and future military posture, including its capacity to take part in collective or multilateral security structures.

THE FOURTH DEFENSE BUILD-UP PLAN

The Fourth Defense Build-Up Plan (DBP), announced in October 1970, represents the most recent stage[8] in an uninterrupted, resolute, and gradual effort to build an efficient, modern, and sizable military capability (see Table 9.1). The total expenditure projected for the five-year period (1972-76) of the Fourth DBP is U.S.$14.44 billion (1971 dollars) or, when forces salary increases are included, U.S.$16.1 billion. This compares with a total budget of U.S.$6.5 billion for the Third DBP (1967-71).[9] In terms of defense expenditures as a proportion of GNP, annual spending during the Fourth DBP will remain below 1 percent of Japan's predicted GNP.

The Fourth DBP places particular emphasis on two areas: upgrading of existing equipment and research and development. The

TABLE 9.1

Evolution of the Self-Defense Forces

1950, August	National Police Reserve established
1951, September	Peace treaty and security treaty between Japan and the United States signed
1952, April	Maritime Safety Force established
August	National Safety Agency established
	National Police Reserve reorganized as National Safety Force and Maritime Safety Force as Coastal Safety Force
1954, July	Japan Defense Agency established National Safety Force renamed Ground Self-Defense Force and Coastal National Safety Force Maritime Self-Defense Force. Air Self-Defense Force and Joint Staff Council established
1956, July	National Defense Council established
1957, May	Basic policy for national defense announced by National Defense Council
June	First Defense Build-Up Plan
1960, January	Mutual Treaty of Cooperation and Security signed with United States
1961, July	Second Defense Build-Up Plan
1962, November	Defense Facilities Administration Agency established
1967, March	Third Defense Build-Up Plan
1970, October	First defense white paper, The Defense of Japan
1972	Fourth Defense Build-Up Plan

Source: Compiled by author.

acquisition of new hardware is expected to absorb approximately 46 percent of the $14.44-billion budget. The Ground Self-Defense Force is to receive more helicopters, surface-to-air (Hawk) missiles, and tanks. The Maritime Self-Defense Force is to have its total tonnage increased from 146,000 to about 246,000 for a force of some 200 vessels. The Air Self-Defense Force will be modernized by the addition of 164 new F-4 Phantom aircraft (130 to be built in Japan) and an increase in the number of Nike surface-to-air missiles. Despite growing labor shortages, the total manpower for the self-defense forces is expected to rise from 259,000 to 285,000 men.[10]

TABLE 9.2

Approximate Strength of the Self-Defense Forces, December 1971

	Authorized Personnel	Equipment
Ground Self-Defense Force	Active: 179,000 Reserve: 36,000 1 mechanized division 12 infantry divisions 3 SAM units 1 airborne brigade 1 helicopter brigade 1 artillery brigade	620 tanks 450 self-propelled artillery 630 armored personnel carriers 90 Hawk missile launchers 220 helicopters 150 other aircraft
Maritime Self-Defense Force	Active: 38,300 Reserve: 300 Ships: about 146,000 tons 4 escort flotillas 2 minesweeper flotillas 5 air wings	11 submarines 1 SAM destroyer 27 destroyers 12 destroyer escort/frigates 20 submarine chasers 2 minelayers 42 coastal minesweepers 5 torpedo boats 3 tank landing ships 49 other landing craft 200 combat aircraft 60 helicopters
Air Self-Defense Force	Active: 41,600 7 fighter bomber squadrons 7 interceptor squadrons 1 reconnaisance squadron 3 transport squadrons 3 Nike unit squadrons	230 F-86 F fighter bombers 160 F-104 J fighter bombers 20 reconnaisance aircraft 50 transport aircraft 26 helicopters 360 trainers 100 Nike launchers

Sources: Japan Defense Agency, The Defense of Japan (Tokyo, 1970); International Institute for Strategic Studies, The Military Balance 1972-73 (London: IISS, 1972).

The proportion of defense expenditure given to research and development in the past has been rather small (just over 2 percent during the Third DBP). The new DBP gives priority to increasing Japanese defense-oriented research and development, particularly in the fields of aircraft and missiles. During 1972-76, of Japan's defense expenditures 3.3 percent will be devoted to research and development --about three times the dollar amount spent during the 1967-71 period but still well below the 10 percent allocation of the United States.[11]

The Fourth DBP is designed to give the armed forces an "autonomous" capability to cope with a limited, localized, and conventional threat to Japan's security through the maintenance of supremacy in the air and on the sea in the area immediately adjacent to Japan. However, for protection against the threat of a large scale conventional or nuclear attack, Japan will continue to rely on the U.S. security umbrella extended by the Security Treaty.[12] Approximately 25,000 American military personnel, mostly engaged in support functions, remain stationed in Japan; and elements of the Seventh Fleet continue to be based at Yokosuka and Sasebo. On Okinawa, under Japanese administration since May 1972, the United States maintains an extensive logistical complex, large numbers of combat aircraft (including B-52 bombers), and 43,000 troops.[13]

THE MAXIMIZATION OF DEFENSE POLICY OPTIONS

The neatly tailored threat of a limited, localized, and conventional attack against Japan (presumably an amphibious assault against Hokkaido by Soviet forces), the ostensible justification for the Fourth DBP, lacks credibility. The steady quantitative and, more important, qualitative improvement of the self-defense forces (see Table 9.2) is being undertaken with a larger purpose in mind. Fundamentally, Japan is seeking to widen its future defense options by creating the potential for a rapid expansion of military power. Japan's massive economic and technological resources, particularly in such fields as shipbuilding, electronics, computers, missilery, and nuclear energy, leave little doubt of Japan's physical ability to realize this potential in a relatively short time. The very existence of this potential is no doubt an important consideration in the strategic planning of both the USSR and the People's Republic of China, and as such adds to Japan's national security.

NOTES

1. For a recent study of Soviet naval activity in the Indian Ocean see Geoffrey Jukes, The Indian Ocean in Soviet Naval Policy. Adelphi Papers no. 87 (London: IISS, 1972).

2. Japan Defense Agency, The Defense of Japan (Tokyo, 1971), pp. 2-3.

3. Quoted in John Emmerson, Arms, Yen and Power (New York: Dunellen, 1971), pp. 50-51.

4. Supreme Court of Japan, Judgement upon Case of the So-called "Sunakawa Case" (Tokyo: General Secretariat of the Supreme Court, 1960), pp. 2-8. Cited in The Defense of Japan, op. cit., p. 28; and in Emmerson, op. cit., p. 53.

5. This phrase is used again and again in The Defense of Japan.

6. The Defense of Japan, pp. 38-40.

7. Ibid., p. 40.

8. The evolution of Japan's military capability from the First to the Third Defense Build-Up Plan is provided in ibid., pp. 36-38 and 83-84.

9. International Institute for Strategic Studies, Strategic Survey 1970 (London: IISS, 1971), p. 35.

10. The data on new hardware for 1972-76 are taken from ibid.

11. This new orientation was outlined by Naomi Nishimura, director-general of the Japan Defense Agency, in a speech delivered on October 11, 1971 at the Foreign Correspondents' Club of Japan. Also, see The Defense of Japan, p. 38.

12. Ibid., pp. 32 and 40-41.

13. Earl C. Ravenal, "The Strategic Balance in Asia," Pacific Community 3 (July 1972): 603.

THE QUESTION OF A
NUCLEAR WEAPONS
CAPABILITY

An elegant shop, but the sweets they sell are tasteless.
Hindu proverb

There has been a great deal of international speculation and concern during the last several years over one particular variable in Japan's present and future defense policy: the possibility that Japan will harness its industrial and technological capabilities to develop and deploy some system of nuclear weaponry to ensure its strategic security and to support its expanding political, diplomatic, and economic interests in the world. Conjecture on the question of a nuclear Japan by foreign observers often has been characterized by an air of inevitability. Yet, a decision by Japan to become a major military power by acquiring even a small nuclear force would have enormously important and perhaps unpredictable ramifications for Japan's relations with the major powers in Asia--the United States, the Soviet Union, and China--and its numerous trading partners there.

JAPAN'S CIVIL NUCLEAR TECHNOLOGY

The white paper on atomic energy published in July 1970 by the Atomic Energy Bureau of Japan's Science and Technology Agency outlined the nation's need for nuclear energy: "With rapid growth of economy, it has become vitally important to secure a great quantity of energy sources stably and cheaply for a long term. To meet this demand, the electric utilities have succeedingly begun to construct large-scale nuclear power plants in parallel with the expansion of fossil fueled plants. In ten years, the rate of nuclear power generation in total electricity supply will reach about 23 percent."[1]

Although its nuclear program was not begun until the mid-1950s, Japan's progress, as in other areas of scientific and technological endeavor, has been spectacular. Of the Western advanced, industrial nations, only the United States and Great Britain surpass Japan in the number of nuclear reactors.[2] In 1971, Japan possessed five operational reactors with an installed capacity of about 1,300 megawatts electric power (MWe). This capacity is expected to reach 15,000 MWe by 1977, and between 30,000 and 40,000 MWe by 1985.[3] The Japan Atomic Industrial Forum predicted in 1971 that the proportion of Japan's energy requirements supplied by nuclear power could be expected to reach 25 percent in 1985, 50 percent in 1990, and 70 percent by the year 2000.[4]

Japan is rapidly achieving self-sufficiency in the production of nuclear reactors. The Tokai reactor, which went critical in July 1966, was only 35 percent domestically produced, but the domestic production percentage for the Shimane number 1 reactor (expected to go critical in June 1974) and the Fukushima number 3 reactor (expected to go critical in December 1974) is projected at 90 percent.[5]

Since Japan lacks commercially exploitable high-grade natural uranium ore, it is dependent on imports that, at present, come largely from Canada. To meet future requirements (perhaps 120,000 tons by 1985), and in an attempt to diversify its sources, the Overseas Uranium Resources Development Company was formed in 1970 to search out and secure foreign supplies of uranium. An agreement with the French Atomic Energy Commission and the government of Niger to participate in a joint exploration for uranium in Niger has been concluded.[6] Similar arrangements may emerge with other countries. Likely candidates for such cooperation are Canada, the United States, Australia, and Indonesia.

For its supply of enriched uranium, Japan now relies entirely on the United States. However, these supplies are unlikely to be sufficient for Japan's rapidly expanding needs. In addition, the overwhelming reliance on a single supplier is a source of concern. The achievement of a self-sufficient uranium enrichment capability is, therefore, a priority item in Japan's nuclear program. Research on both the gas diffusion and the gas centrifuge processes has been conducted for several years; and, according to the Stockholm International Peace Research Institute, 10 experimental gas centrifuges were operational in early 1972.[7]

However, the economic viability of a domestic uranium enrichment facility has not been established yet. Furthermore, since uranium enrichment technology clearly has both civil and military applications, an enrichment facility located on Japanese soil almost certainly would generate both domestic and foreign criticism. Japan, therefore, is engaged also in an attempt to diversify its current dependency on U.S. sources of enriched uranium and has expressed interest in a French offer for the joint production of enriched uranium in a facility to be constructed in Australia or Europe before the end of the decade.[8] Similar joint ventures have been discussed with Canada and the United States. Indeed, even the USSR apparently has offered to sell Japan enriched uranium.[9]

There are two principal reasons for the high priority which the nuclear development program has received in Japan. Japan's rapidly expanding economy requires cheap, clean, and, most important, secure and stable long term energy resources. The nuclear program represents an attempt to lessen Japan's almost total dependence on Persian Gulf oil,[10] and to increase self-sufficiency in the field of energy. Second, Japan's civil nuclear program clearly has military implications that are designed to increase the options available for Japan's future security policy. Growing self-sufficiency in the peaceful use of nuclear power will provide Japan with the technological capability necessary to move rapidly into a nuclear weapons program, should the momentous decision to do so ever be taken.

It is estimated that Japan's production of plutonium will reach 3,000 kilograms in 1975 and 15,000 by 1980.[11] This relative abundance of plutonium, a substance that is created by an operational nuclear reactor and readily lends itself to the fabrication of tactical nuclear devices, together with the difficulties that Japan likely will encounter in attempting to generate an independent uranium enrichment capability, has led to speculation that Japan will develop a defensive tactical nuclear capability.[12] It should be remembered also that Japan possesses an impressive missile technology, having launched three earth satellites. (The first was on February 11, 1970, two months before China became the fifth nation in space--after the Soviet Union, the United States, France, and Japan.) The experimental solid-fuel MU rocket reportedly could be developed into a missile with a range of 4,000 kilometers and a payload capability of 5,000 kilograms.[13] In addition, the Japanese satellite program is to be supplied with the U.S. Thor rocket (produced under license in Japan) by 1975.[14]

PRESSURES FOR A NUCLEAR JAPAN

Pressure to include the development of a nuclear force in Japan's national security strategy exists for two basic reasons. First, nuclear weapons are perceived as conferring on their possessor an enviable degree of international status and influence. In part, this is so because nuclear weapons symbolize the summit of achievement in the field of advanced technology. More important, it is a demonstrable reality of international relations that the world's "first-rate" powers all possess nuclear arsenals. As nationalism and confidence continue to flourish in Japan, the view that Japan is a "second-rate" power whose influence in the world is not commensurate with its economic might because it does not possess a nuclear force could become more prevalent.

Hard considerations of strategic security constitute the second source of likely pressure for a Japanese nuclear force. Japan is faced with two potentially hostile nuclear powers in Asia, both within reach of the intermediate-range ballistic missiles. From Tokyo's perspective, the credibility of the American nuclear guarantee to Japan has been placed in some doubt by the Nixon Doctrine and the president's unilateral effort at detente with Peking. It will be asked, particularly if China deploys an ICBM force capable of reaching targets in North America, whether the United States realistically can be expected to risk nuclear retaliation in the defense of Japan. Pressure for Japanese strategic autonomy through the development of an independent nuclear force is therefore likely to increase.

Most experts agree that, although a sizable diversion of resources would be required, Japan possesses the economic and technological capability (assuming continued growth) to embark on a nuclear weapons program. It generally is estimated that an annual expenditure of $1 billion for 10 years (over and above existing and projected defense spending) would provide Japan with a "modest" nuclear force.

The forces operating to constrain a Japanese decision to a nuclear force are largely political, diplomatic, and strategic in nature.

Domestic Constraints

Although the 1970 defense white paper maintained that strictly defensive nuclear weapons would not contravene article IX of the Japanese constitution, the possession of such offensive weapons as long-range bombers and ICBMs was rejected, and Japan's adherence to its three-point nonnuclear policy (the nonproduction, nonpossession, and nonintroduction of nuclear weapons) was reaffirmed. In addition, the 1955 Basic Law on Atomic Energy continues to limit nuclear programs to peaceful purposes.

A Japanese decision to develop nuclear weaponry therefore would require a reversal of the government's declared nuclear policy, an amendment to the Basic Law on Atomic Energy, and possibly a revision of the constitution. Despite growing nationalism, opposition to such dramatic and unavoidably visible changes in Japanese policy likely would be massive.

Strategic Constraints

The Japanese archipelago, long and narrow with heavy concentrations of industry and population in a few sprawling urban complexes (20 percent of Japan's population is located in the three conurbations of Tokyo, Nagoya, and Osaka), is singularly vulnerable to nuclear attack. A relatively small number of thermonuclear weapons would inflict destruction on a scale that would destroy Japan as a viable 20th century nation. Even if Japan could create an assured second-strike capability through the deployment of a sea-based nuclear force (ground-based missiles could not be assured invulnerability on Japan's limited territory)--and the costs of such a capability ensure that it will remain the monopoly of the two superpowers--the vulnerability of Japanese industrial and population centers would tend to erode the credibility of the Japanese deterrent. The assured destruction of a small number of enemy targets in retaliation for what would no doubt be tantamount to the destruction of Japanese society would not appear to constitute a rational or effective national security policy.

A defensive (as opposed to deterrent) nuclear strategy--that is, an antiballistic missile (ABM) system or a combined ABM/sea-based deterrent system--may be appealing to Japanese defense planners if Japan decides to develop a nuclear capability. However, high costs, technological difficulties, and Japan's vulnerability to nuclear attack would still be important considerations. Given Japan's small area, even the testing of nuclear devices (which would have to be underground since Japan adheres to the partial test ban treaty) would present enormous difficulties.

In the short to medium term the U.S. nuclear guarantee will continue to be available to Japan at a bearable political cost and, as such, will diminish the necessity for an independent Japanese nuclear capability. Despite the often enunciated perception that the credibility of the U.S. guarantee has been eroded by recent American policies and an international atmosphere characterized by detente and negotiation, the security of Japan remains of vital interest to the United States.[15] In consequence, the American nuclear shield will continue to afford protection to Japan.

International Constraints

A decision to proceed with the development of a Japanese nuclear force would have profound effects on Japan's principal external relationships. In Southeast Asia, a region vital to Japan in terms of trade, natural resources, and sea routes, such a decision would catalyze an already growing fear of Japanese economic and military strength,[16] thereby jeopardizing years of Japanese effort to cultivate goodwill in an area where memories of the excesses of imperial Japan are never far below the surface.

The recent improvement in relations between Peking and Tokyo and the massive increase in Sino-Japanese trade expected by many over the next decade in Japan[17] no doubt would be threatened also if Japan opted for a nuclear weapons program. Although some growth in Japan's military strength might be welcomed by China as a counterweight to the growing Soviet military capability in Asia and the Pacific,[18] an independent Japanese nuclear weapons program almost certainly would compete with the Chinese program and, therefore, would be perceived by Peking as a significant threat to Chinese security-- since parity with the Chinese force probably would be the objective of a Japanese nuclear effort.

The adverse ramifications for Japan's relationship with the United States also would have to be weighted carefully by Japanese decision makers if Japan chose to embark on an independent nuclear weapons program in an international environment that did not differ dramatically from the present one. Although the American government has expressed the hope that Japan would endeavor to assume a greater share of its own defense burden according to the principles of the Nixon Doctrine, the United States continues to extend its nuclear umbrella under the mutual security treaty. Furthermore, the United States has opposed publicly the proliferation of independent nuclear capabilities and has urged the Japanese government to ratify the Nuclear Nonproliferation Treaty.[19]

Adverse reaction from the Soviet Union also could be expected if Japan were to decide to create a nuclear force. Prospects for an improvement in Russo-Japanese relations, including the possible return of the four northern islands and potential Japanese involvement (in terms of capital and technology) in the proposed development of Siberian natural resources, would be endangered. Indeed, the USSR almost certainly would attempt to apply political and, depending on the state of Japan's relations with Peking and Washington, military pressure to frustrate a Japanese nuclear weapons program.

A JAPANESE PROTONUCLEAR POSTURE

The fundamental parameter in Japan's future security posture remains the U.S.-Japanese relationship. Japan's only credible deterrent against the USSR and, for some time to come, against China, is the American nuclear umbrella. Although no guarantee can be considered absolutely certain in the field of international affairs, the American commitment to the security of Japan (based on hard calculations of national interest) would seem to present risks to any potential adversary sufficient to ensure Japan's vital strategic defense.

Given the U.S. nuclear guarantee and the present international environment characterized by detente and rapprochement between traditional opponents, a decision to create an independent Japanese nuclear force--a course that would entail tremendous economic and political costs (both domestic and international) without guaranteeing any significant improvement in Japan's security--seems unlikely in the near term. However, the desire to be accorded an international status commensurate with its global economic influence will generate growing pressures for strategic autonomy. Japan therefore appears to be pursuing a policy designed to create a protonuclear[20] capability. That is to say, Japan will seek to improve its potential to become a nuclear weapons power by continuing to place a considerable priority on rapid progress in the civil nuclear program. As Japan's civil capability is steadily augmented, the period of time necessary to field a nuclear force will diminish progressively. One observer has estimated that, by 1975, Japan could deploy a force of perhaps 10 nuclear Poseidon-type submarines within five years of the decision to do so, and that the time necessary to implement such a decision could be cut to three years by 1980.[21] However, given the constraints, Japan's growing potential to transform its status from that of a near-nuclear nation to a nuclear weapons power is likely to be used only if the international environment undergoes a dramatic change for the worse.

NOTES

1. White Papers of Japan 1970-71: Annual Abstract of Official Reports and Statistics of the Japanese Government (Tokyo, 1972), p. 19.

2. For a complete list of nuclear power and research reactors, location, type, output, and date of criticality, see ibid., pp. 22-24.

3. The Near Nuclear Countries and the NPT (Stockholm: SIPRI, 1972), p. 36.

4. Ibid. The percentage of Canada's energy requirements to be supplied from nuclear sources is projected to reach 35 percent by 1990. Energy Supply and Demand in Canada (Ottawa: National Energy Board, 1969), p. 15.

5. White Papers of Japan 1970-71, p. 22.

6. The Near Nuclear Countries and the NPT, p. 37.

7. Ibid., p. 36. According to the International New York Herald Tribune (August 23, 1972), the Japan Atomic Energy Commission stated on August 22 that a gas centrifuge enrichment plant would be built and operational by 1985.

8. The Near Nuclear Countries and the NPT, p. 37.

9. Ibid.

10. It is estimated that by 1975, of Japan's petroleum requirements 99.9 percent will be imported from the Persian Gulf. International Institute for Strategic Studies, Strategic Survey 1971 (London: IISS, 1972), p. 60.

11. The Near Nuclear Countries and the NPT, p. 37.

12. Washington Post, August 31, 1971, p. 7.

13. The Near Nuclear Countries and the NPT, p. 41.

14. Ibid.

15. U.S. Foreign Policy for the 1970's: The Emerging Structure of Peace, A Report to the Congress by Richard Nixon, February 9, 1972 (Washington, D.C.: U.S. Government Printing Office, 1972), p. 32.

16. For example, Japan recently has sent a roving envoy to southeast Asian nations in response to growing apprehension over Japan's Fourth Defense Build-Up Plan. "Japan's Defence Budget Soars," Montreal Star, January 2, 1973.

17. For example, Mitsui Bussan, a leading Japanese trading company, has forecast that Sino-Japanese trade will increase from $900 million in 1971 to $10 billion by 1982. Japanese government economists predict that trade between the two countries will quadruple by 1980. "Japanese Business Hopes for Trade Boom with China," Toronto Star, September 25, 1972.

18. According to one account, Chou En-lai stated during Tanaka's visit to China in September 1972 that he could visualize a situation in which China would come to Japan's aid, even alongside American forces, if the Soviet Far Eastern fleet were deployed on a regular basis in the east China Sea or if the Soviet fleet engaged in direct military operations against Japan. Toronto Globe and Mail, December 14, 1972, p. 3.

19. In his 1972 foreign policy report to the Congress, Nixon reaffirmed the American commitment to shield nations vital to U.S. security, thereby "discouraging nations from developing their own nuclear capability." U.S. Foreign Policy for the 1970's: The Emerging Structure of Peace, op. cit.

20. The term appears in Zbigniew Brzezinski, The Fragile Blossom: Crisis and Change in Japan (New York: Harper & Row, 1972).

21. Ibid., p. 108.

11

RELATIONS WITH THE PEOPLE'S REPUBLIC OF CHINA

To convert a setback into a success should be like riding
a horse at the edge of a precipice. Be not so careless
as to whip it even once.

Epigram from the Ming Dynasty

THE RELATIONSHIP IN HISTORICAL PERSPECTIVE

Japan's foreign policies and ambitions over the past 100 years
have reflected a continuous preoccupation with China. The reasons
for this phenomenon are to be found largely in the realms of economics and geopolitics. However, it is important to note that the Japanese fascination with China is fueled by other powerful factors. Both
countries are Asian. For the Japanese, the bonds of racial kinship
are fortified by an awareness that the roots of Japanese civilization
are to be found in classical Chinese civilization. It is principally
from Chinese civilization that Japan's own religion, culture, philosophy, ethics, and written language have evolved. In short, China is
Japan's Greece.

During the postwar period, Japan's relations with China have
been influenced overwhelmingly by the primacy of the Japanese-American relationship in Japan's foreign and security policy. Although
the United States was committed firmly to the containment and isolation of the People's Republic of China, Japan had little choice but to
conclude a peace treaty with the Nationalist regime of Chiang Kai-
shek on April 28, 1952, thereby recognizing the Taipei government
as the sole legitimate government of China. It had become clear to
the then prime minister of Japan, Shigeru Yoshida, that a refusal on
the part of Japan to extend full diplomatic recognition to the Republic

of China would jeopardize ratification by the U.S. Senate of the San Francisco peace treaty, which was to end the occupation and restore sovereignty to Japan. Yoshida's decision to seek normal diplomatic relations with Chiang Kai-shek's government was communicated by letter to Secretary of State John Foster Dulles on December 24, 1951. The key points of the letter are these.

> The Japanese Government desires ultimately to have a full measure of political peace and commercial intercourse with China which is Japan's close neighbor.
> My government is prepared as soon as legally possible to conclude with the National Government of China, if that government so desires, a Treaty which will reestablish normal relations between the two Governments in conformity with the principles set out in the multilateral Treaty of Peace. The terms of such bilateral treaty shall, in respect of the Republic of China, be applicable to all territories which are now, or which may hereafter be, under the control of the National Government of the Republic of China. . . . I can assure you that the Japanese Government has no intention to conclude a bilateral treaty with the Communist regime of China.[1]

Japan's official posture toward China since 1951 generally has been supportive of and consistent with American policy. The primary concern of successive Japanese governments (at least until Nixon's July 1971 announcement of his intended visit to the P.R.C.) has been to avoid taking any official position on China that could produce undesirable ramifications for Japan's relationship with the United States. By pursuing a policy that claimed to separate politics from economics, Japan, in fact, has been able to develop lucrative trade relations with both the Republic of China and the People's Republic of China (see Table 11.1). Although this activity sometimes has resulted in friction between Tokyo and Taipei (as in 1963) or fluctuations in Peking's willingness to trade with Japan (as in 1958), on balance Japan has been able to reap substantial economic gains from its trade with both Chinas, while maintaining both normal diplomatic relations with Taipei and unofficial contacts with Peking.

On November 21, 1969, Nixon and Sato made public a joint communique[2] that declared, the "mutual security interests of the United States and Japan could be accommodated within arrangements for the return of the administrative rights over Okinawa to Japan." In addition, the communique went on to state that the "security of the Republic of Korea was essential to Japan's own security" and that "the maintenance of peace and security in the Taiwan area was also a most important factor for the security of Japan."

117

TABLE 11.1

Japan's Trade with the Republic of China and the People's Republic of
China, 1964-71
(in millions of U.S. dollars)

	1964	1965	1966	1967	1968	1969	1970	1971
P.R.C.	310	470	621	558	550	625	825	900
Republic of China	279	375	403	465	622	787	953	1,200

Sources: For 1964-69: Shinkichi Eto, "Features Characteristic of the Economy of China," in Peace Research in Japan 1971
(Tokyo: Japan Peace Research Group, 1971), p. 27; for 1970:
John K. Emmerson, Arms, Yen and Power (New York: Dunellen,
1971), p. 209; for 1971: newspaper reports, for example, Toronto Star, September 25, 1972.

    The Chinese reaction to the promised reversion of Okinawa
(the agreement finally was signed by Japan and the United States
in November 1970) and the inclusion of Taiwan and South Korea in
the Japanese defense perimeter was both voluminous and forceful.
The theme of Peking's propaganda barrage, motivated by the fear
that Japanese political and economic influence on Taiwan would be
augmented further after the return of Okinawa to Japanese control,
predictably centered on the revival of Japanese militarism, albeit
under the aegis of American imperialism. The New China News
Agency immediately denounced Japan for what it described as a re-
militarization designed to make Japan the "gendarme of Asia."[3]
However the zenith of the verbal tirade came when Chou En-lai
met Kim Il-Sung in Pyongyang, North Korea, in April 1970. The
joint communique that the two leaders released on April 7 strongly
denounced Japanese militarism. "The two sides vehemently con-
demn Japanese militarism which, revived again as a dangerous
force of aggression in Asia under the active patronage of U.S. imperialism, is embarking on the road of open aggression against
the Asian people with a delusion to realize the old broken dream
of 'Greater East Asia Coprosperity Sphere' with the backing of
U.S. imperialism and in conspiracy and collusion with it."[4]
    Peking's sensitivity to the linking of Taiwan and South Korea
with Japanese security interests was underscored further on April
19, 1970, when the difficult negotiations on the Sino-Japanese trade

agreement finally ended. The Chinese successfully pressed for the inclusion of the following paragraph in the joint communique: "The purpose of the U.S. and Japanese reactionaries in stepping up military collusion is obvious, that is, to perpetuate the forcible occupation of China's sacred territory of Taiwan Province and prevent the Chinese people from liberating Taiwan; to perpetuate the forcible occupation of South Korea, obstruct the reunification of Korea and even invade anew the Korean Democratic People's Republic."[5] As the communique was being released, Chou En-lai announced his "four principles" on trade. Essentially, the P.R.C. would no longer trade with those Japanese firms that (1) traded with South Korea or Taiwan, (2) had large capital investments in South Korea or Taiwan, (3) supplied weapons or ammunition to the American military in Indochina, or (4) had large amounts of American capital invested in them.

Then, on July 15, 1971, Nixon announced to a surprised world that Kissinger had conferred secretly with Premier Chou En-lai and that the president himself would visit the People's Republic of China early in 1972. The old international system appeared to be disintegrating in an atmosphere of detente and negotiation between those who only a short time ago had been irreconcilable opponents. The Chinese leadership had decided to seek rapprochement with the United States to counterbalance a growing threat from the Soviet Union in the aftermath of the serious Ussuri River fighting of 1969 and the increase in Soviet army divisions stationed in the Sino-Soviet border area and in Mongolia. The United States, for its part, wished to increase its leverage in the Strategic Arms Limitation Talks with the Soviet Union, while simultaneously hoping to enlist Chinese aid in an attempt to extricate itself from the quagmire in Indochina.

Nixon's announcement of his impending mission to China was received with utter shock and dismay by the Sato government in Tokyo. An American decision to seek an improvement in U.S.-P.R.C. relations normally would have found great support in Tokyo. However, the president had chosen to act unilaterally, without consulting America's oldest and closest Asian ally on a matter of vital interest to it. In consequence, the trust and good faith with which the Sato government had conducted its relations with the United States were undermined seriously. A reappraisal of Japan's own policy toward China as well as a change in Japan's political leadership became inevitable.

The crowning blow came in the joint communique signed by the president and Chou En-lai in Shanghai. The Chinese denunciation of the revival and expansion of Japanese militarism was alleviated only nominally by the affirmation that the United States continued to place the highest value on friendly relations with Japan.

Contrary to early Japanese fears that the U.S. overtures toward China were totally inimical to Japanese interests, Nixon's initiatives, in fact, have had the effect of increasing Japan's foreign policy options. For example, during 1972 Tokyo received Soviet Foreign Minister Andrei Gromyko's overtures for improved relations and for joint ventures in a massive Siberian development scheme, dispatched an official foreign ministry mission to Hanoi (the Japanese have pledged to aid in the reconstruction of Indochina and hope to increase their exports to this area), extended official diplomatic recognition to the government of Bangladesh, and dispatched a parliamentary delegation (not officially approved) to North Korea to negotiate an increase in trade. Most important, Japan moved to normalize its relations with the People's Republic of China.

The new Japanese prime minister, Kakuei Tanaka, and his cabinet took office on July 7, 1972. Peking responded favorably. After almost three years of constant abusive propaganda directed at Tokyo, Premier Chou En-lai commented, "The Tanaka Cabinet was inaugurated on July 7 and with regard to foreign policy it has announced that it will endeavor to realize a normalization of relations between Japan and China. This is certainly to be welcomed."[6]

Tanaka lost little time in responding to Peking's conciliatory gestures. The prime minister and senior officials began a five-day visit to China on September 25, 1972. Speaking at a banquet in his honor on the opening day of the tour, Tanaka apologized for the destruction his country had perpetrated on China during the 1931-45 period, "I hereby express our profound self-reflection for having imposed great trouble on the Chinese people during the regretfully unfortunate period of relations between our two countries."[7]

Four days later, on September 29, Chou En-lai and Tanaka signed a joint communique normalizing relations between Japan and the People's Republic of China. The communique stated, among other points, that

2. The Government of Japan recognizes the Government of the People's Republic of China as the sole legal Government of China.

3. The Government of the People's Republic of China reaffirms that Taiwan is an inalienable part of the territory of the People's Republic of China. The government of Japan fully understands and respects this stand of the Government of China and adheres to its stand of complying with Article 8 of the Potsdam Proclamation.
. . .
8. To consolidate and develop the peaceful and friendly relations between the two countries, the Government of

the People's Republic of China and the Government of
Japan agree to hold negotiations aimed at the conclusion
of a treaty of peace and friendship. [8]

At a news conference following the signing of the document that
was telecast live to Japan by satellite, Japan's foreign minister,
Masayoshi Ohira, declared that the peace treaty that Japan had signed
with the nationalist government in 1952 was no longer valid and that
the Japanese embassy on Taiwan would be closed. In Tokyo, however,
Trade Minister Yasuhiro Nakasone told a press conference that Japan
wished to continue cultural and economic relations with Taiwan. [9]

The normalization of relations with the P.R.C. clearly has fur-
thered certain Chinese and Japanese objectives. Although any analysis remains tentative so soon after this historic and potentially far-
reaching event, certain conclusions emerge.

On the Chinese side, the legitimacy of Peking's claim to represent the sole government of all China has been augmented considerably
by the extension of formal recognition from America's major Asian
ally and the world's third largest economic power. As such, the nationalist government on Taiwan has been further isolated, both from
the world community in general (the People's Republic of China gained
possession of China's seat in the United Nations on October 25, 1971)
and from Japan in particular. The normalization of Sino-Japanese
relations no doubt will tend to generate further pressure for other nations to do likewise, particularly in Asia. And, indeed, Australia
and New Zealand announced on December 22, 1972 that they would
place their relations with Peking on a normal footing.

Although the Chinese have consistently emphasized self-sufficiency, the potential access to advanced Japanese technology and the
likely long term financial credits that the normalization of relations
has generated must be considered an important gain for Peking.

With respect to security concerns, the normalization of relations
represents a major Chinese victory. Peking has weaned Japan away
from the United States, but not to the point where Japan feels so in-
secure that it feels the necessity to attempt strategic autonomy. At
the same time, the establishment of diplomatic relations with Tokyo
has preempted (at least for the moment) the possibility of a Soviet-
Japanese coalition and, as such, has considerably increased Chinese
security. One report of Tanaka's talks with Chou En-lai in September 1972 suggests the Chinese premier told the Japanese prime minister that he welcomed a reasonable increase in Japanese military
strength as a counterweight to Soviet power in Asia and that he could
visualize circumstances in which China might aid Japan militarily,
perhaps even alongside U.S. forces. [10]

For the Japanese, the normalization of Sino-Japanese relations represents a major success for their new, more independent foreign policy, a policy that increasingly will endeavor to influence world events (particularly in Asia), rather than merely reacting to them. Together with the Sino-American detente, the rapprochement with Peking has considerably enhanced Japan's national security by promoting an international environment characterized by negotiations, compromise, and flexibility, and by increasing the prospects for stability among the major actors in the Asian theater.

With respect to Soviet-Japanese relations, the reconciliation with the P.R.C. is likely to improve Japan's bargaining position. The USSR clearly is unhappy about the rapid improvement in Sino-Japanese relations. This fait accompli represents a major failure for Soviet Asian policy, a policy that appears to have as its central objective the military and political containment of the People's Republic of China. The possibility of a working coalition between China—with its vast natural, political, and military resources—and the economic and technological might of Japan therefore must be the source of enormous anxiety in Moscow.

Soviet attempts to entice Japan into the vast development scheme for Siberia during the last few years (stepped up after Nixon's announcement that he would travel to China) so far have failed, largely because the Russians apparently have overestimated the price Japan is willing to pay for the resources (particularly oil and natural gas) Siberia offers. The USSR consistently has taken a tough stand on the question of Japan's claim to the disputed northern islands, a matter of tremendous emotional force in Japan. In the aftermath of the Sino-Japanese rapprochement, the Soviet Union again has hardened its position on the northern territories and resumed its charges of a reviving Japanese militarism, after having taken a more conciliatory posture in early 1972. [11] Although the Japanese would certainly wish to improve their relations with the USSR if this can be accomplished at a reasonable cost (since this would, in turn, increase Japan's bargaining position with Peking), the Soviet Union clearly has more to gain than Japan in any improvement of relations between the two countries as it seeks to avoid being isolated in the four-power maneuvering with Japan, China, and the United States in the Asian theater.

In normalizing its relations with Peking, Japan has in fact "leapfrogged" the United States, now the world's only major nation not to have recognized officially the Peking government. The rapidity and scope of Tanaka's initiatives (of which the United States was informed in advance) do not appear to have met with adverse reaction in Washington. However, the Sino-Japanese rapprochement is likely to improve Japan's overall bargaining position with the United States since the prospect of too close a coalition between Asia's two most important and powerful nations is not likely to be welcomed in Washington.

As noted earlier, there has been a great deal of speculation in Japan that the normalization of Sino-Japanese relations will result in a massive increase in Sino-Japanese trade, with estimates ranging from the $10 billion in 1982 of Mitsui Bussan, to a more conservative government prediction that Sino-Japanese trade will quadruple by 1980.[12] It is extremely difficult to evaluate these predictions. Optimists cite the following considerations: (1) that China's long-standing indifference to foreign trade is likely to disappear as Peking seeks to rationalize and hasten the development of its economy; and (2) that the Japanese government seems to be willing to make available long term, low interest loans to enable China to purchase large quantities of Japanese goods, particularly advanced technology equipment.

Those who are more skeptical about the scale of the expected increase in Sino-Japanese trade point to other factors: (1) that Japan will encounter tremendous competition, particularly from Britain, France, West Germany, and, increasingly, the United States for China's markets; (2) that China is essentially an underdeveloped country with a GNP approximately two-fifths of the Japanese GNP and a much more modest growth record; (3) that although China is a massive market in terms of population size, the low level of income limits the scope for the sale of consumer goods; (4) that political considerations in the past have played a key role in China's trading relations and, consequently, the China market promises continued elements of uncertainty and instability that increase the risks involved in trade relations; and (5) that China consistently has emphasized self-sufficiency, engaging in trade not out of any belief that it is mutually beneficial to have such relations with other countries but rather to acquire specific necessities. Pessimists therefore argue that China is not likely to wish to increase its dependence on trade at all and certainly not with Japan, which already accounted for 20 percent of China's total trade in 1971. (Japan's trade with China represented only 2 percent of its total trade in 1971.)

It seems that all that can be said with certainty so soon after the normalization of Sino-Japanese relations is that trade is bound to increase. The extent of that increase will become more apparent over the next year or two and could be affected by a myriad of events. The course of Sino-American relations, to cite one variable, certainly will influence the scale and composition of Sino-Japanese economic relations.

THE FUTURE OF THE SINO-JAPANESE RELATIONSHIP

Japan's rapidly improving relationship with the People's Republic of China is not to be seen in terms of a coalition or an alliance.

It is best viewed in the context of the fluid situation in Asia, which demands flexibility and continuous maneuvering among the principal actors--the United States, the USSR, China, and Japan. Though Japan clearly is drawn to China on the basis of an emotionally powerful mixture of history, common cultural and linguistic roots, and a sense of shared destiny, a prime objective in furthering its relations (both political and economic) with Peking will be to improve its bargaining position with the USSR and the United States. This is not to say that Japan will not value its relationship with China for its own sake. Rather, Japan will have to (and will prefer to) operate in a multilateral setting rather than in the context of an exclusive bilateral alliance with a particular great power, as has been the case over the past 20 years. Japan, therefore, will endeavor to minimize dependencies and maximize options. With respect to its growing relationship with Peking, Tokyo certainly must consider the possibility that the post-Mao Tse-tung leadership in China could move to heal the Sino-Soviet rift. Therefore, an attempt to improve relations with the Soviet Union almost certainly will be made. Relations with the United States will continue to remain the crucial element in Japan's foreign and security policy considerations, but they are not likely to be as all-pervasive as in the past.

NOTES

1. U.S. Department of State, Bulletin 26 (January 28, 1951): 120.

2. U.S. Department of State, Bulletin 61 (December 15, 1969): 555-58.

3. New China News Agency (Peking), November 23, 24, and 28, 1969. Cited in John Emmerson, Arms, Yen and Power (New York: Dunellen, 1971), p. 214.

4. Pyongyang Times, April 13, 1970, p. 11. Cited in Emmerson, op. cit., p. 271.

5. The full text of the communique was published by the New China News Agency, April 19, 1970. Cited in Emmerson, op. cit., p. 216.

6. This statement was broadcast by Radio Peking and appeared in the New China News Agency (international service) on July 9, 1972, and in Jen-min Jih-pao (Peking) on July 10, 1972. Cited in Shinkichi Eto, "Japan and China--A New Stage?", Problems of Communism 21 (November-December 1972), p. 1.

7. "Japanese and Chinese Premiers Meet to Normalize Relations," Toronto Star, September 25, 1972.

8. See The London Times, September 30, 1972; Problems of Communism 21 (November-December 1972), p. 13 for text of communique.

9. "Japan is 79th nation to recognize Peking," Toronto Star, September 29, 1972.

10. Toronto Globe and Mail, December 14, 1972, p. 3.

11. Ibid., January 15, 1973, p. 2.

12. "Japanese Business Hopes for Trade Boom with China," Toronto Star, September 25, 1972.

12

RELATIONS WITH THE USSR

Many think that an accomplishment can be accelerated
by vigor; but haste often causes delay. So that superior
man tempers his levity with gravity.

Epigram from the Ming Dynasty

RUSSIA'S ASIAN STRATEGY

Politically and diplomatically, the Soviet Union has been on the
offensive in Asia for several years. The Soviet attempt to increase
its influence in this theater stems from three factors. The first and
most important consideration is the worsening of Sino-Soviet relations, particularly after armed clashes along border areas in 1969.
The USSR also has attempted to take advantage of the decline in British influence in Asia as a result of that country's withdrawal of
forces from that region in 1971. Finally, the Russians eagerly have
sought possibilities for extending their own presence in the area as
the long-expected scaling-down of the American posture on and around
the Asian mainland became more certain.

The Soviet diplomatic offensive has taken many forms. In south
Asia, the USSR has scored a triumph of sorts by forming stronger
links with India. The Indian victory during the 1971 war with Pakistan has strengthened these ties and has served to augment the image
of Soviet influence on China's southern flank. In Indochina, particularly in Hanoi, the USSR has attempted to profit by the disenchantment
with Peking that the thaw in Sino-American relations has generated
among the region's liberation movements. Elsewhere in Asia, the
Soviet Union has moved to establish diplomatic relations with Malaysia and Singapore (two of the three nations adjacent to the strategi-

cally vital Malacca Straits) and trade relations with the Philippines. It is not unlikely that, in its attempt to encircle China militarily and diplomatically, the USSR will endeavor to form diplomatic and perhaps security links with Taiwan. If the American security guarantee to the nationalist regime were abrogated either by the United States (in favor of much improved relations with Peking) or by the nationalist government itself (having decided that, in light of the growing Sino-American rapprochement, the guarantee is no longer credible), a Soviet-Taiwan coalition based on a mutual fear of Chinese power could appear attractive to both parties. As Taiwan's sense of isolation increases, such an option will become more attractive to Taipei. Unofficial exchanges of visits between Taiwan and the USSR already have taken place.[1] The fear that Soviet influence will be sought actively by Taipei might induce Peking to encourage the continued maintenance of American forces on the island.

Finally, as part of its Asian strategy, the Soviet Union has revived the proposal for an Asian collective security arrangement, first enunciated by Leonid Brezhnev in June 1962[2] and elaborated during March 1972. Its principal elements included the renunciation of force, peaceful coexistence, economic, scientific, and cultural relations on the basis of mutual benefit, noninterference in internal politics, and the inviolability of national boundaries. The proposal has been received cautiously by Asian nations both because of its vagueness and because of the perception that it is designed to suit the requirements of a Soviet stragegy to contain the People's Republic of China.

Japan constitutes a critical element in the Soviet Union's strategy. Concern over the unexpected Sino-American rapprochement led the Russians to step up their approaches to Tokyo. In January 1972, Soviet Foreign Minister Andrei Gromyko visited Japan for the first time since 1966 in an attempt to capitalize on the disenchantment that Nixon's new China and economic policies had produced in Japan. Gromyko's visit included consultations with then Prime Minister Sato, Foreign Minister Takeo Fukuda, and Trade and Industry Minister Tanaka. The joint communique[3] issued at the end of Gromyko's stay left the impression that a new spirit of cooperation had been inaugurated between the two countries who, despite the resumption of diplomatic relations in 1956, were still legally at war with one another. The two sides agreed that talks would begin before the end of 1972 to establish terms for a peace treaty. Gromyko took a conciliatory stand on the question of the northern islands (two islands in the Southern Kuriles, Kunashiri and Etorofu, and two islands off the north coast of Hokkaido, Shikotan and Habomai).[4] This territory, taken by the Soviet Union when it violated the neutrality pact with Japan in 1945, had been the principle obstacle to the negotiation of a peace treaty. The two parties also agreed "to continue making efforts towards the development of economic co-operation," presumably a reference to the possibility of Japanese participation (in the form of capital and technology) in the development and exploitation of Siberian natural resources.[5] Finally, both sides agreed to hold "regular consultations at the level of foreign ministers of both countries at least once a year," alternately in Tokyo and Moscow.

As of early 1973, the Soviet attempt to strengthen its ties with Tokyo to counter the warming of Sino-American relations appears to have met with little success. The Japanese continue to approach with caution the Soviet proposal for joint development of Siberian resources. The ultimate blow, however, came in late September 1972 when Prime Minister Tanaka visited Chou En-lai, a meeting that resulted in the normalization of Sino-Japanese relations and opened the prospect for increases in the flow of Japanese capital and technology to China. It now seems reasonably clear that the appearance of a change in Soviet-Japanese relations that Gromyko's visit gave (both sides had an obvious interest in such an impression as a means to strengthen their respective positions in the aftermath of the Sino-American rapprochement) provided Tanaka with added leverage in his overtures to Peking and helped to make possible the normalization of relations less than three months after he became prime minister.[6]

Fundamentally, the shift to a more conciliatory approach toward Japan during late 1971 and 1972 reflects the Soviet preoccupation with the encirclement and containment of China. To avoid being isolated by potentially anti-Soviet coalitions, the USSR hoped to create a counterweight to the developing Sino-American rapprochement and to preempt a possible Sino-Japanese working alliance by improving relations with Japan and by drawing Japanese capital and technology into the development of Siberian resources.

Since a Sino-Japanese coalition is no doubt considered to constitute a serious potential military threat to the USSR, the pursuit of a policy of rapprochement is designed to preempt or at least to dilute the flow of Japanese capital and advanced technology to China by tying down resources in Siberia. If successfully implemented, this strategy offers several attractions to the Soviet Union.

By assisting in the development and exploitation of the vast untapped resources (particularly energy resources) of Siberia through the introduction of Japanese capital and technology, the Soviet economy would receive a much needed stimulus, thereby adding to the overall national security of the USSR. Development in Siberia also would encourage the settlement and population of vast areas now only sparsely inhabited. This would strengthen the Soviet presence in the Siberian area, which is contiguous with the Chinese frontier.

Since a principal element in the Soviet proposals concerning Japanese involvement in Siberia call for the building of a 6,600-kilometer oil pipeline from Anzhero-Sudzhensk in West Siberia to the port of Nakhodka on the Sea of Japan along a corridor roughly parallel to the Trans-Siberian Railway, the capability and operational range of the nearly 50 red army divisions now stationed in the Sino-Soviet border area (early 1973) and the Soviet navy's Pacific fleet would be augmented considerably.

The growing Soviet military capability in the Far East is directed principally at the People's Republic of China. However, in view of Japan's economic, industrial, and technological might, the Soviet Union recognizes the potential for conflict with Japan in the longer term. As such, Soviet military power should be seen as being deployed primarily against China, but with Japan as a secondary target.[7] With this consideration in mind, the Soviet proposal for Japanese involvement in Siberia in return for natural resources would offer the added advantage of conferring on the USSR physical control over a significant quantity of Japan's strategically vital resources, principally natural gas and oil.

In seeking to adjust its relations with the USSR, Japan's strategy will be based on three fundamental considerations. From the point of view of Japanese national security, Tokyo seeks to improve its relations with Moscow since the USSR is perceived by Japan as the principal potential military threat to its security. As the postwar bipolar structure, under which Japan's security was guaranteed by one great power (the United States) against another (the USSR), evolves into a fluid multipolar system, the need to achieve rapprochement with former opponents will become more pressing.

Second, the recent rapid normalization of Sino-Japanese relations was facilitated by the increased leverage that accrued to Prime Minister Tanaka as a result of an improvement--or the threat of improvement--in Japan's relations with the USSR. However, in future dealings with Moscow, the Japanese will need to be particularly sensitive to the possibility that changes (substantive or illusory) in Soviet-Japanese relations may be perceived as hostile by China and that Peking will respond by taking action detrimental to Japanese national interests. The large-scale participation by Japan in the Siberian development scheme, with its direct ramifications for Chinese security, is likely to fall into this category.

A third factor is the considerable extent to which the Soviet and Japanese economies are complementary. The USSR would like access to Japanese capital, technology, consumer goods, and assured long term markets for its surplus raw materials. Japan wishes to diversify its export trade and its source of supply of essential resources, particularly energy, to minimize the susceptibility of the Japanese economy to the impact of international tensions.

These conflicting considerations promise to make the management of Japan's relations with the USSR and the P.R.C. an extremely difficult task.

THE FUTURE OF SOVIET-JAPANESE RELATIONS

The Japanese neither like nor trust the Russians. They still are angered by the ruthless Soviet abrogation of a neutrality agreement in 1945 that resulted in the seizure of the northern islands and the brutal mistreatment of hundreds of thousands of Japanese prisoners in Manchuria. The politically, economically, and culturally dominant elements that mold Japan's weltanschauung are the West, as represented by the United States and the European community, and, in a category all its own, China. Soviet military and economic power will continue to be an important concern to Japan's leaders. Japan, however, will be inclined to approach its relations with the USSR on the basis of hard calculations of national interest, seeking to maintain peaceful coexistence and economic relations. To the extent that it furthers Japan's national interests at an acceptable level of risk, Japan will attempt to capitalize on Soviet-American and, more important, Sino-Soviet rivalries in an effort to improve its own position with respect to the three major powers. However, Japan will place a premium on flexibility, maneuverability, and the maximization of options in its dealings with the United States, the USSR, and China. In both the economic and political realms, Japan will be acutely sensitive to the ramifications that its relations with the Soviet Union will have on its relations with China and the United States. Japan's interaction with the three great powers will more and more tend to take place within the framework of simultaneous negotiation and rivalry, both tacit and explicit.

The Soviet Union has chosen to attempt to advance its relations with Japan by proposing the joint exploitation of Siberia, where there are natural resources of direct interest to Japan. In particular, it is the Soviet proposal, first made in March 1966, for joint Japanese-Russian development of the Tyumen oil fields and the construction of a pipeline to Nakhodka on the Sea of Japan that has been of greatest interest to Japan. The reason for this interest is not difficult to find. As Table 12.1 indicates, Japan's level of dependence on imported supplies of vital resources exceeds that of any other industrialized nation. Japan imports 99.9 percent of its oil, mostly from the Persian Gulf. This oil is transported to Japan by tanker and therefore must pass through the increasingly congested (minimum width is four nautical miles and minimum depth two and one-half fathoms[8]) and strategically vulnerable Malacca Straits.[9] Access to

TABLE 12.1

Raw Material Imports: Japanese Demand and Dependence

| Material | Unit of Measure | 1975 (Estimated) | | | Average Increase 1969-75 (percent) | Extent of Dependence on Foreign Sources, 1970 (percent) |
		Demand	Domestic Supply	Import (percent)		
Copper	1,000 tons	1,420	225	82	9.8	Philippines 43.3 Canada 33.1
Lead	1,000 tons	303	163	46	7.7	Peru 31.2 Canada 26.9 Australia 24
Zinc	1,000 tons	1,149	494	57	11.1	Peru 42.6 Australia 17.8 Canada 14.6
Aluminum	1,000 tons	2,000	--	100	15.5	(Bauxite) Australia 49.9 Indonesia 24.6
Nickel	1,000 tons	160	--	100	13.0	New Caledonia 90.6
Iron ore	1,000 tons	200,000	18,000	91	12.8	Australia 27.9 India 16.4 Peru 10.4 Chile 9.3
Coking coal	1,000 tons	106,000	12,600	92	12.0	United States 47.8 Australia 39.0
Petroleum	1,000 kiloliters	323,000	800	99.9	11.1	Mostly Persian Gulf
Natural gas	million cubic meters	9,500	2,510	73.6	26.1	--
Uranium	short tons	15,660	--	100.0	--	--

Source: International Institute for Strategic Studies, Strategic Survey 1971 (London: IISS, 1972), p. 60.

131

Tyumen oil would not eliminate Japanese dependence on Persian Gulf oil, but it would certainly further Japan's policy of diversifying sources of supply.

To date, Japanese participation in the development of Siberian resources has been limited to the joint development of forest resources and the construction of a port complex in the Bay of Wrangel.[10] Japan understandably is reluctant to provide the Soviet Union, the nation Japan perceives as the principal potential military threat to its security, with direct control over the flow of any portion of its imported strategic resources, particularly oil. However, if the conditions affecting the price and stability of Japan's present sources of oil in the Persian Gulf were to deteriorate significantly, Japan could be forced to pay the political and strategic costs--including those that large-scale Japanese participation in Siberian development could have for Sino-Japanese relations--to diversify its sources of supply to the greatest extent possible.

If Japan is to participate in the exploitation of Siberian natural resources, perhaps the most attractive possibility from Japan's point of view would be a tripartite arrangement among the USSR, the United States, and Japan. It was announced on November 3, 1972 that precisely such an arrangement was under consideration by the three governments.[11] The proposal (no final decision had been made public by early 1973) involves the expenditure of $10 billion for the construction of two pipelines to carry natural gas (valued at $45 billion over the full term of the agreement) to liquification plants at Soviet ports. Japan would be allocated one-half of the natural gas (one billion cubic feet per day) flowing through a pipeline, which would terminate at Nakhodka, near Vladivostok. From there a fleet of tankers would carry the liquified gas to Japan for distribution.

This type of multilateral arrangement for the development and exploitation of Siberian resources clearly raises the possibility of yet another source of economic conflict between Japan and the United States. However, it has the dual advantage, for Japan, of minimizing the security risks inherent in purchasing large quantities of strategic resources from the USSR on a unilateral basis and furthering Japan's objective of diversifying present dependencies in the supply of vital natural resources. The economic interdependence that a scheme of the proposed scale inevitably would generate, together with the political pressure that the United States would bring to bear in the unlikely eventuality that the USSR were to decide to interrupt the gas flow, makes this type of arrangement highly attractive to Japan. Moreover the adverse political effects that Japanese participation in Siberian development could have on Sino-Japanese relations would be diffused by American involvement in projects of this sort.

NOTES

1. John K. Emmerson, <u>Arms, Yen and Power</u> (New York: Dunellen, 1971), p. 245.

2. For a discussion of this proposal and reaction to it see ibid., pp. 245-48.

3. Text may be found in <u>Pravda</u>, January 28, 1972.

4. For a discussion of the Northern Territories issues, see Emmerson, op. cit., pp. 230-37.

5. An excellent analysis of Japanese participation in Siberian development can be found in Kiichi Saeki, "Ventures in Soviet Diplomacy--Toward Japanese Cooperation in Siberian Development," <u>Problems of Communism</u> 21 (May-June 1972).

6. Toronto <u>Globe and Mail</u>, January 15, 1973, p. 2.

7. Soviet long range reconnaissance and surveillance aircraft make regular runs off both the Japanese shoreline and the Chinese coast on electronic intelligence gathering missions. See Toronto <u>Star</u>, January 12, 1973, p. 8.

8. T. B. Millar, "The Indian and Pacific Oceans: Some Strategic Considerations," Alelphi Papers no. 57 (London: Institute for Strategic Studies, 1969), p. 17.

9. A pipeline across the Kra Peninsula has been proposed but not yet established as feasible. The Lombok Straits, in Indonesian waters to the south of the Malacca Straits, is a possible alternate route; but the cost of transportation would be increased considerably. International Institute for Strategic Studies, <u>Strategic Survey 1971</u> (London: IISS, 1972), p. 60.

10. For details, see Saeki, op. cit.

11. Toronto <u>Star</u>, November 3, 1972, p. 1.

CONCLUSION:
A SUMMATION AND PROJECTION
OF CHINESE AND JAPANESE
BEHAVIOR FOR THE 1970s

The wise man keeps one foot firm, and moves the other.
Without making sure of your next move, do not give up
your present place.

Epigram from the Ming Dynasty

BASIC ASSUMPTIONS OF THE STUDY

In attempting to project the direction of Chinese and Japanese
behavior and national policies over the remainder of the decade, we
have made the following fundamental assumptions with respect to the
international environment within which the two states will be required
to operate.

1. The central strategic interface will continue to be characterized by Soviet-American military bipolarity.
2. The international system is evolving toward political multipolarity.
3. The overall Soviet-American rapprochement is likely to be
improved further on the basis of a growing common interest in the
maintenance of stability and the status quo. Should appreciable Soviet-American economic and technological interdependence develop,
this tendency will be strengthened considerably.
4. The Sino-American detente will continue, although Taiwan
will present difficulties for the United States if official diplomatic relations with the P.R.C. are sought in Washington. The scaling down
of American military power encircling the People's Republic of China
has removed the principal irritant from Sino-American relations
from Peking's point of view. At the same time, Peking sees the im-

provement in relations with Washington and a continuing American military presence in the Asian-Pacific region as a counterweight to the increase in Soviet military and diplomatic activity in Asia. The United States, on the other hand, will use the relationship to increase its leverage in dealings with the USSR as well as to facilitate the continued withdrawal of American military forces from the southeast Asian quagmire.

5. The Sino-Soviet dispute, a principal potential source of instability in Asia, can be expected to persist. A rapprochement seems unlikely even after Mao has passed from the scene. Protracted political and perhaps military confrontation will dominate the relationship.

6. Asia will continue to exhibit a strong propensity for instability and violence. Traditional ethnic-religious conflicts, political instability, continuing problems of economic development in the noncommunist nations of south and southeast Asia (due to uncontrolled population growth and declining terms of trade), and great-power rivalries are among the complex reasons for this state of affairs.

7. The Nixon Doctrine does not portend American isolationism. The U.S. military presence in the Asian-Pacific region will remain potent, although its purpose and composition will change. The doctrine does, however, represent a guideline against automatic U.S. commitments that are not directly related to vital American national interests.

P.R.C. FOREIGN POLICY PARAMETERS

Given this environment, the foreign policy of the People's Republic of China will be conditioned by seven basic parameters during the 1970s.

1. A sinocentric mentality: the Chinese perception of themselves, their culture, their nation, and its position in the states system will be dominated by an implacable sense of their own social superiority. This fundamental psychological disposition serves as an important support for the P.R.C.'s system of totalistic social conformity; however, with respect to China's foreign relations, this abiding devotion to Han culture may be interpreted abroad as arrogant, petty chauvinism. Thus the phenomenon of sinocentrism conceivably could obstruct the P.R.C.'s attempts to expand and strengthen relations with other nations in the global "intermediate zones."

2. A preoccupation with the export of political culture: in following the dictates of redirected nationalist sentiment and the imperatives of Mao Tse-tung Thought, Chinese foreign policy decision makers will

tend to focus their efforts on those nations most likely to be receptive to the central imperative of the Maoist cultural universe--nationalist anticolonialist revolution. In this respect, the export of Maoist ideology is a necessary process for the continuing validation of Maoist theory. The export of revolutionary writings will continue to be seen as a much more important process than the export of material assistance.

3. An obsession with ideological purity: because of its uniquely totalistic qualities, Chinese revolutionary practice involves an unparalleled use of guilt and existential redefinition of self in the inculcation of the communists' world view. The resultant impact on the mental life of the Chinese is manifest as a hitherto unequaled attitudinal uniformity, extending through all political strata of society. The very perception of attitudinal deviations from the established social norms induces severe guilt or anxiety in most members of the society. Therefore it is reasonable to expect that Chinese decision makers will partake of the generalized obsession with maintaining an unswerving dedication to established social principles (that is, the precepts of Marxist-Leninist-Maoist thought). Thus we may also expect that P.R.C. foreign policy will continue to be characterized by a certain xenophobic avoidance of entangling alliances, which might generate pressures for extensive social or economic intercourse with alien societies. Chinese decision makers will strive to prevent the introduction of "bourgeois" or "revisionist" influence into the P.R.C.

4. The will to autarky: mistrust of foreigners, the emphasis on Spartan, revolutionary asceticism, and the low priority assigned to the improvement in the Chinese standard of living will tend to perpetuate the traditional Chinese emphasis on the creation of a largely self-sufficient economic system.

5. Demographic stability: with a population that will probably reach more than 1 billion people by the year 2000, the P.R.C. will be forced to adhere to strict population control measures. Because of the truly totalitarian nature of their social system, restrictive measures can and probably will be carried through. Thus, unlike south Asia, the P.R.C. may be spared the worst excesses of the operation of Malthusian constraints: starvation, epidemic, and chronic social disorder. Unlike south Asian nations, China will not require massive economic aid to stave off a collapse of the domestic social structure.

6. An emerging capacity for strategic autonomy: already possessing a rudimentary first-generation nuclear capability and the necessary personnel and institutional framework for an expanded weapons development program, the P.R.C. is in a sound position to expand and diversify its strategic nuclear forces. Through harden-

ing its present IRBM systems and its projected ICBM system, and by pressing ahead with the development of a modest submersible seaborne deterrent force, the Chinese could acquire a credible second-strike capability with respect to both the USSR and the United States. This is a possible, but not a probable, development. Achievement of this degree of strategic autonomy is entirely contingent on the continued limitation of ABM deployment in the United States and the USSR, the success of future SALT negotiations in restraining the deployment of MIRV (Multiple Independently Targeted Re-entry vehicles) or FOB (Fractional Orbiting Bombardment) systems, and the rate of economic investment by the United States and the USSR in the qualitative improvement in "software" capabilities, such as electronic monitoring and intelligence. Substantial improvement in this capability could nullify totally the Chinese systems (even SLBM-carrying submarines) by rendering them susceptible to preemptive first strikes. To date the Chinese have demonstrated that they have the prerequisite will to divert a large portion of the national output toward the acquisition of a modern, weapons-oriented, scientific establishment. Whether they will continue to invest in their nascent deterrent at previous rates of expenditure now that they can see the possibility of supplementary security arising from successful "united front" diplomacy is debatable. But where security matters are concerned, we believe the Chinese leadership rarely is swayed by economic considerations alone. Therefore, they probably will opt for a condition of maximal strategic autonomy. This choice would be consistent with past behavior. Furthermore, the deployment of what appears, to third parties, to be a credible nuclear deterrent remains a substantial symbol of China's great-power status.

7. Revived political structures: in spite of the rise in influence of the People's Liberation Army as a result of the Cultural Revolution, it is probable that the Chinese communist party eventually will reassert control over the military. The principal effect of the recent period of militarization well may be an appreciation of the value of the military as a stabilizer for the entire social system, that is, as an instrument for moderating the excesses caused by rapid shifts in the internal balance of power. The party as the fount of theoretical insight should regain soon its appropriate position of dominance.

P.R.C. FOREIGN POLICY GOALS

In light of these operative constraints, we believe the Chinese foreign policy will seek to achieve the following goals over the next decade.

I. The Sino-Soviet relationship

  A. At a maximum, the attainment of ideological and political hegemony in the world communist movement; at a minimum, substantial recognition of the validity of the Chinese revolutionary experience either through the successful dissemination of Mao Tse-tung Thought on its own merits or through the more expedient approach of plying nationalist bourgeoisie with economic aid.
  B. The neutralization of Soviet containment policy through the attempted elimination of Soviet influence in North Korea, North Vietnam, and southeast Asia in general.
  C. International recognition of Peking's claim to Soviet-held territories in the Far East and west of Sinkiang.

II. The Sino-American relationship

  A. Continued diplomatic isolation of the nationalist regime prior to a withdrawal of the last vestiges of a concrete military presence on Taiwan by the United States and a negotiated surrender of Taiwan to Peking's suzerainty.
  B. A continued deescalation of the American military presence in Asia--but only if the USSR undertakes a reduction in forces on the northern borders. Short of that goal, the Chinese perceive it to be in their own interest that the United States maintain a substantial military presence in the western Pacific.
  C. Exploitation of opportunities for access to the latest developments in aeronautics, communications, electronics, and computer technologies, as a result of the current phase of detente and cooperation in Sino-American and Sino-Japanese relations.

III. Revolutionary objectives

  A. An increase in influence in Africa to exploit the "revolutionary contradictions" inherent in the blatant neocolonialism of white rule in Rhodesia and South Africa, and the "unabashed colonial exploitation" prevalent in Angola, Mozambique, Portuguese Guinea, and the Spanish Sahara. A renewed trade/aid offensive across North Africa also could be expected. The recent overtures (and loans) to Ethiopia point to more northerly aspirations on this continent.
  B. Acquisition of a diplomatic foothold in Latin America through a concerted attempt to develop Sino-Latin American trade.

C. A renewed effort to penetrate the Middle East in an effort
to negate Soviet influence in this strategically vital zone.
Secondarily, the Chinese will attempt to create problems for
the USSR in the long term through the creating of yet another
military front on its south-central frontiers. If this is in
fact a hidden objective in the P.R.C.'s Middle Eastern strategy, China and the USSR may offset each other's influence in
this strategically vital zone of confrontation.

JAPANESE FOREIGN POLICY: OBJECTIVES AND PROSPECTS

For the remainder of the 1970s, Japan's vital national interests
will necessitate seeking the following six basic objectives:

1. the maintenance of general international stability;
2. the preservation of a credible U.S. nuclear guarantee;
3. the avoidance of conflict with the Soviet Union and the People's
   Republic of China;
4. secure sea routes;
5. the diversification and maintenance of secure and stable sources
   of supply of raw materials; and
6. the continued availability and expansion of secure markets.

In view of these objectives, we believe that Japan's national policies over the remainder of the decade will take the following direc-
tions.

1. The domestic environment: despite its global economic influence, Japan remains an insular and inwardly looking nation, highly
preoccupied with domestic problems. Japan's successful, single-
minded pursuit of economic growth has left in its wake enormous social, economic, and ecological problems whose solution will affect
profoundly the structure of the Japanese economy. A permanent shift
in the pattern of national priorities, objectives, and resource allocation will take place over the remainder of the decade as Japan
moves to create a high-welfare economy. Massive expenditures by
the public sector on social overhead capital will take place in such
fields as social and health care, housing, transportation, and environmental control. The shift of resources from the private to the public sector will slow Japan's economic dynamism, but average growth
rates between 6 and 10 percent over the remainder of the decade
likely will be achieved.

2. International economic activity: Japan can ignore no longer the political antagonism caused by the disruption of foreign economies, which is the product of its global economic dynamism. Although trade represented only 11.2 percent of Japan's GNP in 1971[1] (only the United States is less dependent on trade), it must be recognized that access to markets and raw materials will continue to remain an absolutely vital element for the security and well-being of the Japanese people. Japan must export to earn the foreign exchange with which to purchase the essential raw materials that Japan lacks. Approximately 75 percent of Japan's imports consist of energy resources and raw materials.[2]

Economic relations with the United States--over 30 percent of Japan's foreign trade is carried on with that nation--will be crucial over the next several years, particularly since continuing Japanese-American economic conflict will tend to erode the credibility of the Japanese-American defense relationship. Prime Minister Tanaka indicated immediately after the Japanese elections in December 1972[3] that his administration would give top priority to efforts designed to reduce Japan's growing trade surplus ($8.97 billion in 1972 compared with a surplus of $7.8 billion in 1971[4]), particularly with the United States. (The United States trade deficit grew to $6.44 billion in 1972--of which $4.1 billion was with Japan--compared with $2.01 billion in 1971, the first deficit since 1888.[5])

If Tanaka's efforts are to have any appreciable impact, voluntary export restraints and orderly marketing practices will have to be applied stringently. In addition, further measures to remove barriers to foreign investment in the Japanese economy as well as import stimulation--particularly in manufactured and agricultural products--will be required. Ultimately, however, the dynamism of the Japanese economy must be slowed if Tanaka's objective is to be realized. This will require structural changes in the Japanese economy (the shift of resources from the private to the public sector), a process that has begun already but will require several years to have any significant impact on the Japanese foreign trade position. In the near to medium term, therefore, Japanese-American economic conflict is likely to continue and the U.S.-Japan relationship, already taut, will be strained further. A new round of unilateral U.S. actions geared to revaluing the yen upward again is virtually inevitable.

The 1970s will witness a massive increase in Japanese overseas investment over the present modest level ($3.43 billion at the end of 1970[6]). Japan's strong position with respect to gold and foreign exchange reserves ($17.9 billion in early 1973[7]) will make such an expansion possible. The attractions of such a program are numerous.

a. secure outlets for Japanese manufactured goods can be created;
b. trade barriers generated by massive imports of Japanese goods can be avoided;
c. the buildup of an embarrassing trade surplus in Japan's favor can be controlled, thereby weakening foreign demands for liberalization of Japanese import policy--pressure for a liberalization of Japan's inward, direct investment policy, however, would tend to increase;
d. greater direct control of sources of supply of raw materials would be possible;
e. high labor costs attending production in Japan might be eliminated by producing in countries with a labor surplus; and
f. heavy industry might be relocated outside Japan to reduce the negative ecological side-effects on Japan's urban-industrial complex.

Finally, during the remainder of the decade, Japan will endeavor to apply its enormous economic power to achieve political and diplomatic influence. Japan's international economic activity--whether it takes the form of trade, aid, or investment--will become an increasingly crucial element in Japan's security strategy. Japan will seek to create stability in Asia through the strengthening of Asian economies. Japan's voice in the political and diplomatic affairs of the Asian-Pacific region is destined to grow in importance as Japan attempts to influence directly the course of events in the area rather than merely reacting to a changing international environement. As Japan's profile rises, the potential for direct involvement in future conflicts will increase proportionately.

3. The relationship with the United States: despite present and potential future economic conflicts and rivalries, the relationship with the United States, with its benefits as well as problems, is likely to remain the central pillar of Japan's foreign and security policies. In the near to medium term there seems to be no viable alternative, for the United States will continue to provide Japan with both its largest export market and the ultimate protection of its nuclear deterrent. The relationship, however, will move toward greater reciprocity and equality and will become less pervasive. The continued existence and credibility of the American security guarantee to Japan will be in the interest of both the USSR and China, insofar as the guarantee tends to contain pressures for the development of an independent Japanese military capability.

4. Defense strategy: although no imminent military threat menaces Japan, the military capabilities of the People's Republic of China and, more important, the Soviet Union, present Japan with serious potential threats to its security over the next decade. A de-

cision to embark on a major military buildup would involve formidable risks, costs, and constraints, without guaranteeing any significant improvement in Japan's security. Japan, therefore, is attempting to widen its future defense options by creating the potential for a rapid expansion of military power. With respect to the self-defense forces, this means qualitative and quantitative improvements in capability-- particularly in the air and maritime forces. With respect to nuclear weapons, Japan will pursue a policy designed to create a protonuclear capability. That is to say, Japan will seek to upgrade its potential to become a nuclear weapons power in a short period of time. The desire to be accorded an international status commensurate with its global economic influence will generate growing pressures for strategic autonomy. However, unless the international environment deteriorates appreciably, these pressures will be resisted. Japan is likely to play a growing role as an international arms supplier, particularly in Asia.

5. Relations with the P.R.C.: Japan is drawn toward China by a powerful mixture of political, economic, sociocultural, and emotional considerations. The normalization of Sino-Japanese relations reflects these considerations as well as a new freedom and independence in Japanese foreign policy. Further improvements in the relationship, particularly in the field of trade, seem likely. Japan will attempt to use the relationship with China to improve its overall position in relation to the USSR and the United States, while maintaining a neutral position in the Sino-Soviet confrontation.

6. Relations with the USSR: Japan is concerned with improving relations with the Soviet Union, the principal potential military threat to its security. However, the Japanese neither like nor trust the Russians. Therefore, Japan will be inclined to approach its relations with the USSR on the basis of hard calculations of national interest and with great sensitivity to any Chinese reaction to changes in the Soviet-Japanese relationship. Japan will continue to remain reluctant to participate in joint Soviet-Japanese projects for the development of Siberian resources, preferring tripartite arrangements involving the United States in order to minimize the security risks inherent in purchasing sizable quantities of strategic resources (particularly oil and gas) from the USSR.

EAST ASIA'S POLITICAL GEOMETRY

In the variable geometry of the Pacific-Asian balance that is usually described in terms of a three-power nuclear triangle or a four-power economic quadrilateral, the following diagram may be useful in illustrating the positions of the four major powers in Asia. With

FIGURE 1

Four Major Powers in Asia

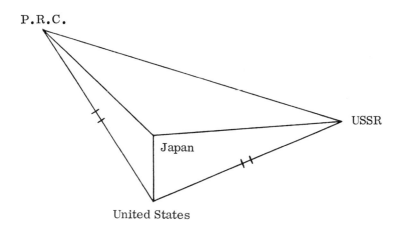

the United States pursuing detente with the USSR to obtain economic
benefits from expanded trade relations (especially in oil and natural
gas) and to promote agreements regarding arms control and disarma-
ment in both SALT and MBFR (Mutual and Balanced Force Reductions)
negotiations, while simultaneously pursuing detente with the P.R.C.
to minimize force deployments in the Asian theaters and to improve
the security of its Asian allies while reducing the cost of this burden,
the Americans are approximately equidistant from the P.R.C. and
the USSR in this hypothetical model. Japan remains very close to
the United States, though leaning more toward the P.R.C. than the
Soviet Union.

In the present configuration of forces, the USSR is in the least
favorable position to capitalize on political maneuvering. It is locked
into a matrix of conflict with the P.R.C.; and it has pursued a strategy
of negotiation with the Japanese that has made too many demands on
Japan, while providing too few incentives for the basis of a long term
entente between the two countries.

It is within this framework that the Chinese and Japanese must
develop their security policies. Clearly, both the present structure
of world power and any future equilibrium are directly dependent on
continued Sino-Soviet antagonism. The Sino-Soviet rift is the founda-

tion of the Nixon-Kissinger approach to building a new age of multilateral diplomacy and balance-of-power adjustments. The rift makes it all possible. As Lao Tzu observed, "Just because the axle moves not, the spokes revolve."

NOTES

1. Organization for Economic Cooperation and Development, Economic Surveys: Japan (Paris: OECD, 1972).

2. International Institute for Strategic Studies, Strategic Survey 1971 (London: IISS, 1972), p. 61.

3. Toronto Globe and Mail, December 12, 1972, p. 11.

4. Ibid., January 24, 1973.

5. Ibid.

6. Strategic Survey 1971, p. 62.

7. Toronto Globe and Mail, February 1, 1973.

POSTSCRIPT
Douglas A. Ross

CHANGES IN THE GLOBAL CONTEXT

Since this study was completed many important changes have occurred in the international system and within several of the major
states. The most significant international development related to
the Arab-Israeli conflict of October 1973--specifically: the use of
the "oil weapon" for the first time; Soviet determination to back the
Arab cause fully despite growing interest in maintaining harmonious
Soviet-American relations; the rapid rise in the price of internation-
ally marketed crude oil, which has caused massive economic disloca-
tion in the noncommunist developed countries (particularly Japan);
the attenuation of the U.S.-European link as a result of the rift over
support of Israel; the undermining of the international monetary system
as enormous oil revenues flow into the accounts of the oil-producing
nations; the development of major problems with balance of payments,
inflation, and recession in all Western, developed economies and the
near crisis in the less developed countries, due in large measure to
the rising cost of energy imports.

In addition to the unresolved political and economic problems pre-
cipitated by the Arab-Israeli conflict, several other globally significant trends became apparent: in the last 12 months a major crisis
in the production and distribution of food developed, and international
recognition of the problem led to the disappointing Rome World Food
Conference in mid-November 1974; Third World nations, particularly
the three in south Asia, continued to be plagued by an expanding population that could not be brought under control (India's population has
increased by over 100 million in the last eight years); major problems in raw material supply have become evident in more than the
petroleum-related industries, particularly in light of the possibility

of further cartelization in international markets and the rapidly expanding competition for such materials between the United States, Japan, and Western Europe. All of these trends bode ill for the non-communist developed countries, particularly as an incipient confrontation between the rich and poor nations can be inferred for the not too distant future. The emerging power of OPEC (and within that group of states the Organization of Arab Petroleum Exporting Nations) countries, as well as the so-called Group of Seventy-Seven nonaligned countries, was made clear at the Rome conference, as was their antipathy toward the "extravagant," resource-consuming populations in Europe, Japan, and North America. In sum, the problems related to the production and trade of energy, food, and raw materials have complicated immeasurably global political and economic relations.

In the strategic weapons context, negotiations to control the Soviet-American race seemed totally bogged down, and qualitative development of successive generations of strategic weapons continued apace. By March 1973, the USSR tested its first onboard computers for its SS-11 ICBM. By the summer of that same year, it had conducted the initial testing for two of the four new ICBM systems that conceivably could be deployed as early as autumn 1975. By January of 1974 tests were conducted with the MIRV-tipped SS-X-19, * which is capable of carrying six warheads--each of which is twice as powerful as the Minuteman III warheads. Through November 1974 tests continued on the SS-X-18 (with 8 warheads), and the mobile SS-X-16 (one large warhead). In addition to MIRV and ICBM development, the USSR began to deploy new "delta" class submarines, each with 16 SLBMs that possess a range of 4,200 nautical miles--sufficient to permit these missiles to attack targets throughout the continental United States while being stationed extremely close to or inside Soviet territorial waters. To counter these developments, the United States has proceeded with development programs of its own, including among others, further development of the 4,600-mile Trident SLBM; continued development of the B-1 (which by the time of its operational deployment may possess a long range, standoff missile); development of maneuverable reentry vehicle (MaRV) warheads and improved terminal guidance systems for all MIRV capable missiles; development of the Trident and Narwhal nuclear submarines; and finally, an already proven capacity to launch Minuteman missiles from airborne C-5A Galaxy cargo aircraft.

To counter what seemed to be an ominous buildup of Soviet strategic strength, the American government also decided to reformu-

---

*Multiple independently targeted reentry vehicles.

late radically its targeting doctrine, shifting away from the "assured destruction" concept to a "counterforce" doctrine that, according to U.S. Defense Secretary James Schlesinger, will maintain the symmetry of the Soviet and American nuclear arsenals--thus bringing the probability of nuclear war to a level "approaching zero." Taken together, the American moves may have forced the Russians to reexamine their own positions on arms limitation and may have led them to reduce their demands at the SALT II talks. Contrary to appearances, real progress has been made in the past six months. Whether this progrsss is due to Soviet concessions cannot be ascertained until the final terms of the Ford-Brezhnev agreement are negotiated. (According to President Gerald Ford's December 2, 1974 press conference, the SALT negotiators are to work out detailed arrangements for a ceiling of 2,400 for the total number of strategic missiles and heavy bombers on each side, with the additional constraint of a figure of 1,320 for the total number of MIRV-capable missiles permissible.) Though the Vladivostok agreement has put a dangerously loose "cap" to the arms race (since it effectively does not slow down qualitative improvements in force deployments), the Soviet-American relationship has received an important stimulus at a time when American congressmen were beginning to doubt Soviet sincerity--because of the Soviet actions in the October 1973 war, because of problems over the question of Soviet Jewish emigration, and because of what many American leaders took to be aggressive behavior by the USSR in escalating the arms race. Unfortunately the so-called "cap" to the arms race was negotiated after MIRV development had been carried out. Whether the world will enjoy increased security against the possibility of a major nuclear conflict involving the superpowers or China with such high numerical ceilings and such clear-cut possibilities for maintaining an unstable first-strike capability against the Chinese by the superpowers remains a dubious prospect.

Nuclear proliferation became a major issue once more with the Indian nuclear test conducted on May 18, 1974. Indian expressions of peaceful intent and a desire to prevent what it termed "technological apartheid" meant nothing to Pakistan. Prime Minister Z. A. Bhutto of Pakistan declared, "If India builds the bomb, we will eat leaves and grass, and even go hungry, but we will have to get one of our own."[1] In November 1973, M. H. Heykal, editor of Cairo's Al Ahram newspaper, charged that Israel already had several bombs (perhaps six to twelve 20-kiloton bombs according to other reports) and proceeded to recommend that the Arab nations develop their own nuclear weapons program well back from Israeli borders in the "strategic depth" of the Arab states.[2] In July 1974 the vice president of the South African Atomic Energy Board declared that "our nuclear program is more advanced than that of India" and, more specifically,

that South Africa possessed a uranium enrichment capability and
could proceed relatively easily with the manufacture of nuclear bombs.[3]
The situation in east Asia is also becoming progressively more ominous at the strategic level. The possibility of Japan's taking up the
nuclear option already has been discounted--but only in respect to
her becoming the sixth or seventh nuclear power. Whether the Japanese aversion to nuclear weapons would remain as strong when there
may be a dozen or more nuclear states is certainly more doubtful.
There is, moreover, the possibility of Taiwan and South Korea decid-
ing to develop atomic weapons, perhaps within a decade--a prospect
the Japanese could view only with grave misgivings.[4]

To sum up, the global strategic context has become much more
indeterminate in the past two years. The two superpowers have continued to match each other in successive rounds of the arms race, and
thus they remain the two most militarily powerful states on the planet.
However, in spite of their massive expenditures on nuclear and conventional armaments, neither alone nor in concert have they been able
to dictate peace to the smaller states in the Middle East, nor to
Greece and Turkey in the Cyprus dispute, nor to the parties in the
continuing struggle in Indochina. And, as elsewhere, the situation
in east Asia reflects the growth of competing centers of power. The
People's Republic of China continues to frustrate Soviet ambitions
concerning the creation of an Asian Collective Security system. The
Chinese, moreover, show no signs of relenting to Soviet military
pressure in the Sino-Soviet border dispute. The Japanese, although
handed a sharp setback with the dramatic rise in the cost of their oil
imports, nevertheless have continued to expand both their exports
and their foreign investments as they search abroad for secure sources
of raw materials. Japanese economic influence and Chinese political-
military influence are both on the rise in Asia in spite of the basic
contradiction between these two forces and in spite of the American
and the even stronger Soviet desire to manage the situation as their
own interests dictate. A polycentric distribution of power and influence is already a reality in east Asia.

THE EAST ASIAN NUCLEAR BALANCE

Regional interaction among the states of Asia is unstable and antagonistic compared with either the existing overall political-strategic
relationship between the superpowers or the regional balance in Western Europe. Whereas continuing talks (at "the Conference on Security
and Cooperation in Europe" and the "Mutual Force Reductions Negotiations") have been established between the opposing sides in Europe
and a dialogue and spirit of accommodation have been created between

formerly bitter opponents, no such pattern of amelioration is present in Asia. War continues in Indochina. The two Koreas have resumed their former habits of mutual recrimination and denunciation following a short-lived minidetente. Japanese-South Korean relations have deteriorated badly in the wake of the Kim Dae Jung affair in 1973 and the attempted assassination of South Korea's President Park Chung Hee in 1974. Japanese-Taiwanese relations have grown acerbic since the signing of Japan's aviation agreement with Peking. Finally, what has been referred to as the major contradiction in Asia--the Sino-Soviet relationship--continues to be the hub of Asian political-military interaction. The Sino-Soviet border talks have stalled, and an end to the military confrontation is nowhere in sight.

Soviet-American relations, on the other hand, remain the most harmonious aspect of great power interaction in Asia; but this is surely because the United States and the USSR have dealt with each other over the heads of the other Asian leaders. Soviet-American concerns focus, naturally enough, on maintaining a meaningful dialogue at the SALT negotiations. Of global significance, the strategic arms limitation talks constitute an area of bilateral concern where both parties can achieve important security gains and future economic benefits. One product of the continuing talks was the Soviet-American Agreement on the Prevention of Nuclear War (June 22, 1973), which stated in article 1 that "the parties agree that they will act in such a manner as to prevent the development of situations capable of causing a dangerous exacerbation of their relations, so as to avoid military confrontations, and to exclude the outbreak of nuclear war between them and either of the parties and other countries." Article 4 provided that "if relations between countries not parties to this agreement appear to involve the risk of nuclear war between the USSR and the USA or between either party and other countries, the Soviet Union and the United States acting in accordance with the provisions of this agreement, shall immediately enter into urgent consultations with each other and make every effort to avert this risk."[5]

The significance of this agreement for the Asian area lies in the provision for immediate superpower consultations in the event of an imminent conflict between the USSR and the P.R.C. Clearly the Soviet Union wants to be assured of an open channel to Washington should they feel compelled to launch a preemptive strike on Chinese nuclear installations. This agreement should be seen as being symptomatic of the Soviet Union's desire to have a relatively free hand in relation to the P.R.C. Above all, the Russians want reassurance that in a time of crisis or overt conflict with the Chinese they would not be subject to American attack. John Newhouse's revelation in 1973 of a Soviet proposal (made in 1970 at SALT I) for a superpower nuclear alliance that clearly would be aimed at the P.R.C. gives cre-

dence to this interpretation of the agreement's value in Soviet eyes.[6]
Relevant also are reports that in 1969 Soviet diplomats inquired in
Western diplomatic circles about American and European reactions
to a Soviet "preventive strike" on China.[7] There have been addi-
tional reports that the original Soviet draft for the Agreement on the
Prevention of Nuclear War also included provision for joint Soviet-
American intervention in the event of a threat to the nuclear peace.[8]
In short, the Soviet Union clearly would prefer dependable American
collusion to undependable negotiations and compromise with the
P.R.C. Short of attaining this collusion, the Soviet leadership will
strive to assure American nonintervention in any Sino-Soviet confrontation.

American aims, especially as articulated by Kissinger, remain
focused on preventing any single power from dominating the Asian
region. The United States therefore is casting itself in the role of
balancer between the Russians and the Chinese. It clearly has an interest in maintaining significant differences and difficulties between
Moscow and Peking, but it has an even greater interest in preventing
a nuclear conflict between the two communist powers. Possibilities
for a "catalytic" spread of any conflict always exist, and certainly
this would be true in the case of any major Sino-Soviet engagement.

A persuasive analysis of a hypothetical Soviet attack was undertaken by Harry Gelber in 1973. He concluded that, since a Russian
preventive strike intending to destroy all Chinese delivery systems
(70 MRBM/IRBM missiles and from 180 to 200 airfields where MiG
19, MiG 21, F-9, and Tu-16 aircraft are stationed) would require--
at a minimum--250 single-warheaded missiles, the prospects for an
attack are unlikely.[9] To coordinate such an attack effectively without "tipping one's hand" and having a few Chinese missiles or aircraft get through to hit Irkutsk, Khabarovsk, or Vladivostok (or even
Kiev, Moscow, and Leningrad) would be a difficult operation of great
risk. Second, the necessary size of such a strike would reduce significantly the Soviet land-based missile capability (against the United
States), and this in itself might persuade the Soviet military to refrain from attacking. Although this latter factor has been somewhat
undermined by the advent of the MIRV-tipped SS-X-17, 18, and 19
rockets, which will probably be deployed in significant numbers
within the next two to three years (a coordinated attack then could be
undertaken with as few as 35 SS-X-18), the fact remains that even an
overwhelmingly powerful attack on all nuclear installations, weapon
systems, and even the command and control system itself (Peking),
still might not guarantee 100 percent success if the Chinese adopt
"fire-on-warning" procedures (as they probably would in times of
acute political crisis with Moscow). Whether the Soviet leadership
would countenance such destruction, albeit limited to a handful of

cities, in return for eliminating the Chinese threat for a few decades is doubtful. Historically the Russians always have been conscious of protecting their own country, having suffered grievously in two world wars in this century alone. In addition, the worldwide opprobrium that would be incurred by the Soviet Union for such "monstrous behavior" could prove disastrous. A nuclear attack conceivably could provoke American intervention on behalf of the Chinese. At the least, it might provoke Japan's nuclearization. Thus, on balance, it appears that there is a low probability of a major Soviet attack and (barring accidents) little likelihood of a Sino-Soviet nuclear confrontation.

On the question of a conventional war between China and Russia, it seems equally reasonable to predict that conflict will be avoided. Most of the 45 to 49 Soviet divisions along the border are understrength, representing a maximum military manpower commitment of about 600,000. From Sinkiang to Manchuria there are about 1 million Chinese troops, but the effectiveness of these troops does not extend much past their own railheads.[10] Conversely, given the difficult terrain in northeast China that greatly favors the defense, a Soviet attack by its heavily armored divisions (which outnumber their Chinese opposites by as much as ten to three) appears unlikely. The Soviet tactical nuclear capability and its commitment of highly mobile, heavily armored forces reflects a need to be able to respond rapidly to any Chinese thrusts across the border at the vulnerable Soviet border cities or the Trans-Siberian railway. Both sides then are thinking in terms of defensive capabilities, although both, perhaps unreasonably so, fear attack. What must be clear to the Soviet leaders is that their goal in east Asia must not be to destroy China as a military and political power, but to exert sufficient and appropriate influence on the Peking leadership to help affect and redirect the continuing policy debates in Peking, thereby helping bring to power a faction or coalition that is sympathetic toward rapprochement with the Soviet Union. Both sides are intent on extracting the maximum political utility from their extant military deployments. Neither is contemplating offensive action seriously. The Soviet Union especially can afford to wait in the hope that Mao Tse-tung will pass from China's political scene in the near future. Thus, China has passed its period of maximum vulnerability in relation to the Soviet Union.

Whether it chooses to continue to pursue a political line radically different from Moscow or not, the Peking leadership can rest relatively secure in the knowledge that the Sino-Soviet strategic calculus is now too complex to warrant the risks entailed in an offensive operation against the Chinese. From this position it will continue to pursue policies that aim to split the superpowers and prevent them from establishing a global condominium. Such splitting tactics are, of course, the traditional mode of communist political-diplomatic operation. However, in the new era of polycentric politics all parties will be playing this game to a greater or lesser extent. Before elaborating on this point in the context of a broader analysis of Chinese and Japanese foreign policies, other recent developments in India will be considered.

INDIA AND NUCLEAR PROLIFERATION

India, not a signatory to the Nonproliferation Treaty, exploded its first nuclear device in an underground test in Rajasthan state on May 18, 1974. Despite the earnest assertion of peaceful intent by Indira Gandhi and various Indian officials, Pakistan's Prime Minister Bhutto (as noted in the previous section) declared Pakistani intentions of acquiring nuclear weapons of its own. Within two weeks of the Indian test, Pakistan's foreign minister was dispatched to Peking seeking nuclear aid. [11] Such aid did not materialize. However Pakistan did secure Chinese support for its subsequent call for a nuclear-free zone in South Asia. How the Chinese leaders really would feel about an Indian nuclear weapons capability is not yet clear. As has been noted by one Indian commentator, R. V. R. Chandrasekhara Rao, the Chinese may see in India's test a genuine desire to maximize political and strategic autonomy and minimize Indian dependence on the 1971 Treaty of Peace, Friendship, and Cooperation with the Soviet Union. Rao observed, "The Chinese leaders can easily visualize . . . Indian calculations for a situation involving foreign aggression where automatic Soviet support is either not forthcoming or is not desired. This type of analysis should to some extent reassure the Chinese, since it mitigates their fears of imminent Indo-Soviet collusion." [12]

In spite of the relative diminution in China's status as the sole Asian nuclear power, the Chinese seem, on balance, to be content with Indian nuclear development, although they clearly would prefer that India shun nuclear arms. But even if the Indian leaders decide to develop nuclear armaments, the Chinese probably would not be too dismayed at such an outcome. In all likelihood they would view such a development as warranting an improvement in Sino-Indian relations, and indeed, as reflecting a desire on New Delhi's part for a more attenuated link with Moscow. What the P.R.C. leaders want from India is not so much nuclear abstention as it is Indian abstention from Moscow's proposed Asian collective security pact. Of course, if possible, it would like to promote both these developments.

What is presently clear is that India has not yet decided to take up the nuclear option. Her armed forces are, at a minimum, several years away from possessing a nuclear capability. Furthermore the Indian airforce lacks the heavy bombers that probably would be necessary to deliver its primitive first-generation bomb. Substantial costs therefore would be entailed in such a decision.

Furthermore, if the Indians are sincerely interested in forestalling any further growth of Soviet or American influence in the Indian Ocean region, as some Indian officials have indicated, India's conventional forces, particularly her naval forces, will have to be upgraded significantly from their present levels (one 16,000-ton aircraft carrier, six submarines, two cruisers, two destroyers, and 22 frigates and destroyer escorts).[13] The Indian government has made additions recently to both the air force and the navy, believing (following the disillusionment of the 1960s) that the most efficient way to earn respect and acquire influence in this evil world is through the accumulation of military might. But India's hope of taking up the strategic slack created by Britain's retreat from east of Suez is a vain one. The Soviet Union has had its policies and its navy directed toward the "power vacuum" in the Indian Ocean for some six years now.[14] The USSR is the principal supplier of the Indian navy's armaments, a fact that guarantees Indian dependence on the USSR, in its need for parts and servicing technology, as well as complete military superiority of the Soviet Union over India, since India's capabilities will be known from first-hand experience. For the next five to ten years the Soviet commitment to the Indian Ocean zone is bound to increase as her naval capabilities increase, primarily because of the probable presence of American Poseidon-carrying nuclear submarines. American ballistic missile submarines no doubt will continue to be stationed in the Arabian Sea and the Bay of Bengal until the long range Trident missile becomes operational.[15] Should deployment of these missiles proceed within the parameters of the Vladivostok agreement, the Soviet need for antisubmarine warfare capability in the Indian Ocean would begin to diminish; and by that time (sometime in the early to middle 1980s), India may find herself with a major role in Indian Ocean security. However such speculation could prove to be irrelevant given the difficulties India will encounter in its struggle toward development and economic self-sufficiency.

If India elects to take up the nuclear option or to try to build up impressive regional naval forces, the effort could strain her already overburdened economy to the breaking point. Such a state of affairs no doubt would be to Peking's advantage, since it would help push India further toward food shortages, extreme social disorder, and communist revolution. On the other hand, if India should choose only to develop nuclear technology and not opt for a full scale nuclear force, she will constitute no threat at all to China. Given India's modest financial resources (a GNP of less than $70 billion for some 600 million people) as well as major technological deficiencies in important software fields such as electronics and computers, even considerable work on bomb and/or warhead research and development would be of little significance militarily. An Indian protonuclear posture, unlike Japan's, would amount to a feeble threat. At best, the Indians might be able to deploy a number of nuclear land mines on borders for defensive purposes or acquire a small number of tactical nuclears for limited offensive purposes.[16]

Reaction in the West of course has been negative. Fears that some other near-nuclear powers could "take the leap" (namely, Israel, Japan, South Africa, Argentina, Brazil, the Koreas, Taiwan, Pakistan, or Egypt) led to Canada's immediate cessation of all nuclear aid to India. American congressional reaction was equally negative and focused additionally on the question of India's development priorities. This critical debate on India presaged a 33 percent reduction in American foreign aid appropriations for India, from $75 million to $50 million for fiscal 1975.[17] However, the most interesting reaction to the test came from India itself. A poll taken by the Indian Institute of Public Opinion (a Gallup affiliate) estimated that 99 percent of Indians believed that the test raised India's status, that 90 percent approved future tests, and that fully 66 percent thought India should acquire nuclear weapons.[18] Clearly the mood of the Indian people is one of asserting the country's claim to great power status and to a predominant role in the security of the south Asian region. Whether such sentiment is in India's long term interests is, however, doubtful. The costs of a significant nuclear force would be heavy, particularly for a country with such serious problems demographically and agriculturally. The decision to develop nuclear technology has been justified by a poorly thought out rationale for adding to the country's technological and scientific expertise. In reality, nationalism, and the political value of catering to this nationalism, lies behind India's nuclear research. Equally symptomatic of this nationalism was the recent and overly hasty incorporation of Sikkim into the Indian federal union, an event that certainly strained Sino-Indian relations and could portend future crises over Nepal and Bhutan.

In sum, India is moving gradually toward nuclearization, though it is probable that it will stop short of a strategically meaningful deployment of modern nuclear-equipped aircraft. Clearly India does not have the financial or technical resources for developing either fusion weapons or ballistic missile delivery systems. An Indian nuclear arsenal would be, at best, a rudimentary affair of regional military significance only, useful solely for defense against Chinese aggression. Nevertheless, the Indian leadership seems determined to make this defense option readily accessible, if only because it can exploit its nuclear program for prestige, status, and domestic political gain. Such a course of action may help Prime Minister Gandhi's New Congress Party politically, but the psychological compensation of such entertainments for the Indian polity can only be a short-run diversion--hardly a long-term substitute for effective governmental planning and expenditures that are urgently needed to brake population growth, expand food production, and develop indigenous energy sources.

CHINA

Recent Foreign Policy Postures

The most significant development in the P.R.C.'s foreign policy over the past two years has been the enunciation of, and the commitment to, its Third World strategy. Such a change was a matter of legitimation, bringing Chinese diplomacy under the authority of the party's official line. It was no more than a matter of policy refinement, since Chinese foreign policy long has been characterized by its efforts to woo the Third World--at least since the Bandung era of the mid-1950s. Chou En-lai's political report to the 10th party congress defined the role the Third World will play henceforth in its foreign policy calculations: "The present international situation is one characterized by great disorder on the earth. . . . Relaxation is a temporary and superficial phenomenon and great disorder will continue. . . . The awakening and growth of the Third World is a major event in contemporary international relations. The Third World has strengthened its unity in the struggle against hegemonism and power politics of the superpowers and is playing an ever more significant role in international affairs. . . . Therefore on the international front our party must uphold proletarian internationalism . . . strengthen our unity with the proletariat and the oppressed people and nations of the whole world and with all countries subjected to imperialist aggression, subversion, interference, control or bullying and form the broadest united front against imperialism, colonialism and neo-colonialism and in particular, against the hegemonism of the two superpowers."[19]

This is China's stragegy for the foreseeable future and as such it marks no major departure from established precedents (notably Lin Piao's exhortations to foment revolution in the Third World "countryside"). The difference from past party lines is that it implies, perhaps, a greater reliance on state-to-state relations and not as much on party-to-party support of "progressive elements" within the Third World nations. The Third World, a somewhat nebulous concept in Chinese usage, includes the economically underdeveloped and the politically nonaligned states of Asia, Africa, and Latin America. The term is defined best by exclusion. All states are eligible for Third World status except the superpowers, and the developed states of the second intermediate zone (Australia, New Zealand, Canada, Japan, and the European states not industrialized or not controlled directly by "the Brezhnev renegade clique").[20] No doubt the Chinese would handle the anomalous situation of South Africa and Rhodesia by denying totally the validity of white governments in these countries and stressing the black Africans' right to Third World status.

From Peking's point of view it is the Third World that will make or break the international revolutionary movement. For it is in the developing countries that the most disturbing, and therefore most revolutionary, changes take place in political, social, and economic life. Rates of change are the crucial factors in present Chinese assessments (as they always have been in Chinese thought in one form or another--see Chapter 1). This conception of a reality based on constant change constitutes the theoretical framework for all pronouncements on foreign policy. In a recent major policy address to the United Nations General Assembly, Chiao Kuan-hua stressed the world's "intense turbulence and unrest," as well as a "further sharpening" of the world's "basic contradictions"--that is, the "contradiction" between the United States and the USSR themselves and the "contradiction" between the superpowers and the people of all other countries.[21]

According to the Chinese view, and rightly so, it is economic and social change that is the "motor of international revolution," the kind of change introduced by the radically transforming effects of new production technologies and the newly awakened nationalisms in the Third World. For the optimists in China's political elite (and all followers of Mao must be nominally optimistic), constant change induces constant pressure for national liberation; and with each national revolution the prospects for "American imperialism" and "Soviet social imperialism" will grow dimmer; but Chinese foreign policy (supposedly based on the Maoist dictum of "never seek hegemony") will become increasingly effective. In short, Peking's scenario of projected global political patterns sees a progressively augmented Chinese influence and a progressively diminished Soviet and American power. It is this kind of simplistic, positive theorizing that has given rise to the policy positions and programs that were enunciated in Chiao's UN address and that illustrate the scope and priority interests of Chinese foreign policy thinking: (1) a constant propaganda barrage against superpower detente, which according to the Chinese has "become a kind of quack medicine hawked by the Soviet leadership

everywhere" and which, in reality, is merely a false peace serving
"the purpose of bigger and more intensified contention"--a chimerical
understanding that masks "the wildest arms race"[22] (2) diplomatic
and covert military support for liberation fronts in Angola, Rhodesia,
South Africa, and Mozambique; (3) unequivocal support for the "restoration of Arab territories" and "Palestinian national rights"; (4)
verbal attacks on the USSR for trying to attain "hegemony in the Mediterranean" and for Soviet efforts "to threaten, cajole, subvert and
undermine the Balkan countries . . . aggravating tension in this region"; (5) denunciation of the "annexation" of Sikkim by India and of
the USSR's south Asian policy (which the Chinese say is aimed at acquiring a corridor to the Indian Ocean) and support for Pakistani and
Iranian proposals for nuclear-free zones in south Asia and the Middle East; (6) a diplomatic attack on international recognition of the
Lon Nol government in Cambodia and American violations of the Paris
Agreement on South Vietnam; (7) a call for withdrawal of all UN
troops in South Korea; (8) a renewed effort to publicize the P.R.C.'s
proposals for "the complete prohibition and thorough destruction of
nuclear weapons and absolutely not the so-called limitation of strategic arms," as well as Chinese demands for "no first use" declarations by the United States and the Soviet Union; (9) unqualified support
for the Declaration on the Establishment of a New International Economic Order and its associated Program of Action, which emerged
from the UN General Assembly's Sixth Special Session in April 1974,
support aimed at promoting monopoly power in the Third World
through fostering cartelization where possible and thereby attacking
what the P.R.C. leaders call "the old order of exploitation and plun-
der" that purportedly was created by the two superpowers through
their aid and trade policies; (10) support for the 200-mile exclusive
economic zone at the Law of the Sea Conference and a concomitant
attack on the Soviet Union and the United States for trying to "emas-
culate" this proposal.

The policy stance reflected in the specific measures of the October UN address clearly demonstrates Chinese contempt for any affili-
ation with either the United States or the USSR, a desire to focus on
and if possible exploit politically the international flash points (such
as Vietnam, the Middle East, and Cyprus) at the expense of Soviet
and/or American policy, and an overall goal of seeking the leadership of the countries of the Third World and common cause where
possible with the states of the so-called intermediate zone. This
bid for leadership should not be construed as a desire to increase
national power and influence in the Soviet manner. Within the terms
of Chinese political culture, the foreign policy of the P.R.C. is
directed genuinely by the principle of "never seeking hegemony."
The principle of fostering state self-determination (albeit communist

if possible) is embedded well in Chinese foreign policy and is likely to remain so--certainly for as long as the P.R.C. is intent on re-dressing its boundaries and restoring the territorial integrity of what the Chinese have begun to call their "sacred socialist motherland." Basically the Chinese crave recognition and status for their economic and political-cultural achievements--not a projection of national power and influence in the hope of securing economic gain and a wholly secure environment.

In terms of Asian great power relationships, the Chinese no longer fear the Russians to the extent they did in the 1969-72 period. Beginning with the 10th party congress (August 1973) and the official campaign to criticize Confucius and Lin Piao, the official party line has been to denigrate the immediacy of the Soviet threat (though not the defense measures thought to be necessary to deter this threat), and to assert that Sino-American detente cannot be construed as a choice of principle but solely as a tactical convenience. Taken together, these two policies illustrate the Chinese leaders' intentions of striking a middle course between the superpowers wherever possible; and where it is not, of leaning to the tactically appropriate side. At the August congress it was Chou En-lai who noted in the political report that "at present, the Soviet revisionists are 'making a feint to the east while attacking in the west' and stepping up their contention in Europe and their expansion in the Mediterranean, the Indian Ocean and everyplace their hands can reach."[23] As evidence of this thesis, Chou pointed to the CSCE and the American "year of Europe" as reflecting the chief American security concerns in the present international balance of power. Chou also went on to accuse the Americans of trying to divert the Soviet "peril" toward China, a gambit rejected by the Soviets because, according to Chou, China is "a tough piece of meat."[24] Yet the report also condemned the Soviet Union for waging an anti-China propaganda campaign meant for the ears of the "monopoly capitalists" in the United States who ostensibly reward the Soviet Union for services rendered.

Recent Economic Trends in China

There is more than an element of truth in such charges, but the P.R.C. itself is open to the same charge. The Chinese, too, have tried to capitalize on the Sino-American normalization of relations by expanding trade with the United States from about $70 million in 1972 to over $750 million in 1973. Similarly, overall Chinese trade has leaped from $4.23 billion in 1970 to $8.79 billion in 1973 (over 90 percent with noncommunist countries according to Japanese government estimates).[25] Trade in 1973 was 64 percent above the 1972 level. This mammoth trade increase is the result of unilateral Chinese moves to try to accelerate the pace of economic development in the P.R.C. Additional impetus was given to the development program through recent decisions to purchase whole industrial plants from Japan, the United States, and Europe--largely on credit. In October 1973, the Chinese signed agreements with the Japanese for the acquisition of a $41 million fertilizer production complex and a $377 million fully automated steel rolling mill. Shortly thereafter they arranged for purchase of a $300 million petrochemical plant from a French consortium.[26] Seeking advanced technology, as in the above purchases, the P.R.C. also has entered negotiations with Rolls Royce in Britain hoping to purchase production rights for its Spey turbofan engine (which powers the Trident and the British Phantom) so China could use it in the follow-on model to the F-9 fighter-bomber.[27]

China's policy on external economic relations certainly has been liberalized in the past two years, as evidenced by both the trade jump and the massive credit it has utilized in the past two years ($1 billion on capital equipment expenditures in 1973 and an expected level of about $1.5 billion in 1974).[28] However it would be wrong to say that the Chinese leadership has abandoned its overall preference for autarky. In fact there are definite political limits to how far this liberalization can go without coming under severe attack from the "militant fundamentalists" in the political elite. Resistance already has commenced against this massive involvement with foreign economies; however, it seems unlikely that the radically autarkic party elements actually will force a cutback in the present trade flow volume for several reasons.

First, the Chinese have much to gain in purchasing plants and equipment from Japan, Europe, and the United States, since this inevitably means that the P.R.C. will be acquiring new productive technologies that can be diffused throughout the economy. Second, such sudden integrated infusions of technology can have an important immediate impact on strategically vital sectors (particularly fertilizer and iron and steel production). As a result of recent purchases, the P.R.C.'s steel production capability is expected to double by 1977 from the 1971 level. A production of some 40 to 45 million metric tons per year by 1977 probably would enable it to surpass British or French production (currently running at 27 and 25 million metric tons per year, respectively). Third, the P.R.C.'s sound balance of payments and currency reserve position easily can permit an expanded reliance on foreign purchases[29]; and beyond that there is the fact that in 1974 the P.R.C. has inquired seriously about the possibility of replacing Taiwan in the International Monetary Fund (IMF), although this will be difficult if the P.R.C. is forced to abide by IMF rules for statistical disclosure. Such a move naturally would help promote China's official status as a developing country and as a fraternal member of the Third World. It also would put an added strain on Taiwan and could increase the difficulty of the nationalist Chinese in obtaining international aid. Yet a fourth consideration stems from the P.R.C.'s continued reliance on foreign grain purchases to even out regional imbalances in domestic production and distribution and to provide insurance against crop failure. China must have access to the international grain markets, and in fact it has given verbal assurances to both Canada and Australia that it will continue to be a reliable market for the indefinite future.

Thus, in spite of the political risks entailed in advocating more economic involvement abroad, it is reasonable to expect that the Chinese leadership, whatever faction comes to power following the departure of Mao and Chou, probably will opt for a maintenance of economic relations with the West at levels close to if not equal to present levels. On balance, the economic interaction has not at all threatened China's capacity for self-reliance. In fact, in many ways this interaction has enhanced self-reliance by providing "the means for a rapidly increased production in the means of production"--for example, more chemical fertilizer production to increase grain production and more steel production to facilitate growth in all steel-using industries.

The P.R.C.'s resource endowment, if developed for export potential, may provide further impetus to widened trade and investment flows. Mainland China's mineral production reached over $5 billion by 1971--trailing only the United States and the USSR in total value. The P.R.C. is well endowed with coal, which may be used for export in the near future--most likely to Japan. The P.R.C. has 80 percent of the world's known reserves of tungsten (important for steel alloys). It is a major producer of bauxite (to the extent that it has substituted aluminum for copper for its electric power grid transmission), as well as a major exporter of important rare minerals such as wolfram and antimony (more alloy materials).[30]

The P.R.C.'s economic prospects brightened still further in 1974 with Chou En-lai's shocking announcement that oil production had climbed to 50 million tons--an apparent increase of 150 percent since 1970.[31] Should production be at only 40 million tons per year (equivalent to 780,000 barrels per day--about one-sixth of Japan's rate of consumption) as some American estimates calculate, it still would leave the P.R.C. with definite prospects for economically significant oil exports that could finance still more imports of equipment, plants, and technology. But in spite of this dramatic rise in China's production and in spite of the potential significance of this development for the P.R.C.'s economy, it still seems doubtful that China has either the capacity or the desire to become a major energy supplier to Japan--unlike the Soviet Union, which appears to have vast reserves in Siberia and which craves Japanese capital and expertise.

Although China has begun to export crude oil to Japan (7 million tons in 1973 with a possible rise to about 25 million tons in 1974) and although the Japanese definitely are interested in helping to develop the Po Hai Bay field near Tientsin, the volume of potential Chinese oil exports could not equal the export potential of the Siberian fields at Tyumen, for example, or even the much smaller scale potential of the Sakhalin Island region now being explored by the Japanese and Russians. By 1975 the Soviet Union will be the world's largest oil producing nation, with exports alone roughly equal to all of China's oil production in 1973. The Chinese eventually may develop equally significant fields in the South China Sea region (some oil analysts rank the region in potential with the Middle East, and American firms already have expressed interest in explorations); but that would be some 10 to 15 years distant, with the lengthy and costly exploration phase yet to be undertaken. For the next decade, China's new-found oil will benefit her economy immensely, both in terms of meeting domestic needs for petroleum products and earning important foreign exchange; but it will not help forge a major economic link with Japan. The Japanese will continue to look toward Siberia for immediately available energy supplies.[32]

To sum up, the Chinese economy is in sound shape and without the problems of domestic inflation presently encountered by most developed countries; and the P.R.C. is in a good position to achieve rapid growth rates in both industry and agriculture over the next five to ten years. With the additional bonus of its newly developed oil production capacity, the Chinese leadership need not concern itself with the problems of the "energy crisis" as other states must but can emphasize the formulation of a sound, coherent, and reliable program for economic development over the course of the next two five year plans. There is but one provision: China will need stable political leadership and administration over the next decade. But the prospects for the P.R.C. obtaining this vital prerequisite of orderly and optimal economic progress are not reassuring. Factionalism and the struggle for power within a new collective leadership may prove to be the order of the day, with all its attendant disruptions are unlikely to cause domestic crises in agriculture or industrial production, given China's rapidly improving status in oil, fertilizer, steel, and mineral production. Possible politically caused dislocations can be expected only to slow the P.R.C.'s rate of economic growth. In short, the Chinese economy now has some safety margin, a cushion, before being shoved to the brink of crisis in food, energy, or resource production--in spite of the great difficulties in maintaining assured supplies of basic necessities for what was admitted recently to be a population of "nearly 800 million."[33] As a result, the urgent desire to lower population growth rates has declined somewhat, although population planning continues to be an important social goal.

Chinese Leadership Factionalism and Future Foreign Policy Options

The current political situation in the P.R.C. is extremely unstable. Mao Tso-tung nears 82. He is said to have suffered a stroke in 1973, although he recovered sufficiently to permit him to preside over the 10th party congress in August of the same year. Mao has been largely in seclusion since May 1971, allowing only a few important visitors to meet with him. Politically he appears to have reduced his activity to that of arbiter between the factions of the Chinese political elite--that is to say, he occasionally will make public pronouncements to support the policies of specific factions. Chou En-lai also has been ill of late, suffering from a heart ailment that has hospitalized him for much of 1974. His illness comes at a difficult time in the history of his party when the waning but still powerful forces of radicalism and egalitarianism have mounted a major attack on Chou himself; his policy supporters in the political bureau and the central committee; and Chou's policies of (1) relative moderation in class struggle, (2) heavy reliance on trade to promote rapid economic development, and (3) conciliatory diplomacy abroad to promote China's regional security.

In one of history's great ironies, Mao and Chou at last have been placed in "dialectical opposition" to one another. Chou's political forces have been largely on the rise since the party congress, and the radical left has been forced to give ground in terms of representation in the party's principal decision-making bodies.[34] Consequently Chairman Mao's occasional interventions in the campaign to criticize Lin Piao and Confucius have been on the side of the radicals.[35] Chou's position has been strengthened by several important political developments in the past year.

First there was a major attack on the power of the PLA leadership--particularly the power wielded by the military region commanders. In December 1973, Chou and other key party officials evidently conducted a major operation designed to reduce the army's power by replacing eight of the eleven commanders and putting two generals apparently sympathetic to Chou En-lai, Li Teh-sheng (also chief political commissar of the PLA and acting chief of staff) and Chen Hsi-lien in charge of the critical Shenyang and Peking military regions, respectively. The fact that Chou conducted this operation apparently did not compromise his generally good relations with the professional military. In fact it may have strengthened his position by putting the military on warning that its powers shortly were going to be attacked by the radical left elements in the party and that, if the professional military elite was to preserve its influence, it would have to align itself with the more moderate bureaucrats, of which Chou is the chief exemplar.

A second major development was the decision to reactivate and radically expand the PLA's militia units and place them all under direct party control. Some estimates of current militia levels are as high as 20 million men. This second action to restore party primacy was undertaken in late 1973, ostensibly for the purpose of creating paramilitary street patrols that could aid with such incidental functions as traffic and fire control, crime prevention, enforcement of the back-to-the-countryside program for urban youth, and so forth. However the prime function of the militia, although not officially stated, was to be always available to the central party organs in times of political rectification campaigns (the cultural revolutions of years to come), so events could not get out of hand as they did after 1967 when massive intervention by PLA regulars was necessary to restore order, thus leading to the party-gun dilemma of 1969-73. The professional military no doubt disapproved of this reorganization of the militia, yet there was little it could do to prevent strengthened party controls. PLA acquiescence, though reluctant, was inevitable.

Of additional significance to the position of the moderates was the rehabilitation of Teng Hsiao-ping in April 1973 and Teng's subsequent elevation to the central committee in August 1973 and to the 10th position in the Political Bureau of the Central Committee in January 1974.[36] Although he is not in the nine-member Standing Committee of the Politburo, Teng's elevation has increased the power of the moderate reform bureaucrats in the Politburo and weakened the position of the radically egalitarian element in the party's central organs. Capable, knowledgeable, and highly experienced in governmental administration, Teng's promotion came just in time to enable him to fill in for Premier Chou En-lai during the latter's periods of hospitalization this year. Should Chou either die in the near term or be forced to cut back his heavy work load, Teng appears to be the logical choice to replace Chou in the performance of key governmental duties.

What has taken place in Peking in recent months have been the opening moves in the struggle for power among what appears to be four rough groupings of political opinion within the party, government, and army organizations. These groupings will be denoted here by the major dichotomy in policy between the radically egalitarian politicos and the hierarchical modernizers. Each of these major groupings can be split again. The radical egalitarians have a militant fundamentalist wing and a conservative leftist wing. The hierarchical modernizers can be divided into reform bureaucrats and the professional military.[37]

Of these four policy trends in the Chinese political elite, it appears that the reform bureaucrats, typified by Chou, now hold the strongest position, though their strength could depend on tacit or explicit collusion with key members of the professional military grouping. On balance then, the coalition of forces represented by the major grouping of hierarchical modernizers seems to be emerging as the dominant force in Chinese politics for now. However, the radical egalitarians cannot be treated lightly, for they have Mao Tse-tung among their number in what has been called here the conservative left wing. In far left field are the militant fundamentalists typified by Chiang Ching (Mao's fourth wife), Yao Wen-yuan, or Wang Hung-wen. Of these three, Yao and Wang represent the youth element in the party's drive to combine the old, the middle-aged, and the young in preparation for Mao's eventual departure. Wang, in his mid-30s, rose to prominence at the 10th party congress, assuming what appears to be the number three party position (although this may be a somewhat symbolic concession designed to appeal to the country's youthful radicals). Without trying to attach too many names to these four alternative opinion clusters in the Chinese political spectrum, the major policy stances within each grouping will be delineated here and assessments of the prospects and implications of each will be made in terms of their future influence on Chinese foreign policy. This is not meant to be an exhaustive analysis but a useful tool for differentiating major trends in China's continuing policy debate. What should be borne in mind is that any given individual could fit under a number of headings. For example, one person could espouse attitudes with regard to economic development or domestic class struggle that put him in the fundamentalist wing of the radically egalitarian segment. On the other hand, his views on trade and the international situation could be placed more appropriately under the reform bureaucrat or professional military policy categories.

The militant fundamentalist position seeks constant class struggle, frequent cultural revolutions (every eight years), frequent purges of crypto-capitalists and crypto-revisionists, self-reliance in all sectors of the economy, and close contact with the masses on the domestic front. With regard to foreign policy it seeks (1) isolationism, since it cannot brook compromise with either imperialism or social imperialism; (2) a recognition of the Soviet Union as the greatest threat to the P.R.C.'s security and to China's ideological purity; (3) strategic autonomy through civil defense and the doctrine of people's war (that is, guerrilla warfare within China after an attack), with much less emphasis put on China's maturing nuclear deterrent; and (4) a greater commitment to party-to-party relations abroad and more liberal support for national liberation fronts (NLFs) without regard to prejudicing state-to-state relations. Militant fundamentalist positions can be recognized presently by repeated calls to "swim against the tide," to be vigilant against the restoration of capitalism, and to vilify former American missionaries (an indirect attack on those who support Sino-American rapprochement). If the militant fundamentalist element in the party, with Mao's help, should assert control over the P.R.C.'s foreign policy establishment, one may expect a return to much of the chaos of the Great Proletarian Cultural Revolution (GPCR), a consequent slowdown in China's growth rates, a cutback in expenditures on the military, and policies of "no truck nor trade with the Yankees" and the West generally. If this happens, China will be in serious trouble economically--but it is an unlikely (in fact the least likely) outcome.

The conservative left comprises attitudes that take a more prudent approach toward radical egalitarianism. On the domestic front, the conservative left seeks party purity, especially in the central committee and the Politburo; effective social integration between the rural and urban sectors; controlled but still powerful GPCR's to ensure psychological uniformity in the society and to promote continued respect for, and adherence to, the egalitarian ideal of communist Chinese society, and institutionalized thought reform processes (exemplified by the May 7 cadre schools). On foreign policy issues this value position espouses (1) independence but not isolationism; (2) the use of united front tactics, but only for short duration and purely military, not economic, purposes; (3) strategic autonomy through people's war plus a reliance on minimum or finite deterrence; (4) avoidance of economic dependence on foreign states in any form--even at the cost of foregoing much-needed technology; and (5) an equal appreciation of the value of international prestige and the value of fomenting NLF insurrections.

Mao Tse-tung's own "conservative left" persuasion is the realistic element on the egalitarian side of the political spectrum. It recognizes certain basic dangers to China's security without lapsing into xenophobic isolationism. This tendency notes tactical advantages and tries to exploit them. It is a more activist foreign policy position, but from the West's point of view it is an exploitative approach. It seeks to divide its opposition and to prevent collusion between the United States and the USSR--through partial rapprochement to split the American commitment to detente and through encouraging European unity and military strength (including the French and British deterrent forces) to force continued division of Moscow's defense efforts. The conservative left tendency has been the dominant trend in Chinese foreign policy for 25 years, and it has accomplished this feat by playing off the representatives of other factions.[38] At present this tendency is seeking to counterbalance the emerging forces on the right, the forces of reaction in Mao's eyes--Chou En-lai's men, the hierarchical modernizers. Should the conservative left line continue to dominate Chinese foreign policy it would prevent further improvement in Sino-American relations, curtail trade flows and external economic involvement generally, and seek independence through maximal self-reliance in economics and defense production and a renewed commitment to guerrilla warfare strategy. This is possible, even probable, if the United States and the West, through economic collapse or policy misadventure, should fail to provide sufficient incentives for maintaining and expanding economic relations. Such an outcome would not be disastrous for Western foreign policy, but it would be far less than optimal.

Just as the militant fundamentalists and the conservative left have a common abiding commitment to the actualization of the egalitarian ideal, so too do the reform bureaucrats and the military professionals have a common and persisting appreciation of the value of hierarchy, stratification, and division of labor in achieving efficiency in the operation of large organizations. The reform bureaucrat and professional military elements together will be referred to as the hierarchical modernizers. Both policy stances are committed to structural efficiency and, therefore, to hierarchy: one in a search for rapid effective economic development, the other in a quest for effective command and control of a complex, vast security bureaucracy.

Domestically, the reform bureaucrat element seeks rapid modernization of the economy, stable predictable rates of social change, institutionalized thought reform to maintain ideological orthodoxy but with due respect for the needs of efficient administration, minimal disruptions in the chain of command (that is, no upheavals on the scale of the GPCR), a respect for bureaucracy, rules, roles, and authority in the economically and strategically vital sectors of the economy, and a fully managed society with a controlled rate of population growth. With respect to foreign policy, the reform bureaucrat mentality espouses (1) activist, maximally flexible, united front tactics with the possibility of entering into security agreements with other states; (2) strategic autonomy and increased national status through rapid economic development that is fostered by considerable economic involvement with the most technologically advanced countries in the world; (3) security against superpower attack through minimum deterrence in the short to medium term leading to a secure second-strike deterrent capability in the long term; and (4) nominal support for NLFs but a great interest in the creation and exercise of political-diplomatic advantage--that is, a balance of power strategy aimed at using the Third World and its manifold resources to constrict the superpowers' capacities, thereby redressing China's strategic and economic disadvantages in relation to the United States and the Soviet Union and promoting the prospects for Chinese-style, nationalistic socialist abroad.

The reform bureaucrat element is the civilian component of the modernizing segment of leadership sentiment and attitudes. It is the most flexible and, to Westerners, the most "rational" and comprehensible stance because it espouses views that most closely resemble the basic attitudes and methodology held by governments in the West and the USSR. Yet these views do not guarantee amity and fellowship toward the other great powers. To understand one another is not necessarily to agree to tolerate one another. The reform bureaucrat point of view in time might be amended to provide for peaceful coexistence on a genuine basis and a transference of the communist/non-communist competition from the political-strategic to the economic dimension. But presently it is not the case nor will it be so, as long as the P.R.C. is an irredentist great power and as long as the P.R.C. can gain increased diplomatic status and influence through revolutionary diplomacy. Chinese leaders, regardless of the factional balance, necessarily must seek to restore the P.R.C.'s "sacred territory." This is in response to a dominant cultural imperative that cannot be ignored. Sinocentrism and a potent nationalism demand it. Equally important, the P.R.C.'s strategy of political alignment with (and possibly leadership of) the Third World nations will continue to be a relevant and rewarding political-diplomatic stance for many years to come; and, for that reason, this strategy will not be discarded lightly. Therefore, for the foreseeable future the reform bureaucrat trend offers little prospect for profound detente with the P.R.C. A Chinese policy-making elite that is dominated by the reform bureaucrat mentality would be flexible, reasonable, and willing to negotiate areas of mutual economic and even joint strategic advantage. But it would not be able to repress the basic drive to restore China's former territories, nor would it reject the P.R.C.'s Third World links, which possess such great potential political advantage for China.

The professional military point of view represents the stance of a somewhat more distinct subsystem in the Chinese political system. It constitutes the basic policy approach of the military service interests, which are reasonably consistent compared with the more readily amendable and the less categorically distinct components of fundamentalism, conservative leftism, and reform bureaucratism. Domestically, the army's weltanschauung tends to promote the forces of stability, structure, and order. It emphasizes heavy industry and advanced weapon systems industries (steel, heavy arms production, electronics, computers, and nuclear research) and advocates minimal interference from the civilian sector in the form of either di-

167

rect party controls over military policies and priorities or civilian demands for the PLA to participate in the psycho-social upheavals of cultural revolution. The professional military has a basic institutionalized tendency to rely on Soviet-type totalitarian social controls (the secret police especially) rather than the uniquely Chinese method of control--the quasi-religious process of thought reform. In spite of the increased role of the PLA from 1969-73, the army cannot be considered to be an aggressive or expansionist force seeking to impose its will directly on the society. As a subsystem, the professional military and most of the men who propound the service viewpoint are imbued with the doctrine of party supremacy as well as a healthy respect for the party's political power. Therefore, they are unlikely to fall heir to Lin Piao's sin of Bonapartism. Because of this basic inhibition, the military has two choices: give selective support to the other factions on a policy-by-policy basis or seek the most congenial coalition partner available. If it chooses coalition politics, its most probable ally would be the reform-bureaucratism school of thought. With regard to foreign policy several convergent interests will become clear.

The professional military espouses (1) an inertial attitude about foreign policy biased toward maintaining established relations rather than creating new ones--first being slow to renounce the Sino-Soviet link, now reluctant to reduce ties with the West; (2) strong support for modern conventional armaments that would be capable of maintaining frontier security at the border with their speed, mobility, and firepower; (3) a flexible response capability against all immediate threats to Chinese territory--that is, conventional tactical nuclear and strategic forces that provide credible deterrence at all potential levels of conflict; (4) an interest in diplomacy and the fruits of diplomatic understanding--increased trade and ready access to the new technologies needed to bring Chinese defenses fully up to date; and (5) an interest in conflict avoidance if China's national security interests and its territorial integrity might be threatened, thus reducing PLA interest in any provocative acts near China's borders and limiting the military's advocacy of support for NLFs in the P.R.C.'s immediate vicinity.

The professional military point of view tends to be more passive in its approach to foreign policy. Like militant fundamentalism it tends toward isolationism, although it is more willing to make limited accommodations with foreign enemies to improve security, accelerate economic growth, or even, perhaps, to gain service influence in a policy-dominant coalition within the P.R.C.'s political elite. In spite of the reform bureaucrats' innate activism compared with the professional military, there is, therefore, a basic identity of interests in the mutual desire to proceed rapidly toward economic development, a joint belief in the value of limited detente with the West to accomplish this goal, and a common respect for the value of a hierarchical chain of command to manage Chinese society effectively. It is not surprising, then, that one of the first major goals of the P.R.C.'s trade offensive was to purchase Japanese fully automated, steel-making technology, a move designed to help double the P.R.C.'s steel production capability within a half decade. This is probably one-half of a bargain struck between the reform bureaucrats and the military. Military support for increased representation of "Chou's men" in the central committee and Politburo might be the other.

The military establishment in any literate and homogeneous society rarely seeks dominance in the social structure. If it comes to prominence, it usually does so by default, as was the case in the P.R.C.[39] The military in China can best serve its own interests by maximizing policy influence on its civilian coalition partner rather than trying to take power for itself and thus incur full responsibility for all domestic and foreign policy decisions. If the PLA again should be thrust inadvertently into a position where it must restore social order, as in the GPCR after 1967, its foreign policy would be characterized by a tendency to preserve the existing conditions, if it is reasonably secure, and if not to seek a rapprochement with any enemy who might negotiate by a tendency to consolidate and expand the development of heavy industry (perhaps even at the expense of agricultural development) and by an innate preference for a quasi-isolationist stance that would exhort other states to revolutionary action but would provide little in the way of substantial military aid.

We thus are confronted with four types of possible policy input in Chinese foreign policy decision making, the various combinations of which show varying degrees of antagonism. It would appear that the military and the bureaucrats are natural allies, as are the two groups who espouse radically egalitarian beliefs.[40] However, this natural dichotomy of Chinese politics might not preclude the militant fundamentalist element from aligning with the military in the interest of implementing an isolationist posture in international affairs. Conversely, the conservative left and the reform bureaucrats might agree to cooperate periodically to implement an activist foreign policy, as they have done from 1970 to 1973. This last period of activist collusion, intended to rectify the very dangerous situation on the northern border through diplomatic initiative and balance of power diplomacy, must be given full credit for a great tactical success. That this coalition dissolved in late 1973 was no doubt the result of the reform bureaucrats' alienating the conservative left by pushing too hard on the trade and technology import programs. Also significant in this regard was the successful campaign to reduce the influence of the PLA that led up to, and culminated in, the actions at the

10th party congress (when military influence in the central committee and the Politburo was drastically cut) and the December 1973 assault on the military's power in the provinces. Following this cut in the military's power base, the necessity for a conservative left-reform bureaucrat coalition was lowered correspondingly.

In the wake of this campaign, the reform bureaucrats appear to be making headway in spite of Chairman Mao's basic distaste for their approach to domestic development and for their lack of interest in permanent revolution. If the newly recreated militia, however, should fall under the sway of the conservatives or the fundamentalists, the reform bureaucrats would be deprived of the effectiveness of their "enforcement branch," the PLA professional class. If Chou and his supporters really are to achieve a predominant influence in the making of Chinese policy they will have to have equal access to this potent weapon for social and political control. If Mao consolidates leftist control over the militia, as it currently appears, Mao and his radically egalitarian successors will be in a position to provide effective countervailing power to the hierarchical modernizers. This no doubt is his goal. He may be attempting for one last time to provide an institutionalized base of support for the radically egalitarian element in the party--something that will persist after his death and will secure the perpetuation of a real "two-line struggle," a permanent state of balance between administrators and mass-line radicals within the ruling elite.

To try to predict the outcome of this power struggle would be as pretentious as it is unreliable. Therefore, this chapter will be confined to a few further remarks on possible changes in the overall trends of the P.R.C.'s foreign policy. Of the seven basic parameters of Chinese foreign policy behavior outlined in the concluding chapter, none requires substantial revision now.

The Sinocentric aspect of Chinese thinking still is plainly evident in Chinese behavior; so much so that in spite of their diplomatic commitment to building an image of humility and fraternity with the Third World states, they have thus far failed to do little more than demonstrate through their archaic repertoire of language and concepts that Chinese society is a unique cultural entity with an extensive culture gap between it and the Third World countries. A preoccupation with exporting political culture, the desire to maintain ideological purity, the will to autarky, and the intention to curb population growth continue to condition Chinese attitudes toward international relations. So, too, does the P.R.C.'s continuing commitment to its strategic weapons program, typified by their unrelenting efforts to develop viable defense and deterrent postures with respect to both superpowers.[41] Revived political structures are already a fact. A diminished military presence in the central party bodies already has been achieved.

Concerning the foreign policy goal orientation of the Chinese political system, a few comments but no basic amendments are in order. China's stand on the border dispute with the USSR remains adamant. It fears Russo-Japanese collusion in the development of Siberian resources and a concomitant consolidation of Soviet power in the Far East, particularly in that part of Siberia south of the Outer Khingan (Stanovoi) Mountains and east of the Ussuri River. For that reason, Peking has exerted pressure on Tokyo not to agree to provide credits for the construction of a second major railway, which the Soviets could use to export Tyumen oil to Japan. Neither will the Chinese be pleased if the Japanese fund a large diameter pipeline to the coast. However, the Japanese view pipeline construction as being of little strategic importance compared with aiding railway construction; and, therefore, they conceivably could go ahead with this project, should the Soviet negotiators lower their price, in the hope that the Chinese leadership would not try to retaliate against Tokyo (perhaps through a sudden drop in Sino-Japanese trade, currently running at an annual rate of about $2 billion). It is arguable that P.R.C. territorial claims in eastern Siberia are more "philosophical" than real;[42] however, the constant Chinese campaign against Moscow's "social-imperialism," the Chinese leadership's persistent demand for realistic negotiations (in which the Soviets presumably would be expected to make major, though not total, concessions to the P.R.C. claim), and the extreme Chinese propaganda measure of attempting to foment a revolt of the ethnic minorities in the USSR would point to a contrary interpretation. The claims are sincere; the P.R.C.'s irredentism is real.

The border dispute should continue to obstruct Sino-Soviet relations at a very basic level. No wholly amiable entente between the P.R.C. and the Soviet Union is possible until the territorial question is satisfied from Peking's point of view. This problem will remain an abiding constraint in Sino-Soviet relations no matter which faction or coalition of factions comes to power after Mao and Chou depart. Should the forces of hierarchical modernization hold sway in the near future, then Chinese policy toward the Soviet Union could grow less hostile and more willing to explore the possibilities for common economic advantage so both could enjoy increased freedom of maneuver diplomatically. But that would be all. With respect to this half of the Chinese political spectrum, the P.R.C·'s foreign policy line is already charted for a path between the superpowers toward the Third World. The present investment in this course of action would not be jeopardized (nor would they risk Japan's possible nuclearization) by refurbishing the Sino-Soviet alliance of 1950, renouncing their territorial claims, and uniting once more against the noncommunist world. Still less would the radically egalitarian party element welcome a Soviet proposal for renewed friendship. The distrust is too great and Mao's example too recent to permit such an ideologically repugnant about-face in Chinese foreign policy.[43] Moreover the United States is unlikely to give strategic cause for such a turnabout.

With respect to the Sino-American relationship, the P.R.C.'s decisional choice is also likely to remain within a fairly narrow span. China will continue to exploit international trade, particularly with the United States and Japan, to her largely unilateral advantage (in terms of helping the country develop quickly and catch up to the superpowers strategically). The Taiwan problem, which has plagued Sino-American relations for so long, should be ameliorated somewhat by the time of President Ford's projected visit to Peking in 1975.[44] It is anticipated that by the end of 1975, U.S. Phantom jets on Taiwan will be removed fully and that part of the vestigial force of some 4,000 men will be redeployed elsewhere.[45] There are grounds, therefore, for predicting continued cordiality in Sino-American relations. Although the problem of establishing full diplomatic relations has yet to be resolved, some progress apparently has been made on the resolution of outstanding financial claims; moreover, there also have been reports that negotiations are under way for joint Sino-American exploration for, and exploitation of, the purportedly immense offshore oil deposits on China's east and southeast coasts.[46] China's sudden renewed interest in the islands of the oil-rich South China Sea tends to support this report. In January 1974 the Chinese navy launched a successful attack and took over the Parcel Islands, hitherto under South Vietnamese control. This aggressive act was accompanied by reiteration of Chinese claims to the Spratly Island group several hundred miles further south (north of Malaysia and west of the Philippines). Such actions reflect Peking's interest in expanding and maintaining its claims of territorial sovereignty wherever oil reserves might be found, even at the risk of American reaction against such moves.

Oil will have an extremely high priority in Peking's foreign policy calculations in years to come. Self-sufficiency would be an adequate goal for the fundamentalists, many of whom no doubt wish to follow a policy of energy resource conservation. In the event of a reform bureaucratic government rising to preeminence this policy would be rejected in favor of an oil export development program designed to contribute greatly to China's economic growth and regional political influence. (The P.R.C. already is exporting oil to Thailand, Hong Kong, and even Taiwan through Hong Kong intermediaries.) In this context, the Sino-American and the Sino-Japanese economic links could be expanded considerably. The key to such a program probably would be a complete withdrawal of American military and diplomatic support of the Taipei government. Peking inevitably would try to link stable oil exports to pry this major foreign policy concession from the U.S.--just as it has attempted to do regarding full normalization of relations.

What Peking cannot obtain (or will not risk) through military pressure, it well may achieve through economic pressure against Taiwan. The Chinese are patient on the Taiwan question; and they will no doubt be content to wage a long term campaign designed to isolate the Taipei government, perhaps to the extent of using a growing diplomatic leverage to create a trade embargo on the nationalist Chinese--in particular a ban on energy resource exports to the island. However such a scheme would depend on three long term projects: (1) the accumulation of much diplomatic weight with the OPEC nations over the next few years; (2) reestablishment of a limited quid pro quo relationship with the Soviet Union (which would be in a position to export oil to the threatened Taiwanese); and (3) inducing a resignation of American support for the Taipei government.

Thus, for the foreseeable future, Taiwan will continue to hinder Sino-American relations. But beyond the Taiwan question, there is considerable scope for mutual economic benefit and strategic advantage afforded by stable, nonoffensive relations between Peking and Washington. Peking will continue to seek American technology and, in times of crop failure, American grain and cotton. Peking will continue to approve of the Japanese-American security relationship to prevent a revival of Japanese militarism and the creation of a Japanese nuclear force. Washington will continue to see in China a countervailing influence to the Soviet military buildup and the prospect of "buying off" the P.R.C.'s commitment to communist insurrection in southeast Asia. This latter hope is in vain.

The P.R.C. will be trying to use the Sino-American relationship to induce the United States to reduce its military support for the Thai government, as well as to totally eliminate American force deployments in Taiwan, South Korea (about 38,000 men), and the Philippines. This will become more evident once the power struggle is resolved in Peking, and once the new leaders can move toward limited compromise with the Soviet Union. The new leadership in Peking in all probability will move toward an attenuation of the Sino-American link in political and strategic terms, although they will do their utmost not to jeopardize expanding economic relations between the two states.

With respect to the P.R.C.'s revolutionary objectives as outlined in Chapter 13, amendments are in order. First, the P.R.C. has continued to support communist dissidents in Burma, Laos, Thailand, and Malaysia. Southeast Asia, from Peking's view, is China's "backyard"; and it naturally would prefer to be adjacent to communist-run countries that would willingly follow Peking's lead in foreign affairs.[47] With American support for these countries waning, Peking may judge that the best means for preventing a growth in Soviet influence in the region is through stepping up its support of communist insurgents. Furthermore, expressions of official Chinese interest in the progress of the Cambodian "liberation struggle" may portend an attempt to bring the Cambodian communist movement under Chinese dominance, away from Hanoi's sphere of control.[48] Thus it appears that Africa has receded to secondary importance as a target for insurrection and subversion and that southeast Asia has been elevated once more to the dubious honor of being Peking's primary target for revolution.

As far as Africa is concerned, it now appears that the P.R.C.'s political-diplomatic Third World strategy with its concentration on effective state-to-state relations has taken precedence over the promotion of rebel insurgency. Peking's support for insurrection in Africa is limited solely to movements attacking Angola, Mozambique, Rhodesia, and South Africa--all popular targets that embody white racism and colonial oppression in the eyes of the Third World leaders. The Chinese are now content to promote sound diplomatic and trade relations with all other African governments. Relations have improved considerably with Zaire and Niger, both former opponents of China's African presence, and are expected to improve with Rwanda and Chad. Though China's relations with Ethiopia are now in doubt following the recent military coup in that country, the Chinese situation in Africa, on balance, is improving rapidly.[49] The Tanzania-Zambia railway is expected to be completed in late 1974, nearly two years ahead of schedule. With both the Tanzanian and Zambian governments extremely satisfied with the success of this project and equally if not more pleased with the demeanor of the Chinese workers, technicians, and army men who worked on the project, it is not inconceivable that the Chinese will engage in further aid projects--perhaps even of this magnitude (in excess of $430 million)--in other parts of Africa. The establishment and maintenance of good relations with the African states will be one of the highest priority goals of Chinese foreign policy for the next decade. The success or failure of their Third World strategy to counterbalance the power of the United States and the USSR will hinge on this campaign.

The P.R.C.'s foreign policy line of recent years has been a successful one, and its projected course of development seems highly propitious from China's point of view. If the Chinese Third World strategy does succeed in appealing to the nonaligned states to step up their unified pressure on the superpowers and other developed countries for more aid and more favorable terms of trade, the P.R.C. will have struck a strong blow at the developed world's eco-

nomic jugular. However, even though this appears to be the strategically appropriate course of action ("avoid strength, attack through
weakness"), the P.R.C. leadership is going to have a difficult time
inducing the vast and diverse conglomeration of Third World states
to formulate common economic policies and adhere to them for a
long duration in the face of economic inducements that the developed
countries themselves surely will offer to try to split this incipient
coalition of the poor. What seems probable is increasing Chinese
influence in the Third World, but the creation of only a loose, somewhat divided, and partially exploitable economic front by these countries.

Finally, although the P.R.C. would like to increase its influence
in the Middle East, it seems unlikely that it will do so in view of the
Arab oil-producing states increasing wealth and their own desire to
exert increased political and military influence. Although Chinese
support is welcomed by the Arab countries, the Arab leaders will no
doubt do their best to oust the existing great power presence in the
Middle East, not add to it. We may therefore conclude that though
the prospects for increased Chinese political-diplomatic influence
are good, a forecast of a highly integrated, Chinese-led federation
of the poor is unconvincing. To obtain even moderate success in its
future policy, the Chinese leadership will need in power a relatively
strong government with a stable policy-making elite that can plan
and orchestrate effective foreign policy maneuvers. Should Chinese
politics and policy making fall under the influence of the isolationist,
antibureaucratic, prorevolutionary, radical egalitarians, this projected rise in the P.R.C.'s global stature and influence will be undermined, if not eliminated totally.

JAPAN

The Oil Crisis and Japanese-American Relations

The Japanese economy, dependent on imports for 99.7 percent
of its oil requirements, suffered an extremely serious blow because
of the drastic price rise in OPEC-supplied petroleum. Total oil import costs in 1972 were about $4 billion. Total costs for oil in 1974
will be in the order of $20 billion. [50] Even though the price rise did
not take full effect until the first quarter of 1974, this phenomenal increase in oil import costs coupled with Japan's high rate of capital
export helped push Japan's balance of payments position in 1973 to a
deficit of some $10 billion. This followed surpluses of $4.7 billion
in 1972 and $7.7 billion in 1971. As a result, the Japanese govern-

ment has had to reassess immediately the projected size of its liberalized capital export program. Equally significant, the government
has had to try to encourage an export drive to offset the negative effects of the oil imports on the balance of payments position. Once
more the Japanese have become conscious of having to export to live,
of having to struggle mightily in an adverse economic situation merely
to hold their position.

With the oil problem undermining Japan's international trade balance (dragging the merchandise trade balance down from a $1.5 bil-
lion to a $2.0 billion monthly surplus to the break-even point), the
Japanese inevitably have turned to export markets to try to shift this
deficit onto other countries. The effects of this type of economic policy, if pursued too long, will damage seriously Japan's international
economic relations. A prolonged effort to run massive trade surpluses
with Japan's major trade partners, the United States, the European
Economic Community, and Canada, will provoke trade protectionism
--particularly in this period of severe inflation and deepening recession in every developed, noncommunist country. In this time of rapidly deteriorating international economic conditions, one might expect
the Japanese to reemphasize their joint interests with the United
States and the other OECD countries. Instead they have demonstrated
an unprecedented independence, choosing bilateralism in their economic relations with the oil exporters and preferring to remain aloof
from entangling economic alliances, hoping to preserve maximum
economic flexibility. This approach is fraught with difficulty and risk
because it conceivably could threaten Japan's greatest foreign policy
priority, the maintenance of free trade in the world economy, by provoking retaliatory protectionism in the other developed noncommunist
states.

In aggregate terms, the Japanese economy has fared well considering the massiveness of the oil shock. As of December 1974, Japan's overall balance of payments figures, including the oil trade,
has shown a monthly surplus since September 1974, and there is some
hope that the country will move out of its overall deficit position by
the end of the year. This is a remarkable adjustment to an extremely
difficult situation. Japan's GNP figure for 1974 will not be as encouraging because it definitely is going to show a decline in output
of about 3 percent--the first decline since the early 1950s. [51] The
GNP for 1974 will be running at a level of about $350 billion at 1974
exchange rates. However, much worse than the fact of a decline in
GNP has been the rampant inflation in the Japanese economy. According to IMF figures for the year ending October 1974, the prices
of consumer goods were rising at a rate of 25.8 percent, the highest
rate of inflation in the industrial world. Wholesale prices continued
to climb at 28.6 percent. When inflation is discounted, consumer

spending has been dropping. As a result the economy has slipped into a zero or "negative growth" mode. With production slipping, unemployment has climbed to 1.5 percent--historically a very high level for Japan--with more layoffs in the automobile, textile, and machinery industries imminent. In the face of these major economic setbacks, the Liberal Democratic Party (LDP) government is beset with serious political criticism. Mainly as a result of problems with the domestic economy (partly because of charges of political corruption), Premier Kakuei Tanaka was forced out of office, to be replaced by one of his former cabinet ministers, Takeo Miki. It is hoped by the LDP leadership that Miki can restore some semblance of party unity through political reforms within the organization that will moderate the factional struggle, while effectively increasing the party's endangered electoral support by restoring its damaged reputation and moving the economy back onto a moderate 6 to 8 percent real growth pattern.

To accomplish this latter task, Miki has retained Masayoshi Ohira as Finance Minister and appointed his other chief rival for party leadership, Takeo Fukuda, to the deputy premiership and the position of head of the Economic Planning Agency. It is assumed, therefore, that the LDP government will pursue its present tight money policies to combat inflation as well as its efforts to reduce oil imports and shift industry toward energy-conserving fields.[52] Fukuda, for one, has been a strong opponent of the high growth mentality prevalent in Japan for the last two decades. Although this leadership may try to steer the Japanese economy through immediate difficulties in a manner that will preserve Japan's low political profile and its reliance on the United States, this program can be accomplished only by overcoming some serious obstacles--namely the damaging political effects that persistent Japanese trade surpluses will have on the leaders of Japan's industrialized trading partners.

The task of maintaining Japan's economic momentum is certainly of great significance in halting the LDP's continuing decline, yet of equal significance will be Miki's efforts to effect genuine political reforms within the party. Recent elections for the upper house demonstrated a further decline in the LDP's support. The party now has a slight majority of six seats in the 252-member upper chamber. However, following the elections severe public criticism of the LDP's massive election expenditures led to pressures to reform the electoral system and tighten the enforcement of campaign expenditure laws.[53] Should Miki's efforts to reform the party fail, it is conceivable that there may be a shift to the left in Japanese politics; and it is not at all sure that such a shift would go the moderate socialist left. In that event, Japan's foreign policy and its relations with the great powers would come under serious review, leading perhaps to a renunciation of the Japanese-American security link and a closer relationship with the P.R.C. However, another more threatening consequence that could be entailed in a move to the left would be a breakdown in the economic system following a leftist attempt to interfere with Japan's overseas economic presence, while overspending on welfare measures at home. Should this admittedly improbable pattern of events come to pass, it would be a short step to a military coup and a return to the authoritarian militarism of the pre-World War II era.

Although one probably can ignore the prospect of extremism in Japanese politics and government, one cannot so easily dismiss the threat of a dangerously inadequate response by the LDP leadership to the massive international financial problems posed by the oil trade. As the French do, the Japanese leaders seem to believe that their best course of action on the oil problem is to pursue a policy to further cooperation between the producing and consuming nations, rather than following the American proposal of increased consumer-nation collusion leading to economic confrontation with the OPEC states in an attempt to drive the price of oil downward.[54] Japanese caution concerning confrontation tactics is understandable.

The United States conceivably could make do with domestic production in the event of an outright halt in oil exports to the developed countries. The United States also has considerable economic leverage of its own by virtue of its position as the world's principal food exporting country. In economic warfare with the OPEC states, it too could turn off an important tap. The Japanese are not so fortunate. They have no big stick but only a few (though very valuable) economic carrots with which to induce favorable policy measures among the OPEC and OAPEC countries. Without strong unequivocal guarantees of proportionately shared use of the OECD countries' own domestic production of oil in the event of unforeseen escalation in the proposed producer-consumer confrontation, it is highly unlikely that the Japanese would choose to participate in the plan. Japan obtains over 70 percent of its energy from oil. Without it, all industry would be shut down for the duration of the oil shutoff (minus the two months of reserve capacity). The United States in contrast, obtains close to 70 percent of its energy from coal, domestically produced natural gas, and hydroelectric and nuclear power generation.[55] To win Japanese and European consent to participate in a major and (in view of the OPEC states' enormous foreign exchange reserves) probably prolonged struggle with the oil-exporting states, the United States probably would have to offer about 20 to 30 percent of American domestic oil production to Japan and perhaps up to 70 percent of it to Western Europe.[56] Although this could be done with sufficient time and planning (present logistical capacity for such a realignment in oil trade patterns is doubtful), the whole operation would require such extensive coordination and cooperation among the OECD countries that the prospects of establishing such a program seem highly implausible. The OPEC operation of arranging common pricing policies and regulating the expansion of oil production was, by comparison, a simple and straightforward matter.

To make a serious and credible threat of economic warfare against the oil-producers in an attempt to force price revisions, the consumer nations' political leadership must be prepared to put the economies of the advanced countries on a wartime footing with provision for emergency rationing of all available energy supplies. In view of the great difficulty that would be entailed in persuading public opinion of the necessity for such an operation, the prospects for such a maneuver are minimal. Accordingly, the probability of a dramatic price rollback is equally low. Therefore, the severe problems of maintaining the stability of international financing of trade and investment flows will remain a crucial and immediate issue in international politics.

Clearly something must be done in the near future to prevent a major economic depression in the West because of the financial conundrum posed by the oil trade. The oil producing states had accumulated 19 percent of world monetary reserves as of September 1974 ($38 billion of $200 billion). If the price of oil remains at 1974 levels (and it probably will increase without countervailing economic pressure), the World Bank estimates that by 1980 the OPEC countries will have accumulated $600 billion in reserves.[57] For the short term there is the immediate problem of recycling the so-called petrodollars and preventing financial crises, especially in Western Europe. Some prudent OPEC members have publicly indicated a willingness to help in this matter.[58] For the longer term there is the question of how to pay off the debt: (1) through commodity transfers, (2) through OPEC asset purchases in the consuming nations' industrial sector, or (3) through a massive, politically negotiated export of capital goods, technology, and infrastructural investment?

The Japanese have opted for all three of these approaches by increasing exports to the Arab states and Iran (with Japanese exports to Middle Eastern states approaching $2 billion per year and increasing at 50 percent per year[59]), by promoting Arab investment in Japanese corporate debentures and overseas companies' stock, by encouraging OAPEC deposits of oil dollars in Japan's foreign exchange banks, and by waging a campaign to win contracts for assured oil supplies in return for Japanese plants, equipment, and technical assistance.[60] Japanese diplomatic strategy, following traditional postwar methods, is to employ a studied and artful ambiguity concerning the purpose of its newly created links with the Arab oil-producing states and Iran when speaking to American representatives who seek to create a united front of consumers. Japan is trying to strike a middle course between the oil-producers' desires and American foreign policy goals. In its own fashion, Japan is evolving gradually a more independent foreign policy that seeks to win accommodation with potentially dangerous adversaries (whether the threat is military or economic) while also trying to impose minimal strains on its traditional allies.

Japanese-American relations are going to be strained, however, and perhaps severely so. American Secretary of State Kissinger's recent proposals reflect basic differences in attitude toward the oil problem. The Kissinger scheme comprises four major points: (1) a joint cutback in oil consumption by the rich consumer nations of about 3 million barrels per day (3 MMBD) to reduce consumers' aggregate demand; (2) the creation of a $25 billion per year loan fund (30 percent of which would be American backed) to be available to the deficit member states (notably Great Britain and Italy) until such time as they can impose conservation measures in their own economy and move toward alternative fuel sources; (3) acceptance by borrowers of economic conditions recommended by fund administrators for rectifying the oil deficit problem; (4) a formal connection between the participating states in this loan fund scheme and the International Energy Agency (established in 1973 to function in the event of another oil embargo).[61] This kind of program is directly at variance with the Japanese attitude, which was reflected in the more moderate comments on the oil problem emerging from the Ford-Tanaka communique of November 1974.

In the Kyoto communique, the United States and Japan pledged themselves to "a new era of creativity and common purpose." President Ford in an earlier speech had stated that the United States would "remain a trustworthy ally" and would "continue to be the supplier of the goods you need." Stressing the theme of cooperation and the benefits of a joint approach to international problem-solving, Ford added, "If shortages occur we will take special account of the needs of our traditional partners. We will not compete with our friends for their markets or for their resources. We want to work with them."[62] Yet for all these promises of goodwill and common purpose, Ford and Kissinger still had to make the significant concession that the Japanese would not have to cut their present level of oil imports to participate in the American plan (about 4.5 MMBD, 45 percent from Saudi Arabia and 42 percent from Iran, the balance from Indonesia, Algeria, and Venezuela). Instead they merely could try to hold their present level of imports or proceed with a slow growth in imports.[63] The Japanese appear to be half in and half out of the American scheme, which no doubt is precisely the position they desire since it postpones the hard decision to commit Japanese policy for the indefinite future.

Japan is thus free to continue in its efforts to obtain a secure inflow of oil through other bilateral arrangements. The Japanese have
resisted American pressure successfully to create a consumers'
monopsony cartel. The Kyoto communique incorporated both positions in fact by noting, first, that Japan and the United States would
seek cooperation among oil consumers to meet energy needs and,
second, that harmonious relations with oil exporters also would be
maintained.[64]

In short, Japanese foreign policy is beginning to show the first
signs of a coherent vision of Japanese self-interest. The vision may
be inaccurate from a North American point of view, but it is unquestionably the view from Tokyo unalloyed with the overt almost servile,
consideration for American foreign policy goals of the predetente
era. The Japanese leadership now has had the opportunity to take
the full measure of Japan's economic vulnerability. Thus the government now realizes that Japan's economic security must be provided
for almost exclusively by Tokyo. Moreover, a new emphasis on conservation is indicated as the guiding philosophy of Japanese decision
makers, both domestic and foreign. The basic postulates of the high
growth, ever-expanding GNP mentality have been repudiated officially.
Japan, therefore, formally has entered a new era with a substantial
redefinition of its national and international goals.

With Tokyo's decision to reach accommodation with the Arab oil
producers in December 1973, Japan became committed to a policy
line that inevitably would create a greater divergence of Japanese interests from American aims. Although this decision seems to portend an increasing degree of antagonism in Japanese-American relations, it does not necessarily presage a rupture. The Japanese political leadership before Tanaka feared any attenuation in the Japanese-
American relationship as a threat to Japan's security. In the post-
Tanaka era, Japanese leadership will take a more mature outlook on
relations with Washington, noting that it always will be in American
interests to provide Japan with the U.S. nuclear umbrella. The new
divergence in economic goals may lead to trade disputes, monetary
policy differences, and so on; but these differences, being economic,
are negotiable. Rational compromise is possible. The United States,
moreover, will be more secure in the long run with a confident, independent, domestically stable ally in Asia rather than a hesitant, in-
troverted satellite. A strong ally can be a force for peace, economic
development, and stability in its own right. A dependent, politically
isolated, internally divided Japanese state would be a major liability
in the global effort to create a structure and age of peace. This fact
is well appreciated by some Americans, particularly, it would seem,
by Kissinger, who has stressed repeatedly the need for maintaining
the economic prerequisites for democracy in the West. It seems rea-

sonable, therefore, to expect that American and Japanese policy makers will treat each other with even greater respect in the future, recognizing that though basic policy differences are inevitable, the two most influential noncommunist economic powers must work together closely and honestly to solve common problems where possible and to reap common gains in their efforts to bring security and economic progress to the Asian region.

On Making a Virtue of Necessity--Expanded Japanese Overseas Economic Involvement

Since the commencement of Japan's capital export program in 1972, long term private sector foreign assets (excluding export credits) have risen from $2.7 billion to $12.6 billion.[65] The outflow of long term equity investment has continued in 1974, although in a somewhat more "orderly" fashion because of the oil trade deficit. Of the $9.6 billion in licensed overseas investment at the end of 1973, 28 percent was in the mining and petroleum industry, 27 percent in manufacturing, and only 11.3 percent in commercial investments. Most of the $1.4 billion invested in Britain was in British Petroleum's Abu Dhabi concession. The pattern of investment of Japanese firms in other countries was similar: investment is aimed largely at facilitating the export of unprocessed or semiprocessed raw materials (particularly oil, coal, or natural gas) back to Japan.

Japan's concern for the security of its oil imports was already evident before the oil embargo associated with the Arab-Israeli conflict. Japanese investment in Saudi Arabia and Kuwait already totaled close to $600 million by the end of 1972. In September 1973 the Japanese obtained contracts for 100 million tons of crude oil (to be delivered over 10 years) and 30 million tons of liquified natural gas (to be delivered over 15 years) in return for a $500 million loan to the Iraqi government.[66] Once the Japanese leadership had resolved definitely to lean toward the Arab side of the Middle East conflict, financial and investment decisions proceeded rapidly. In November of 1973 the Japanese obtained a contract for 200 million barrels of Saudi Arabian oil in exchange for (among other things) the construction of a truck assembly plant and an integrated steel mill. In December, following the Arab announcement of a 25 percent cut in exports, Tanaka sent a mission headed by Miki, then Deputy Premier, to the Arab states with generous aid offers and instructions to fully explain Japan's position on the Arab-Israeli dispute. By December 25, after Tokyo had called for an Israeli response to UN resolution 242, the embargo was eased. By January, Sheik Yamani of Saudi Arabia and the then foreign minister of Japan, Ohira, were toasting "a very beautiful arrangement . . . a very happy marriage which will have no divorce" between their two countries.[67] The basis of the agreement involved Saudi money and oil flowing to Japan in return for technical assistance and capital investment. By 1974 the Japanese government also was committed to developing an expanded capacity for importing oil through wholly Japanese companies, rather than the American and Dutch oil firms on whom Japan relies for the transport and delivery of 70 percent of its present imports.

In January 1974 the Japanese government offered $280 million in reconstruction aid to the Egyptian government--primarily aimed at helping to open the Suez Canal.[68] In February the Japanese government provided a $1 billion loan to Iraq for the construction of a refinery and a gas liquefaction plant. In return the Japanese obtained 1.1 billion barrels of Iraqi oil to be delivered over 10 years.[69] Iran also received a billion dollar loan as an "advance for imports." Similarly Saudi Arabia and Kuwait sought further Japanese assistance in constructing whole petrochemical industries. Lack of fresh water (as well as roads, utilities, and housing) appeared to be the chief obstacle to even more rapid Japanese success in meeting these requests. By the end of fiscal 1973, Japanese corporations, following the government's lead, had established their presence in Algeria (Fujitsu is to build a $276 million telecommunications system), Syria (a $100 million loan from Japan to build an oil refinery), and Iraq (Japanese corporate investment totaling $1 billion in cement, fertilizer, and natural gas concerns). Japanese oil firms already operate in Egypt, Abu Dhabi, and Qatar; and the Japanese concluded an offshore oil exploration agreement with North Yemen in the spring of this year.[70]

The Japanese response to the harsh economic realities of the mid-1970s, particularly in its efforts to build bridges to the Arab World, systematically is a natural and perhaps unavoidable move. From Tokyo's point of view this course appears to entail the least risk and the greatest potential economic and political payoff. With the third largest and the most dynamic, but the most vulnerable, economy in the world, the Japanese leaders are well aware that Japan is on the road to global influence if not global power. But they also know that because of Japan's self-abnegating position with regard to military power, the instruments in Japan's political arsenal most likely are going to remain purely economic. The natural focus of Japanese foreign policy, therefore, is bound to shift to ease and accommodate the strains imposed by the Arab states on Japan's economic system. In view of the possibility of a total embargo should North America and Western Europe choose to stand and fight OPEC, a major political-diplomatic effort by the Japanese to reach an accord with the Arab leaders is a logical and prudent step. The first stages of this new Japanese-Arab entente conceivably may pave the way for an era of unprecedented economic involvement between two peoples so large and so different. The Arab states surely would view an increasing Japanese presence in their economies with much less misgiving than either an American or Soviet role. Japanese-aided economic development and Japanese direct investment in the Arab states, therefore, most certainly will expand in the near future if the initial wave of projects proves successful and mutually satisfactory.

The Japanese, besides achieving an enhanced security of supply for their energy sources for the next decade, will be more than happy to undertake a major role in helping the 120 million people of the Arab countries to industrialize and prosper. The Japanese leadership has been frustrated over the last five years because of Japan's still modest international stature. Japan's economic miracle, although acknowledged as such by European and American academics, has received scant popular commendation in other Western countries and has provoked anger, not respect, from foreign governments threatened by Japan's economic dynamism. Success within the rules of established economic patterns resulted only in the United States and the European countries forcing two major yen revaluations on the Japanese (the second one the yen "float" of February 1973). Moreover, American failures to consult Japan adequately over American monetary policy and an increasing wave of protectionism and resentment because of Japanese exports of automobiles, steel, electronic goods, textiles, and so on, have left the Japanese feeling somewhat alienated, even distrustful, of the United States and Western Europe. This factor, too, contributed to the Japanese decision to opt for cooperation not confrontation with the Arab states. As in the past, Japan's foreign policy flows directly from economic necessity. There are however, some troubling contradictions in Japanese foreign policy that remain unresolved.

Despite the great increase in Japanese exports to the Arab states and despite the inflow of Arab money into the Japanese economy, without a recycling mechanism the only way that Japan is going to be able to bring its oil deficit into "equilibrium," as the Japanese say, is through greatly expanded exports to its traditional trading partners. Preliminary estimates have already put Japanese exports for 1974 at $54 billion, up from $36.8 billion in 1973--a monumental increase even after the effects of inflation are discounted. [71] Although, through their competitive and effective business practices the Japanese might win even larger shares of European and North American markets, as this statistic seems to indicate, such tactics will be viable for a matter of months, not years. The OECD oil importers cannot all run surpluses with each other. As a group they will run up annual trade deficits with the oil exporters of between $60 billion and $100 billion.

A Japanese attempt to shift its own $15 billion to $20 billion deficit onto the gravely threatened European economies and the recession-inflicted American economy inevitably will provoke trade restrictions. The Japanese recognize this fact and have therefore done their best to placate Washington and the European capitals, but within the already established parameters of Japan's economic foreign policy.[72]

Japan's immediate goal is thus one of persuading the United States and Western Europe to move to the bargaining table with the OPEC states where some mutually acceptable recycling mechanism can be created that will continue to function even in the event of a consumers' boycott by Europe, Canada, and the United States in late 1975 or 1976. The Japanese badly need the prompt establishment of such an institutionalized financial framework if they are not to be forced into launching an "export offensive" that would damage relations with all other OECD countries.

Besides establishing a new, potentially profitable, and mutually beneficial relationship with the Arab states, Japan has strengthened its economic links to many other countries--particularly the raw material exporting nations but also the United States and Europe, where the Japanese hope to create a significant financial role for themselves. As indicated in Chapter 13, Japan's massive foreign exchange holdings made possible the mammoth outflow of long term private investment. The close to $13 billion in foreign assets that the Japanese now hold is highly diversified geographically, although economically concentrated strongly in the resource and manufacturing industries.

In addition to the already enumerated oil and petrochemical investment projects in the Arab states, the Japanese have invested fairly heavily to develop food production capacity in southeast Asian countries. Current investment is promoting the production of tea, peanuts, and corn in Indonesia, corn in Thailand, and grain, sorghum, beef, and oil seed in Australia[73]--all with a view to developing an export capacity in these countries that would help alleviate Japanese dependence on American exports of agricultural products. (Japan imports about 50 percent of its wheat, over 50 percent of its corn, and 92 percent of its soybeans from the United States.[74]) In addition to the flow of private sector investment that amounts to between 20 and 40 percent of new investment in Singapore, Malaysia, the Philippines, Indonesia, and Thailand, Japan also provides between 20 and 47 percent of the aid that these countries receive.[75]

With such an important and increasingly visible presence in southeast Asian states, it is not surprising that the Japanese often are condemned as "Asian imperialists." The past two years have seen consumer boycotts of Japanese goods in Thailand and student riots in Djakarta during former Premier Tanaka's visit to Indonesia in January 1974 because of popular concern over Japanese economic domination.

Japan continues to buy 85 percent of Philippine production of chrome, copper, manganese, and lumber; 100 percent of Thailand's fluorite production; 67 percent of Thai rubber production and 100 percent of its corn exports; 100 percent of oil and gas exports from Malaysia and Brunei; 50 percent of all of Australia's mineral exports; and 80 percent of India's iron ore exports.[76] Japan also supplies southeast Asian states with a large proportion of their important imports (chemical fertilizer, synthetic fibers, plastics, and so on). Over 30 percent of Thai and Indonesian imports come from Japan, as well as 30 percent of the Philippines' imports and about 20 percent of Singapore's imports.[77] Although Japan itself is not absolutely dependent on any southeast Asian state for specific commodities (there are alternative supply sources in Latin America, Africa, and North America), the Japanese do have a vital interest in the maintenance of political and economic stability in southeast Asia--in direct contradiction to the P.R.C.'s recently revised support for national wars of liberation in the southeast Asian zone. Japanese and Chinese foreign policies will be engaged, therefore, in a powerful and strategically important struggle over the political future of this region, with Japan supporting the already established governments of the Association of Southeast Asian Nations and China placing a predominant emphasis on support of communist insurgency, with a secondary priority accorded to improving diplomatic and economic relations with these countries.

In view of this developing trend, it is supremely important that the Japanese make every effort to upgrade their contribution to the economic development of the southeast Asian countries and, thereby, to undercut the pervasive resentment of the Japanese economic presence that now exists. But to date such effort by the Japanese has been lacking. It is utterly improbable that the Japanese or Japan's economic foreign policy will be able to contain the emergent nationalisms of southeast Asia through economic support of overtly "reactionary" or "counterrevolutionary" regimes. The Japanese must do their utmost to cater to popular demands to speed up economic development in these states. If Japan's role in southeast Asia continues to be seen by the native people of the region as "imperialistic" and counterproductive to economic and social progress, the already uncertain struggle to preserve free market economies will be lost irrevocably. The Japanese need stable, economically progressive societies in southeast Asia, not merely to facilitate the importing of raw materials but, more significantly, for the long term regional power balance. The countries of ASEAN are weak and the Southeast Asia Treaty Organization (SEATO) arrangement moribund. A Japanese foreign policy that was maximally supportive of southeast Asian security would focus logically on promoting the strength of the ASEAN countries--economically through better terms of trade and increased investment and more generous aid, and militarily through exports of the armaments thought necessary by local governments and perhaps even military assistance training programs (although the latter measure probably would require a major shift in public opinion in Japan). Evidence of intentions to establish such supportive programs is, by and large, nonexistent.

There is, on the contrary, evidence of a weakening Japanese commitment to the southeast Asian countries. In September 1974 a group of Japanese companies decided to postpone indefinitely a $450 million petrochemical project in Thailand, citing financial problems, new environmental constraints, and political and social instability.[78] Significant also is the fact that Japanese trade missions are now usually headed for Latin America, not south and southeast Asia. In September 1974, Tanaka signed a $3.2 billion agreement with the Brazilian government for the construction of aluminum and pulp and paper plants. Japanese investment in Mexico, Canada, and Australia also is expected to grow rapidly. Chiko Nishiwaki, director of Japan's International Resources Development Institute, stated during a visit to Canada this year that "the Japanese mining industry is seriously studying the economic and technological possibilities of smelters and refineries at or near the mine site. . . . We would expect a good return on our investment but we wouldn't insist on an equity based one. Frankly Japan wants Canada as a long-term stable supplier and we're willing to co-operate within the host country even to the fabrication of similar products."[79]

It is possible that the Japanese business community is prepared to turn their backs on southeast Asia, not wishing to place Japan's limited foreign investment money into high political risk zones. From this point of view, Japanese interest in developing oil and petrochemical production based on the Athabasca tar sands in western Canada, increased agricultural and mineral exports from Canada and Australia, and oil exports in return for industrial assistance from Venezuela and possibly Mexico, seems rather ominous. The recent Japanese agreement with the Soviet government over east Siberian resource development also fits into a pattern of increasing Japanese concern for stable long term supply. The Japanese want to diversify their import dependency to be sure, but they also seem to want diversification away from southeast Asia specifically.

Although a fear of political instability and communist takeover may hinder investment growth in countries such as Thailand and Taiwan, the Japanese have shown no reluctance to trade with their communist neighbors. Trade with the P.R.C. is now over $2 billion per year with an additional flow of Japanese capital goods and technology to the mainland purchased by the Chinese on credit. Trade with the USSR has continued to grow; but, more important, agree-

ment was reached in March 1974 concerning the terms of the first
phase of Japanese participation in Siberian development. Total value
of the initial agreement is $1,050 million. Credits to this amount
will be extended to the Soviet government, which will then proceed to
purchase some $940 million worth of Japanese equipment. Lumber
and pulp (total investment $500 million) and South Yakutian coking
coal resources ($450 million) will be developed for export to Japan.
Soviet coal exports to Japan will begin in 1983 and will run for 20
years at a rate of about 7 million tons per year. With the $100 mil-
lion Japanese contribution to financing gas exploration (and equal
participation by two American companies, El Paso, and Occidental
Petroleum) Soviet development of east Siberian gas fields should proceed rapidly, providing Japan with yet another "assured" source of
supply. [80]

Japanese success in winning reasonable terms for coal and gas
development in the Yakutsk region has not been matched by equivalent
success in negotiations over Japanese access to Tyumen oil exports.
The first Soviet proposal to the Japanese would have involved a second major railway line with new double capacity tanker rolling stock
at an estimated cost of $6.3 billion. The Japanese, aware of Peking's
extreme displeasure over such strategically significant projects,
declined this proposal. The second Soviet offer involved construction of a large diameter pipeline to Nakhodka as well as a refinery
complex in that port (probable total cost over $5 billion). The Japa-
nese were interested in the pipeline construction, but only if they
could buy crude oil--not refined products. As a result, negotiations
over Tyumen energy exports to Japan have been discontinued for the
time being.

In spite of the size of the Yakutian basin project, it is still too
early to say that the Japanese have decided to pursue full scale
Siberian development despite Chinese objections. Moscow might be
able to induce such a shift provided it offered a sufficiently irresisti-
ble price. So far the Russians have shown little inclination to soften
their terms. They know, after all, that the Japanese are almost desperate for oil and that there is little point in getting locked into a
long term deal with Tokyo when the price of oil could climb still
higher. The Japanese are reluctant too because of the outstanding
problem of the four northern islands. To date, the Soviet leaders
have refused to discuss return of the southern Kuriles fearing perhaps that such a concession to Japan might weaken the Soviet hand
in dealings with Peking at the Sino-Soviet border talks. It can be expected, therefore, that Moscow will remain intransigent on this issue until the Sino-Soviet territorial dispute is resolved. It is equally
probable that the Japanese will be extremely reluctant to move into
Siberian resource development on the scale desired by Moscow until

there is a thaw in Sino-Soviet relations--or perhaps until Moscow feels sufficiently secure in eastern Siberia to return the islands to Japanese control. There is, therefore, a significant interdependence among the Sino-Soviet and Russo-Japanese territorial disputes and the timing and extent of Japanese participation in Siberian development.

An overview of events of the last 21 months indicates that the pattern of Japan's economic involvement abroad reflects a predominant concern for helping Japanese industry maintain and improve its security of supply for basic raw materials--especially energy resources. In accordance with this prime policy goal the Japanese have embarked first of all on a new and extensive relationship with the Arab states, the so-called "beautiful marriage." Second, Japan simultaneously has downgraded its emphasis on southeast Asian countries. Until the governments of Malaysia and Thailand fully demonstrate their capability of containing communist insurgents, until the war is ended in Cambodia and Vietnam, and until the political climate in Indonesia grows less hostile to Japan's economic presence, Japanese aid, trade, and investment in the region will continue to decline in terms of their relative, though not absolute, contribution to Japan's overall external economic relations. The P.R.C.'s renewed interest in the region probably has contributed importantly to this development, as has the oil crisis, which developed at a time when Japan otherwise might have redoubled efforts to support the governments and economies of this region. Third, the Japanese need for energy resources was allowed to take precedence over the Sino-Japanese relationship to the extent of permitting joint Russo-Japanese exploitation of Siberian lumber, coal, and gas. Fourth, to keep open the possibility of a greatly expanded access to Russian, and to a lesser degree, Chinese resources, Japan has pursued a policy of trade expansion with the USSR and the P.R.C. To help maintain the present peace in Sino-Japanese relations, Tokyo even went as far as to sign an aviation agreement with Peking, effectively forcing Japan Air Lines to surrender its most profitable air service, the Tokyo-Taipei route. Economic security for the future, harmony with the resource-rich communist giants, and a new accord with the oil rich states of the Third World are thus the priority themes of Japan's recent economic foreign policy.

What is now needed is a successful campaign to legitimate Japan's position in closer proximity to the Arab world by persuading the United States and European policy makers that this is indeed a reasonable and defensible posture. If this maneuver can be accomplished without provoking American antagonism and retaliation (trade protectionism and/or a unilateral move to abrogate the Japan-U.S. Security Treaty), Japan's diplomatic flexibility will be enhanced, its economic security increased, and its future claim to great power status strengthened. The immediate means to this end is American acquiescence in the establishment of a jointly administered recycling facility for the growing flood of "petrodollars." Creating the necessary institutional framework for financial stability in the oil trade thereby would obviate the need for deficit-diverting tactics that could only offend Japan's trading partners and inspire protectionist retaliation.

In the present context Japan's position on energy policy is, this author would argue, both a rational response to Japan's immediate foreign policy problems and what might prove to be but a preliminary phase in the development of a constructive and vital role in the preservation of the security of the noncommunist states. This sanguine, speculative theory is based on the following reasoning.

A concerted effort to attack the monopoly power of the oil-producing countries inevitably would require a major cutback in consumption by the developed countries to try to reduce aggregate demand, to reduce the revenues of the needier OPEC countries, and thereby to bring about an eventual return to price competition in the international marketing of oil. Such a program would involve a major effort to conserve energy in the developed consumer nations. In Western Europe and North America energy conservation measures could have an important effect on aggregate noncommunist demand for oil (per capita energy consumption in the United States is about twice the level in Sweden). The United States imports about 7 million barrels per day of oil, and Western Europe imports at a rate of about 14 MMBD. Japan, on the other hand, imports only 4.5 MMBD, and its oil use is not as readily contractable. (Only 6 percent of Japanese electric-generating stations could be converted to coal, and the Japanese government estimates that it could effect no more than a 6 to 8 percent reduction in overall demand.)

It would seem, therefore, that it would be in Western interests to try to exclude Japan from its confrontation strategy with OPEC. The Japanese would be a drain on a common oil pool of the OECD states since they are unable to reduce their own consumption to any significant degree. Why, therefore, should Japanese survival be threatened for at best a marginal contribution to Kissenger's proposed confrontation with the oil producers? Canadian and American domestic oil production of about 11 MMBD certainly could help alleviate shortages in Europe (and perhaps even in Japan). But whether this same 11 MMBD could be stretched to cover even the basic emergency needs of North America and Western Europe alone, should OPEC retaliate with a major oil export embargo of indefinite duration is doubtful. If Japanese emergency deficits of some 4 MMBD also had to be provided for, the viability of emergency relief would be degraded significantly, and thus the credibility of any price rollback campaign would be undermined severely. Furthermore, there are other difficult questions concerning first, the resilience and adaptability of the Japanese economy, and second, Japan's ability to handle high unemployment without falling victim to political extremism (of the left or right). The viability of the Japanese state must be maintained; and, contrary to views held by Herman Kahn and others, the Japanese socioeconomic experiment is a fragile one that must be protected against the severe battering of an all-out economic war. Without oil the Japanese economy and soon the Japanese social and political order would be plunged into utter chaos. The kind of leadership that would emerge from this chaos would be, in all probability, wholly inimical to Western democratic ideals. Encouraging the Japanese to find another path, separate from that of North America and Europe is, in this author's opinion, the optimal approach to the situation.

In political-diplomatic terms, a present "schism" in the West over oil policy could lead to further future benefits. The European states and the United States have been compromised already to a large extent in their relations with the Third World. The stigma of "neocolonialism" is attached firmly to nearly all their efforts to improve the lot of the less developed countries. The Chinese and the Soviets do their utmost to perpetuate that stigma. Unfortunately, in their first overseas contacts the Japanese showed a distressing tendency to emulate their Western predecessors by exacting maximum economic benefits from the less developed countries without helping them to advance economically or to solve their enormous social problems. As a result, Japanese businessmen already are called "economic animals" (and other more loathsome epithets) in some parts of the Third World--especially southeast Asia. However, they have not done irreparable damage yet to their reputation. The Japanese lack of delicatesse still could be put down at this stage to the inexperience of international novices, which the Japanese still remain. There is, moreover, a major effort already under way directed by Japan's powerful Ministry of International Trade and Industry (MITI) to improve Japanese corporate behavior abroad.

Under the MITI guidelines established in 1973 and 1974, Japanese companies must do their utmost to find local partners for overseas ventures (an upper limit of 75 percent Japanese ownership has been set for overseas operations). Companies are expected to pay closer attention to local culture and customs, to promote more local personnel up the corporate hierarchy (there should be 30 local people for every Japanese in companies as a whole, with no more than 50 percent of the executives being Japanese), to reinvest a higher percentage of profits in the countries concerned, and to make every effort not to disturb local markets and cause supply shortages.[81]

In brief, MITI policy makers are attempting to transform the "ugly Japanese" into model overseas investors and ambassadors of goodwill for Japan, knowing that Japan's future economic relations with Third World countries may depend on the outcome of this program. It is in Western interests generally to encourage the Japanese to expand their relations with the less developed countries of Asia and the Middle East in the hope that by having had the opportunity to learn from the mistakes of previous Western "imperialisms" and, more important, by having the tremendous incentive of providing for Japan's future economic security through the establishment of a lasting relationship with the Third World based on mutual benefits, the Japanese may (1) significantly help many less developed countries toward the goal of rapid, self-sustaining economic growth (and possibly demonstrate that underdeveloped countries can achieve significant social and economic development without abandoning the market economy or liberal-democratic government); (2) improve the image of the noncommunist democratic countries among the peoples of the Third World by demonstrating truly nonpredatory economic behavior; (3) act as a counterweight to growing Chinese diplomatic and political influence in the south and southeast Asian regions; and (4) impart a coherent, more altruistic, and therefore more meaningful element to Japanese foreign policy, which has hitherto suffered from the dullness and stifling inhibition of economic pragmatism.

Japan's present situation was summed up succinctly by Takuji Shimano, professor of economics at Gakashuin University: "The bigger the Japanese economy becomes, the more it depends on world peace, even if we must sacrifice something at home to maintain that peace. Japan can be an economic power but it cannot be a military power because the economy cannot live even one day without raw materials from overseas."[82] Of necessity the Japanese must strive to become leading spokesmen for, and demonstrators of, the value of international economic interdependence.

The Japanese thus seem destined to become the new Western internationalists, the new proponents and supporters of peaceful economic and social change in the Third World. The task they face is an enormous one because the present forces of political, social, and economic ferment in the less developed countries clearly are directed against the achievement of peaceful progress. To move toward this goal, Japan will need tolerance and forbearance from the leadership and peoples of the other developed countries. For the near to medium term, Tokyo may appear to be diverging from, and even to some extent obstructing, the aims and interests of the other developed Western states (particularly with respect to energy policy); but this should be regarded primarily as a transitional phase in which a short term divergence in policy-making goals prepares the way for a more efficient long term division of labor between Japan on the one hand (as economic internationalist and policy ally of the Third World states) and the United States and Western Europe on the other (as guarantors of the strategic security of the liberal-democratic world).

To accomplish such a program would be to transform Japan's economic problems into political-strategic benefits for the entire Western world. If the Japanese can refocus their national policies and recast their national goals to suit such a long term strategy, they would indeed be making virtue from harsh necessity.

JAPAN AND CHINA: REGIONAL POWERS AND EMERGING GLOBAL ACTORS

It now appears that both Japan and the People's Republic of China have entered officially a new age of global influence and responsibility. Because of China's military capability, its great population, and its determination to lead the cause of the Third World peoples in their struggle for a "just division of the world's wealth," the Chinese political elite now has a legitimate claim to great power status and an important position in the vital international political debates yet to come. The Japanese, although clearly lagging behind the Chinese in the struggle for political-diplomatic influence, are acquiring more status and respect despite their own self-deprecating posture. Because of the great impact of expanding trade and overseas investment, because of its technological dynamism and dangerous military potential, and because of an emerging political and economic interdependence with the Arab states and the resource-exporting countries of the Third World, Japan seems destined for a great power role in international affairs.

At present the principal threats to the attainment of global influence by both countries are domestic in nature. The factional struggle for power within the P.R.C. undoubtedly will have a major impact on China's foreign policy goals and even could reverse the present trend toward increased political-diplomatic influence by reverting to the isolationism and autarky of militant fundamentalism. Similarly the factional struggle for power in Japan's Liberal Democratic Party could result in an unqualified victory for the low profile, low growth school of thought championed by Miki and Fukuda, in which case Japan's political and economic impact abroad could be reined in rather than expanded over the next decade. Even if the high growth faction should predominate, Japan's role in international affairs, to attain an optimal impact, still would require the formulation and articulation of a basic set of principles and goals whereby Japanese interests could be strengthened systematically. The present haphazard reli-

193

ance on the random benefits of foreign economic intercourse weakens Japan's foreign policy. For both the Chinese and the Japanese, the present opportunities and potential for increased regional power and global influence are good. What is required in both cases to realize this potential is a quick resolution of their respective power struggles and a clear-cut, policy-making predominance for the proponents of increased international involvement.

With respect to the present perception of threats in Peking and Tokyo, several comments are in order. The Chinese leadership, for the most part, recognizes that the chief military threat to the P.R.C. emanates from Moscow. Moscow is also the only probable source of attempted political sabotage or internal subversion of the Chinese political elite. The Lin Piao affair will condition Chinese threat perceptions for many years to come; and Lin Piao tried to escape to the Soviet Union, not to Okinawa or Guam. Finally it is Moscow, not Washington, that is trying to encircle China diplomatically through collective security proposals for Asia. The Chinese leadership will do their utmost, therefore, to render Moscow's influence minimal in the political debate in China by waging a continuous propaganda campaign against Soviet-style "revisionism" and "socialist-imperialism" within the P.R.C. while exerting every effort toward deterring "adventurist" military intervention and obstructing Soviet "containment" policy.

The second major threat to Peking's international goals and interests is Soviet-American collusion at Chinese expense. Chinese foreign policy will reflect, therefore, an important desire to split any incipient Soviet-American entente by maintaining a sufficient number of positive links with one of the two military superpowers (currently the United States) to forestall such ominous collusion. Interim tactical agreement with the United States over regional security arrangements in the western Pacific, as well as the increased level of economic intercourse with the United States, stem from the need to prevent superpower collusion. It is important to note that Chinese foreign policy realistically could redirect this alignment in favor of the Soviet Union--provided the outstanding problems of the Sino-Soviet relationship are ameliorated to some extent by Soviet concessions. This, however, does not appear to be a trend of events that can be expected.

The third major threat perceived by the Chinese is the rising influence of Japan, both as a regional and a global actor. Increased Japanese economic influence in southeast Asia, if successfully redirected toward the national development of these countries, would threaten China's immediate goal of promoting communist revolution throughout Indo-China and the southeast Asian archipelago. To date this threat seems negligible because of Japanese reluctance to assume a major role in promoting the political stability and economic progress of the southeast Asian countries. Present Japanese aversion to a politicized foreign policy toward southeast Asia is not, however, sufficient reason to ignore the "Japan factor" in Peking's foreign policy calculations for the medium to long term. Japan's potential role in Asia must be circumscribed if the P.R.C. is to become the principal arbiter of regional security. The best way to approach that goal is to inhibit the success of the "hawkish" or self-assertive elements in Japanese politics and to supply whatever political ammunition possible for the Japanese advocates of extensive relations and maximal detente with China. This program cannot be undertaken in an overt fashion but will be attempted through economic means, offering increased resource exports (especially oil) and an increased share of the China market to Japanese industry. Peking will say nothing to raise Japanese fears of attack (or Chinese-instigated subversion) and even could join the United States in urging Japan to expand its capacity for self-defense by building up its maritime forces to a limited degree to act as a counterweight to the threatening growth of the Soviet Union's Pacific fleet.

With Japanese concern over military security waning, Tokyo's perception of threats to Japan's security are almost exclusively economic. Hypothetical military threats or nuclear blackmail by the P.R.C. or the USSR no longer seem credible to many Japanese, who feel that the American guarantee of Japanese security is inevitable with or without the U.S.-Japan Security Treaty and that neither the Chinese nor the Russians would want to risk a major confrontation with the United States over Japan, thus destroying the basis for a lucrative detente with America. There is, moreover, little that either the P.R.C. or the USSR could or would want to obtain from Japan by force that could not be won by economic diplomacy. From this point of view, a judiciously steered middle path between Chinese and Soviet strategic and economic interests should in itself guarantee Japan's sovereignty and security. Budgetary cuts in the Fourth Defense Buildup were enacted in 1972 and 1973, probably because of such attitudes as well as the increasing pressure on governmental fiscal resources that resulted from former Premier Tanaka's commitment to improve the quality of life in Japan and to introduce basic social welfare amenities. [83]

Japanese aversion to nuclear weapons remains as strong as ever and popular antinuclear sentiment received a boost with the disclosure that American warships have not been unloading nuclear arms before entering Japanese ports--possibly with the explicit, secret consent of the Japanese government. [84] Renewed controversy over the constitutionality of the Self-Defense Forces also has developed during the last 15 months because of the September 1973 judicial decision over

the legality of an Hokkaido missile base.[85] In short, the trend of
popular political opinion continues to run against the improvement of
Japan's contribution to its own military security, despite the rational
and articulate arguments favoring such improvement by a number of
Japanese academics and defense analysts.[86]

With Japanese concern for strategic matters largely in abeyance,
the threat perceptions of the Japanese leadership focus on two dominant concerns: (1) maintaining security of supply for oil and other
raw materials and (2) maintaining access to overseas markets in
North America and the United States. To pursue these goals, the
Japanese have elected to diversify economic dependence on major
resource exporters, to achieve important bilateral understanding with
the Arab countries while attempting to maintain stable, though less
secure, relationships with the United States and the European Community. There are several contingent threats to Japan's economic
well being and political stability that presently must cause governmental concern and anxiety in Tokyo. A list of these possible threats
would include: (1) a total oil embargo to all developed states by the
OPEC countries; (2) a major recession or depression in the OECD
countries, whether caused by uncontrolled inflation, an exacerbated
oil crisis, or both, leading to protectionism in Europe and North
America and the loss of absolutely vital export markets for Japanese
industry; (3) revival of isolationism and quasi-autarkic sentiment in
the United States as a result of such imponderable factors as the
post-Vietnam depression regarding commitments abroad; (4) possible American and European protectionism induced solely by an unresolved oil crisis; (5) an inability to purchase raw materials abroad
at prices that make exporting to Japan's traditional overseas markets
feasible because of extensive cartelization in international commodity
markets; (6) an inability to sell Japanese exports abroad because of
a rate of inflation in Japan that might continue to remain worse than
that experienced by other developed countries; and (7) political extremism at home caused by an unfavorable popular response to such
possible measures as wage controls or the postponement of new welfare measures and environmental improvement programs.

The basic aims of Japanese foreign policy are being reexamined
and reformulated in light of such threats. Some of the threats, such
as possible massive depression in the OECD countries or wholesale
cartelization of resources, are improbable. However, they are having a large, perhaps disproportionate, effect on Japanese political
thinking, if only because the Japanese are not accustomed yet to the
idea of applying economic sanctions themselves or of exerting overt
political power alone or, more reasonably, in conjunction with the
other developed states. As an antimilitarist, polite, "face-saving"
people, the Japanese have an inordinate propensity for avoiding out-

right conflict with other states.[87] They excel in ambivalent and ambiguous policy making designed to appeal to everyone. In a period of acute international crisis, however, they would be in grave danger of pleasing no one and of being left in a vulnerable political-diplomatic isolation.

It would seem, therefore, that the Japanese require a systematic elaboration of foreign policy goals and commitments, not only to improve the effectiveness of their foreign policy decision making but also to make clear to their American and European economic partners that Japan has a present appreciation of, and respect for, Western security goals in relation to the communist countries. Only in the context of a clearly stated commitment to the long term interests of the liberal-democratic countries can the Japanese reasonably expect fair and cooperative treatment from the United States, Canada, and the European community, given a major rift over energy policy toward the OPEC states. Only by making a major effort to explain the Japanese position to its Western partners will the Japanese successfully accommodate expanding Third World demands without seriously damaging relations with Japan's major trading partners.

Both Japan and the P.R.C. are regional powers in Asia. Both are engaged in the definition of viable global political roles. China, as a military great power that lacks a correspondingly well-developed economic base, and Japan, as a most influential economic power in the Asian region that lacks the basic capacity to defend itself and its overseas commerce, are two anomalies of uneven development in the states system. Because of their respective deficiencies, each must seek allies if they are to further their respective goals. Neither country is in the same category of power as the two superpowers: neither is likely to become a superpower with the passage of time. The P.R.C. is dedicated to the overthrow of the status quo in the international system. Japan is motivated equally strongly to support and maintain the existing institutionalized modalities of international intercourse. As two complex decision-making structures, they have fundamentally antithetical aims for their immediate environment and for the pattern of development of the entire global political system. But because they possess only partially developed national capabilities, both the Chinese and the Japanese have come to appreciate the value of limited rapprochement in the face of threats to their sovereign interests and political autonomy posed by both the Soviet Union and the United States.

Conflict in Asia between China and Japan probably will be avoided because of a mutual understanding of the strategic interdependence between the two countries. Both countries will compete with the instruments at their disposal for influence (and in the P.R.C.'s case, despite protests to the contrary, even hegemony) in the east Asian

197

region. But neither will challenge the direct and vital interests of the other because both countries have an abiding interest in the permanent abbreviation of Japan's military capabilities. One may expect a continuing desire by the Japanese political leadership (as long as the LDP is in power) to rely on the American security guarantee, thus permitting an indefinite postponement of the rearmament question. It seems reasonable to predict also that the Chinese leadership will continue to look favorably on the Japan-U.S. security arrangement as a hedge against increasing Soviet influence in Tokyo. Whether this liberal attitude would continue if Chou En-lai's reform bureaucrats were displaced from the ruling elite in Peking is, however, doubtful. A swing to radical egalitarianism in the P.R.C. (especially to the militant fundamentalist element) probably would damage the jointly shared perceptions of tolerance and peaceful coexistence that now exist in Sino-Japanese relations.

Given the present configuration of global forces, the Chinese and the Japanese need each other's presence to act as a check to future superpower encroachment on the Asian domain. China is Japan's Asian counterweight to the overwhelming threat that the USSR would present were it the sole dominant power in the east Asian zone. Japan's presence as the great Asian capitalist country will preempt any major renewal of American economic and strategic interest in the region--except to deny to the Soviet Union the possibility of unopposed regional hegemony. From Peking's point of view, it will be much less difficult to overcome Japanese efforts to stabilize governments in southeast Asia than to defeat an equivalent American effort backed by the Seventh Fleet and counterinsurgency training and assistance programs to these states. With the present state of play in southeast Asia and an unequivocal Chinese commitment to revolution that is only halfheartedly countered by Japanese political sentiment, the Chinese-directed, Chinese-supported "liberation" of all the Indochinese peninsula, including Burma and Thailand, seems a probable pattern of events. Japanese efforts to support governments in this area and Japanese economic investment in this zone, will tend to be directed therefore toward the Philippines, Indonesia, Malaysia, and Singapore.

To conclude this essay, it must be emphasized that it is unlikely that either country will develop a mix of policies that will engender an entirely optimal increase in regional and global political-diplomatic influence. The present disarray within the domestic political subsystems of each country will not be resolved easily; nor can one count on the emergence of strong, decisive leadership following the present power struggles. Both Japan and the P.R.C. are handicapped by their domestic political strife. The foreign policies of each country will suffer as a result because of the lack of long term policy planning.

With factional struggle precluding strong, coherent, political leadership, China's foreign policy has fallen into the hands of day-to-day bureaucratic administration--a situation that tends to perpetuate existing policies and allows only modest incremental changes within the overall framework of the official party line. Similarly, the current struggle for power among the handful of factions that Miki must try to bind into a precarious unity for the LDP's very political survival has undermined the capacity of the Japanese political system to determine a new national consensus.

To date the Japanese leadership has demonstrated little in the way of a capability for formulating long range programs that could promote effectively Japan's regional security and its global influence in a systematic fashion. During the past two decades the Japanese have not been forced to analyze alternative futures, nor have they needed to be overly concerned about immediate security needs. Such considerations were for their American allies. This is no longer the case. The Japanese are in extreme need of an indigenously developed set of foreign policy principles to guide them through the difficult decade ahead. They still are waiting for leaders to step forward with the programs that will match the problems and the threats that have already materialized. The Chinese are more fortunate, since their present foreign policy program probably will continue to fit their political-strategic situation for many years to come, with or without united leadership. Barring a return to the extremism of the Great Proletarian Cultural Revolution, the P.R.C. is firmly set on a course that can only lead to expanded power and influence. In comparison with Japan, the threats the Chinese must face are fewer in number, less complex, and more amenable to solution through application of sheer willpower and determination. For this reason and because of an apparent weakening in Japanese resolve, the Chinese seem certain to widen their lead over the Japanese in terms of regional power and global political-diplomatic influence. Only one qualification needs to be added to this prediction. The Japanese are capable of reversing this present trend--and with surprising abruptness--but only if they can devise the extensive changes in the conceptual guidelines of their foreign policy that clearly are required.

In any case, it seems probable that in the contest for influence and a preeminent position as the leading actor in the Asian drama, victory probably will fall to the country that can settle quickly and effectively its political conflicts and focus an undivided effort on a systematic campaign to guide the destiny of the east Asian region. The best outcome that either country can hope for, however, is a qualified victory. Preeminence is possible; total dominance is not.

1. Toronto Star, July 27, 1974.

2. Ibid., November 23, 1973.

3. Toronto Globe and Mail, July 12, 1974.

4. See, for example, George H. Quester's speculatively perceptive analysis in "Taiwan and Nuclear Proliferation," Orbis 18, no. 1 (spring 1974): 140-50.

5. Full text reprinted in Survival 15, no. 5 (September-October 1973): 243-44 (emphasis added).

6. John Newhouse, Cold Dawn (New York: Holt Rinehart and Winston, 1973), p. 189.

7. Hannes Adomeit, "Soviet Risk-Taking and Crisis Behaviour: From Confrontation to Coexistence," in Adelphi Papers, no. 101 (London: IISS, 1973), p. 37.

8. New York Times, July 22, 1973.

9. Harry Gelber, "Nuclear Weapons and Chinese Policy," in Adelphi Papers, no. 99 (London: IISS, 1973), pp. 34-36.

10. See, for example, the balance of forces as described in Strategic Survey 1973 (London: IISS, 1974), pp. 65-69.

11. Toronto Globe and Mail, May 30, 1974.

12. R. V. R. Chandrasekhara Rao, "Proliferation and the Indian Test: A View from India," Survival 16, no. 5 (September-October 1974): 211.

13. The Military Balance 1974-75 (London: IISS, 1974), p. 54.

14. For a record of the early visits and an analysis of their significance, see Geoffrey Jukes, "The Indian Ocean in Soviet Naval Policy," Adelphi Papers, no. 87 (London: IISS, 1972).

15. The maximum range of the Poseidon and Polaris A-3 missiles is about 2,880 miles. Trident will have a reach of some 4,800 miles.

16. The suggestion regarding the possible use of nuclear land mines is drawn from Ryukichi Imai, "Proliferation and the Indian Test: A View from Japan," Survival 16, no. 5 (September-October 1974): 214.

17. Toronto Star, October 30, 1974.

18. Ibid., July 31, 1974.

19. Chou En-lai, "Report to the Tenth National Congress of the Communist Party of China," as in Peking Review 16, nos. 35-36 (September 7, 1973): 22-24 (emphasis added).

20. For a concise analysis of Chinese relations with the Third World, see Peter Van Ness, "China and the Third World," Current History 67, no. 397 (September 1974).

21. Chiao Kuan-hua, Chairman of the P.R.C. delegation to the United Nations General Assembly's 29th Session, in his opening speech on October 11, 1974. As reprinted in Peking Review 17, no. 41: 9-16.

22. Ibid., p. 10.

23. Chou En-lai, "Report to the Tenth National Congress of the Communist Party of China," as in Peking Review 16, nos. 35-36 (September 7, 1973): 22. (Hereafter called "Report.")

24. Ibid.

25. Financial Times (Toronto), July 22, 1974; and Ottawa Citizen, September 5, 1974.

26. New York Times, October 9, 1973.

27. Andrew Wilson in the London Observer, January 27, 1974.

28. Christian Science Monitor, July 22, 1974.

29. The P.R.C. is the recipient of several hundred million dollars per year in foreign currency through money sent to the mainland from overseas Chinese, a fact that would permit significant annual trade deficits indefinitely. London Times, October 5, 1973.

30. Ibid.; see also, Christian Science Monitor, September 15, 1973.

31. Chou En-lai to Japanese Foreign Minister Masayoshi Ohira as reported in the New York Times, January 4, 1974.

32. Some 60 percent of Soviet energy resources lie in Siberia. Current Soviet production for 1974 is estimated to be approximately 450 million metric tons. It also is developing massive port facilities at Vostochny near Vladivostok to add to the present port facilities at Nakhodka. See Report of the Round Table on "Siberia and Its Natural Resources," NATO Review 22, no. 4 (August 1974): 23-25; also the Toronto Star, September 21, 1974; and the Toronto Globe and Mail, November 15, 1974.

33. See the Chinese address to the World Population Conference in Bucharest (August 1974) reprinted in Peking Review 17, no. 35 (August 30, 1974): p. 9. Significant for its betrayal of Chinese apprehensions concerning its enormous population, the Chinese delegation unsuccessfully sought to delete all printed references to the size of its own population. Toronto Star, August 19, 1974.

34. There is, of course, considerable dispute concerning the policy preferences of specific members; however there does seem to be substantial agreement that Chou's position in the Politburo and in its standing committee was strengthened as a result of the 10th party congress. See John Burns, Toronto Globe and Mail, September 1 and 6, 1973; Michael Oksenberg and Steven Goldstein, "The Chinese Political Spectrum," Problems of Communism 23, no. 2 (March-April 1974): 1-13; and Henry S. Bradsher, "China: The Radical Offensive," Asian Survey 13, no. 11 (November 1973). For a somewhat dissenting view that stresses a mutually offsetting factional balance because of the increased power of the "Nanking-Shanghai regionalists," see Thomas W. Robinson, "China in 1973," Asian Survey 14, no. 1 (January 1974).

35. Party moderates even have been forced to criticize Mao Tse-tung himself because of the gravity of the attacks from the radical left. See Robert Elegant, "Thoughts of Mao under Attack," Toronto Star, July 30, 1974.

36. Toronto Globe and Mail, January 15, 1974.

37. The discussion that follows derives some of its terminology and much of its analysis to Oksenberg and Goldstein, op. cit., but equally to the overall analytical method and insights provided by Franklyn Griffiths in his highly useful study, Genoa Plus 51: Changing Soviet Objectives in Europe, Wellesley Paper 4 (Toronto: Canadian Institute of International Affairs, June 1973).

38. See, for example, Oksenberg and Goldstein, op. cit., pp. 9-13.

39. Parris Chang, "China's Military," Current History 67, no. 397 (September 1974): 101.

40. See, for example, the argument that the military and the bureaucrats are natural allies in Ting Wang, "The Succession Problem," Problems of Communism 22, no. 3 (May-June 1973): 23-24.

41. ICBM development continues unabated according to the International Institute for Strategic Studies report of September 1973. Toronto Star, September 7, 1973.

42. See O. Edmund Clubb, "China and the Superpowers," Current History 67, no. 397 (September 1974): 100.

43. Donald Zagoria's insightful analysis confirms this argument. See "Mao's Role in the Sino-Soviet Conflict," Pacific Affairs 47, no. 2 (Summer 1974): 139-52.

44. Toronto Globe and Mail, November 30, 1974.

45. New York Times, May 20, 1974, with regard to the F-5 for Phantom exchange to be completed by the end of 1975; and Toronto Globe and Mail, November 30, 1974, on projected forced reductions on Taiwan.

46. Toronto Star, May 21, 1973.

47. Armaments, training, and assistance to guerrilla soldiers and radio facilities in China itself for rebel movements to use have all been provided to communist insurgents in southeast Asia--despite Ne Win's confirmed neutralism and Bangkok's somewhat more tolerant attitude toward Peking. See Robert A. Scalapino, "The Asian Policies of the PRC," Current Scene 12, no. 10 (October 1974); and J. M. van derKroef, "Guerrilla Communism and Counterinsurgency in Thailand," Orbis 18, no. 1 (Spring 1974).

48. Toronto Star, April 3, 1974.

49. Bjorn Kumm, "A Liberation Railway Picks Up Steam," Toronto Globe and Mail, July 12, 1974.

50. The 1972 figure: Toronto Globe and Mail, January 8, 1974; the 1974 figure: The Financial Post, September 21, 1974.

51. Toronto Globe and Mail, December 10, 1974.

52. Ibid.

53. Some LDP candidates spent as high as 900 million yen ($3 million) to win election in the upper house. The party as a whole spent $250 million on the election--money that comes almost totally from the large corporations. Jack Cahill, Toronto Star, September 14, 1974.

54. See Reuter report of Premier Miki's first policy speech to the Diet, Toronto Globe and Mail, December 16, 1974.

55. James Schlesinger's figures for 1972 indicate that the United States obtains 25 percent of its energy from coal, 38 percent from natural gas, and 4 percent from hydroelectric and nuclear generating sources. See Schlesinger's contribution to J. J. Murphy, ed., Energy and Public Policy (New York: The Conference Board, 1972), p. 72.

56. American oil production has continued to drop steadily from its peak level of 9.64 million barrels per day (MMBD) to 1974's 8.95 MMBD and an estimated 8.6 MMBD for 1975. American Petroleum Institute figures as in Toronto Star, November 11, 1974. American consumption, by contrast, was about 16 MMBD in 1973 and probably will be somewhat below that level in 1974. The United States, therefore, is approaching 50 percent dependence on foreign supplies of oil.

57. Toronto Star, November 4, 1974.

58. Sheik Ahmed Yamani, Saudi Arabian Oil and Mineral Resources Minister, repeated his concern for maintaining international economic stability, most recently in Geneva. Toronto Globe and Mail, December 16, 1974.

59. Andrew Carvely and Susan Stone, "Japan Cements Special Links to Arab Bloc," Toronto Globe and Mail, April 30, 1974.

60. Toronto Star, September 12, 1974 and September 16, 1974.

61. Hyman Solomon, "U.S. decision to confront OPEC," Financial Post, December 7, 1974.

62. Toronto Globe and Mail, November 24, 1974.

63. Ibid., November 21, 1974.

64. Ibid.

65. Financial Post, September 21, 1974.

66. Manchester Guardian, November 3, 1973.

67. Toronto Star, January 3, 1974.

68. Carvely and Stone, op. cit.

69. Christian Science Monitor, February 6 and 11, 1974.

70. Carvely and Stone, op. cit.

71. Financial Post, September 21, 1974.

72. This enormous increase in exports may turn out to be a "cosmetic" measure in which Japanese overseas inventories have been inflated--without a matching increase in sales.

73. New York Times, August 28, 1972.

74. Ibid., July 1, 1973.

75. Ibid., January 13, 1974.

76. Ibid., August 28, 1972.

77. Ibid., January 13, 1974.

78. Toronto Globe and Mail, September 27, 1974.

79. Toronto Star, March 26, 1974.

80. See London Times, August 16, 1973; and Le Monde, August 24, 1974.

81. See London Times, August 16, 1973 and July 15, 1974; also Le Monde, August 24, 1974.

82. Takuji Shimano's comments as quoted in New York Times, July 1, 1973.

83. Le Monde, December 9, 1972.

84. Toronto Globe and Mail, October 8, 1974; see also Russell Brines, Christian Science Monitor, November 19, 1974.

85. See for example Ichiji Sugita, "Japan and Her National Defence," Pacific Community 5, no. 4 (July 1974): and Kazutomi Uchida, "Japan's National Defence and the Role of the Maritime Self-Defence Force," Pacific Community 6, no. 1 (October 1974).

86. See Mizuo Kuroda's perceptive analysis of Japan's "lack of principles," lack of commitment, and lack of systematic goal elaboration in his article, "Some Basic Elements of Japan's Foreign Policy," Pacific Community 5, no. 3 (April 1974): 387-91 especially.

87. Ibid.

CHINA

Aide, W. A. C. "China's West Asian Strategies." Paper presented to the Australian Institute of International Affairs Conference: China and the World Community, June 1972, Melbourne.

_____. "One World Restored? Sino-American Relations on a New Footing?" Asian Survey 12 (May 1972).

Andrigo, R. F. "Doing Business with China." Canada Commerce 135 (November 1971): 15-18.

Australia, Department of Trade and Industry. "Australia's Trade with the People's Republic of China." Paper presented to Australian Institute of International Affairs Conference: China and the World Community, June 1972, Melbourne.

Barnett, A. Doak. Cadres, Bureaucracy and Political Power in Communist China. New York: Columbia University Press, 1967.

Barnett, Robert W. "China and Taiwan: The Economic Issues." Foreign Affairs 50 (April 1972).

Barrymaine, Norman. The Time Bomb: Today's China from the Inside. New York: Taplinger, 1971.

Bedelski, Robert E. "Institutional Legitimacy and External Affairs in Modern China." Orbis 16 (Spring 1972): 237-56.

Bell, Coral. "The Foreign Policy of China," in The Foreign Policies of the Powers, edited by F. S. Northedge. London: Faber, 1968.

Ben-Dak, Joseph D. "China in the Arab World." Current History 59, no. 349 (September 1970): 147-52.

Bradsher, Henry S. "The Sovietization of Mongolia." Foreign Affairs 50 (April 1972).

Bueschel, R. M. Communist Chinese Air Power. New York:
Praeger, 1968.

Bullard, M. R. "Current Trends in the PRC." Military Review 52
(September 1972).

Butwell, Richard. "China and Other Asian Lands." Current History
63, no. 373 (September 1972).

Chang, Parris H. "China's Scientists in the Cultural Revolution."
Bulletin of the Atomic Scientists 25 (May 1969).

Chen, Kuan-I. "The Outlook for China's Economy." Current History
63, no. 373 (September 1972).

Chen, Nai-Ruenn, and Walter Galenson. The Chinese Economy under
Communism. Chicago: Aldine, 1969.

Chen, Pi-Chao. "The Political Economics of Population Growth:
The Case of China." World Politics 23 (January 1971).

"China's New Status in Oil." Survival 14 (March/April 1972).

Clubb, O. Edmund. China and Russia, The Great Game. New York:
Columbia University Press, 1971.

_____. "China and the United States: Collision Course?" Cur-
rent History 59, no. 349 (September 1970).

_____. "Sino-Soviet Relations and the Economic Imperative."
Current History 63, no. 373 (September 1972).

Committee of Concerned Asian Scholars. China! Inside the People's
Republic. New York: Bantam Books, 1971.

Communist China and Arms Control: A Contingency Study 1967-76.
Stanford: Hoover Institution on War, Revolution and Peace,
1968.

Cooley, John K. East Wind over Africa: Red China's African Offensive. Rev. ed. New York: Walker, 1966.

Dewenter, John R. "China Afloat." Foreign Affairs 50 (July 1972).

Dubnic, Vladimir Reisky de. "Europe and the New U.S. Policy Toward China." Orbis 16 (Spring 1972): 85-104.

Dunn, John. Modern Revolutions. London: Cambridge University Press, 1972.

Durdin, Tillman. "The New Face of Maoist China." Problems of Communism 20 (September-October 1971).

Dutt, Vidya Prakash. China and the World. New York: Praeger, 1966.

Eto, Shinkichi. "Features Characteristic of the Economy of China," In Peace Research in Japan 1971. Tokyo: Japan Peace Research Group, 1971.

_____. "Postwar Sino-Japanese Relations: 1949-1970." Paper presented to the Peace in Asia Conference, June 1972, Kyoto.

Fairbank, John K. "China's Foreign Policy in Historical Perspective." Foreign Affairs 47 (April 1969).

_____. "The New China and the American Connection." Foreign Affairs 51 (October 1972).

_____. "The People's Middle Kingdom." Foreign Affairs 44 (July 1966).

_____. "The State That Mao Built." World Politics 19 (July 1967).

Fan, K., ed. Mao Tse-tung and Lin Piao: Post-Revolutionary Writings. Garden City, N.Y.: Anchor Books, 1972.

FitzGerald, C. P. The Birth of Communist China. New York: Praeger, 1966.

_____. China: A Short Cultural History. London: Cresset Press, 1935.

_____. "Reflections on the Cultural Revolution in China." Pacific Affairs 41 (Spring 1968).

FitzGerald, Stephen. "China and Australia." Paper presented to the Australian Institute of International Affairs Conference: China and the World Community, June 1972, Melbourne.

_____. "Impressions of China's New Diplomacy: The Australian Experience." China Quarterly, no. 48 (October-December 1971).

Franke, Wolfgang. China and the West. New York: Harper & Row, 1967.

Gayn, Mark. "China Convulsed." Foreign Affairs 45 (January 1967).

Gelber, Harry S. "Nuclear Weapons in Chinese Strategy." Problems of Communism 20 (November-December 1971).

George, A. L. The Chinese Communist Army in Action: The Korean War and Its Aftermath. New York: Columbia University Press, 1967.

Giap, Vo Nguyen. People's War, People's Army. New York: Praeger, 1962.

Gibson, J. M., and D. M. Johnston, eds. A Century of Struggle: Canadian Essays on Revolutionary China. Toronto: Canadian Institute of International Affairs, 1971.

Gittings, John. "Military Control and Leadership, 1954-64." China Quarterly, no. 26 (April-June 1966).

_____. Survey of the Sino-Soviet Dispute 1963-67. London: Oxford University Press, 1968.

Godson, R. G. "China Trade Winds Are Blowing." Canada Commerce 135 (November 1971).

Gurtov, Melvin. "Sino-Soviet Relations in Southeast Asia: Recent Developments and Future Possibilities." Pacific Affairs 43 (Winter 1970-71).

Halperin, Morton H. China and the Bomb. London: Pall Mall Press, 1965.

_____, and John W. Lewis. "New Tensions in Army-Party Relations in China, 1965-66." China Quarterly, no. 26 (April-June 1966).

_____, Helmut Sonnenfeldt, and Oran K. Young. "Sino-Soviet Relations and Arms Control." China Quarterly, no. 26 (April-June 1966).

Harrison, John. China since 1800. New York: Harcourt Brace and World, 1967.

Hinton, Harold C. Communist China in World Politics. New York: Houghton Mifflin, 1966.

_____. "Conflict on the Ussuri: A Clash of Nationalisms." Problems of Communism 20 (January-April 1971).

Ho, Samuel P. S., and Ralph W. Huenemann. Canada's Trade with China: Patterns and Prospects. Montreal: The Canadian Economic Policy Committee, Private Planning Association of Canada, 1972.

Holmes, Robert A. "The Sino-Burmese Rift: A Failure for China." Orbis 16 (Spring 1972).

Hsieh, A. L. Communist China's Strategy in the Nuclear Era. Englewood Cliffs, N.J.: Prentice-Hall, 1962.

Hsu, Kai-yu. Chou En-lai. Garden City, N.Y.: Doubleday, 1968.

Huck, Arthur. The Security of China. London: Chatto and Windus, 1970.

Hunt, Kenneth. "Security Systems in East Asia." Paper presented to the Peace in Asia Conference, June 1972, Kyoto.

Jackson, Basil. "China and Russia Next in PBEC?" Financial Post, October 14, 1972.

Johnson, Cecil. Communist China and Latin America: 1959-67. New York: Columbia University Press, 1970.

Johnson, Chalmers. "How China and Japan See Each Other." Foreign Affairs 50 (July 1972).

Jukes, Geoffrey. "Soviet Views of China." Paper presented to the Australian Institute of International Affairs Conference: China and the World Community, June 1972, Melbourne.

Kahin, George McTurnan. The Asian African Conference: Bandung, Indonesia, April 1955. Ithaca, N.Y.: Cornell University Press, 1956.

Kintner, William. China's World View 1972. Philadelphia: Foreign Policy Research Institute, 1972.

LaFeber, Walter. "China and Japan: Different Beds, Different Dreams." Current History 59, no. 349 (September 1970).

Lewis, John W. "The Study of Chinese Political Culture." World Politics 18 (April 1966).

Li, Dun J. The Essence of Chinese Civilization. Princeton, N.J.: Van Nostrand, 1967.

Lifton, Robert Jay. Revolutionary Immortality. New York: Random House, 1968.

Liu, Leo Yueh-Yun. China as a Nuclear Power in World Politics. Toronto: Macmillan, 1972.

Logoreci, Anton. "China's Policies in East Europe." Current History 63, no. 373 (September 1972).

Lowenthal, Richard. "Russia and China: Controlled Conflict." Foreign Affairs 49 (April 1971).

MacFarquhar, Roderick. Sino-American Relations 1949-71. New York: Praeger, 1972.

Mao Tse-tung. Basic Tactics. New York: Praeger, 1966.

_____. Quotations from Chairman Mao. Peking: Foreign Language Press, 1972.

_____. Selected Works. Vol. 1. New York: International Publishers, 1954.

_____. Selected Works. Vol. 2. London: Lawrence and Wishart, 1954.

_____. Selected Works. Vol. 3. London: Lawrence and Wishart, 1954.

_____. Selected Works. Vol. 4. London: Lawrence and Wishart, 1956.

_____. Selected Works. Vol. 5. New York: International Publishers, 1963.

_____. Six Essays on Military Affairs. Peking: Foreign Language Press, 1971.

Mehnert, Klaus. China Returns. New York: New American Library, 1972.

Meisner, Maurice. "Maoist Utopianism and the Future of Chinese Society." International Journal 26 (Summer 1971): 535-58.

Melby, John. "Great Power Rivalry in East Asia." International Journal 26 (Summer 1971): 457-68.

_____. The Mandate of Heaven. Toronto: University of Toronto Press, 1968.

Michael, Franz. "Is China Expansionist: A Design for Aggression." Problems of Communism 20 (January-April 1971).

_____. "The New United States-China Policy." Current History 63, no. 373 (September 1972).

Murphy, Charles H. "China's Nuclear Deterrent." Air Force Magazine, April 1972.

Nakamura, Kikuo. "The Taiwan Straits." Papers presented to the Peace in Asia Conference, June 1972, Kyoto.

Nelsen, Harvey. "Military Forces in the Cultural Revolution." China Quarterly, no. 51 (July-September 1972).

Ness, Peter Van. "Mao Tse-tung and Revolutionary Self-Reliance." Problems of Communism 20 (January-April 1971).

_____. Revolution and Chinese Foreign Policy. Berkeley: University of California Press, 1971.

Pollack, Jonathan D. "Chinese Attitudes Towards Nuclear Weapons 1964-69." China Quarterly, no. 50 (April-June 1972).

Powell, R. L. "The Military and the Struggle for Power in China." Current History 63, no. 373 (September 1972).

_____. "The Power of the Chinese Military." Current History 59, no. 349 (September 1970).

Prybyla, Jan S. "China's Economy: Experiments in Maoism." Current History 59, no. 349 (September 1970).

_____. The Political Economy of Communist China. Scranton, Pa.: International Textbook Publishers, 1970.

_____. "The Soviet Economy." Current History 63, no. 374 (October 1972).

Pye, Lucian W. "China in Context." Foreign Affairs 45 (January 1967).

_____. The Spirit of Chinese Politics. Cambridge, Mass.: Massachusetts Institute of Technology Press, 1968.

Ra'anan, Uri. "Chinese Factionalism and Sino-Soviet Relations." Current History 59, no. 349 (September 1970).

Rawski, Thomas G. "Foreign Contacts and Industrialization." International Journal 26 (Summer 1971): 522-34.

Robinson, Thomas R. "The View from Peking: China's Policies Towards the U.S., the USSR, and Japan." Pacific Affairs 45 (Fall 1972).

Salisbury, Harrison E. Orbit of China. New York: Harper & Row, 1967.

_____. War Between Russia and China. New York: Norton, 1969.

Schram, Stuart. Mao Tse-tung. Harmondsworth, England: Penguin Books, 1966.

_____. The Political Thought of Mao Tse-tung. New York: Praeger, 1970.

Schurmann, Franz, and Orville Schell, eds. Communist China. New York: Vintage Books, 1967.

Schwart, H. China. New York: Atheneum, 1965.

Snow, Edgar. Red Star over China. New York: Grove Press, 1938.

Stoessinger, John G. Nations in Darkness: China, Russia and America. New York: Random House, 1971.

Subrahmanyam, K. "Defense Preparations in India and China." Bulletin of the Atomic Scientist 24 (May 1968).

Sun Tzu. The Art of War. New York: Oxford University Press, 1971.

Terrill, Ross. "China and Southeast Asia." Paper presented to the Australian Institute of International Affairs Conference: China and the World Community, June 1972, Melbourne.

_____. "The 800,000,000: China and the World." The Atlantic 229 (January 1972).

_____. "The 800,000,000: Report from China." The Atlantic 228 (November 1971).

Tuchman, Barbara W. "If Mao Had Come to Washington: An Essay in Alternatives." Foreign Affairs 51 (October 1972).

Tung, William L. The Political Institutions of Modern China. The Hague: Martinus Nijhoff, 1964.

Watson, Francis. The Frontiers of China. London: Chatto and Windus, 1966.

Whiting, Allen S. China Crosses the Yalu. Stanford, Calif.: Stanford University Press, 1960.

_____. "China and East Asian Security." Paper presented to the Peace in Asia Conference, June 1972, Kyoto.

_____, et al. "China's New Diplomacy." Problems of Communism 20 (November-December 1971).

_____. "The Sino-American Detente: Genesis and Prospect." Paper presented to the Australian Institute of International Affairs Conference: China and the World Community, June 1972, Melbourne.

Wilson, Ian. "Chinese Views of the USSR." Paper presented to the Australian Institute of International Affairs Conference: China and the World Community, June 1972, Melbourne.

Yahuda, Michael B. "Chinese Foreign Policy: A Process of Interaction." Paper presented to the Australian Institute of International Affairs Conference: China and the World Community, June 1972, Melbourne.

_____. "Kremlinology and the Chinese Strategic Debate, 1965–66." China Quarterly, no. 49 (January–March 1972).

Zagoria, Donald S. The Sino-Soviet Conflict 1956–61. Princeton, N.J.: Princeton University Press, 1962.

JAPAN

Adamo, L. J. "Japanese Treaty Patterns." Asian Survey 12 (March 1972).

Akagi, Roy Hidemichi. Japan's Foreign Relations 1542–1936. Tokyo: Hokuseido Press, 1936.

Bieda, K. The Structure and Operation of the Japanese Economy. Sydney: John Wiley and Sons Australasia Publishing, 1970.

Brzezinski, Z. The Fragile Blossom: Crisis and Change in Japan. New York: Harper & Row, 1972.

Curtis, Gerald L. "Conservative Dominance in Japanese Politics." Current History 60, no. 356 (April 1971).

Ellingsworth, Richard. Japanese Economic Policies and Security. Adelphi Papers no. 90. London: International Institute for Strategic Studies, October 1972.

Emmerson, John K. Arms, Yen and Power: The Japanese Dilemma. New York: Dunellen, 1971.

Eto, Shinkichi. "Japan and China--A New Stage?" Problems of Communism 21 (November–December 1972).

Haas, Anthony. "Japan–New Zealand Economic Relations." Pacific Community 4 (October 1972).

Harako, Rinjiri. "Japan–Soviet Relations and Japan's Choice." Pacific Community 4 (October 1972).

Japan Defense Agency. The Defense of Japan. Tokyo, 1970.

Japan's Economic Expansion and Foreign Trade 1955 to 1970. Geneva: GATT, 1971.

Japan, Ministry of Foreign Affairs, Economic Affairs Bureau. Statistical Survey of Japan's Economy 1970. Tokyo, 1971.

Kahn, Herman. The Emerging Japanese Superstate. Englewood Cliffs, N.J.: Prentice-Hall, 1970.

Kamiya, Fuji. "Japan and the Stabilization of the Korean Peninsula." Paper presented to the Peace in Asia Conference, June 1972, Kyoto.

Kanazawa, Masao. "Japan and the Balance of Power in Asia." Pacific Community 4 (October 1972).

Kavic, Lorne. "Canada-Japan Relations." International Journal 26 (Summer 1971).

Kawata, Tadashi. "Japanese Trade Policy and Structural Adjustment." Paper presented to the Peace in Asia Conference, June 1972, Kyoto.

Kishida, Junnosuke. "Non-nuclear Japan." Paper presented to the Peace in Asia Conference, June 1972, Kyoto.

Klein, T. M. "The Ryukyus on the Eve of Reversion." Pacific Affairs 45 (Spring 1972).

Kubo, Takuya. "Revaluation of Japan-United States Security Treaty." Paper presented to the Peace in Asia Conference, June 1972, Kyoto.

Levine, S. B. "Japan's Growth Economy: Joy and Anguish." Current History 60 (April 1971).

Maxon, Yale. Control of Japanese Foreign Policy: A Study of Civil-Military Rivalry 1930-45. Berkeley: University of California Press, 1970.

Mishima, Yukio. Sun and Steel. Translated by John Bester. New York: Grove Press, 1970.

Miyamoto, Ken'ichi. "Urban Problems in Japan." Japan Institute of International Affairs. Annual Review 5 (1969-70).

Miyazaki, Isamu. "Japanese Economy in the 1960s." Japan Institute of International Affairs. Annual Review 5 (1969-70).

Morton, W. S. "Educational and Cultural Trends in Japan Today." Current History 60, no. 356 (April 1971).

Mushakoji, Kinhide. "The Changing Japanese Foreign Policy Attitudes in the 1960s." Japan Institute of International Affairs. Annual Review 5 (1969-70).

Ogawa, Iwao. "Nuclear Submarines: Comment from Japan." Bulletin of the Atomic Scientist 24 (April 1968).

Olson, Lawrence. Japan in Postwar Asia. New York: Praeger, 1970.

Organization for Economic Cooperation and Development. Economic Surveys: Japan. Paris: OECD, 1972.

Osamu, Miyoshi. "Multipolarized Asia and Japan's Choice." Paper presented to the Peace in Asia Conference, June 1972, Kyoto.

Ozawa, Terutomo. Transfer of Technology from Japan to Developing Countries. New York: UNITAR, 1971.

Passin, Herbert. "Socio-Cultural Factors in the Japanese Perception of International Order." Japan Institute of International Affairs. Annual Review 5 (1969-70).

Peace Research in Japan 1971. Tokyo: Japan Peace Research Group, 1971.

Pringsheim, Klaus. "Japan's Position in East Asia." Paper presented at a conference on Japan and Superpowers--Friend, Partner, Rival, February 18-19, 1972, Saskatoon.

Reischauer, Edwin O. Japan: The Story of a Nation. New York: Alfred A. Knopf, 1970.

Royama, Michio. The Asian Balance of Power: The Japanese View. Adelphi Papers no. 42. London: Institute for Strategic Studies, 1967.

Saeki, Kiichi. "Japanese Options in the 1970s." Paper presented to the Peace in Asia Conference, June 1972, Kyoto.

_____. "Ventures in Soviet Diplomacy--Toward Japanese Cooperation in Siberian Development." Problems of Communism 21 (May-June 1972).

Sohn, Jae Souk. "The Korean Peninsula." Paper presented to the Peace in Asia Conference, June 1972, Kyoto.

Storry, Richard. A History of Modern Japan. Harmondsworth, Middlesex: Penguin, C. Nichols and Co., 1960.

Tatu, Michel. "The Emergence of a New International System." Paper presented to the Peace in Asia Conference, June 1972, Kyoto.

Taira, Koji. "Japan's Economic Relations with Asia." Current History 60, no. 356 (April 1971).

Ueno, Hiroya. "A Long-Term Model of Economic Growth of Japan, 1906-1968." International Economic Review 13 (October 1972).

Unger, Jonathan. "Japan: The Economic Threat." Survival 14 (January-February 1972).

"U.S.-Japanese Political and Security Relations: A Conference Report." Orbis 16 (Spring 1972).

Wakaizumi, Kei. "Japan and Southeast Asia in the 1970's." Current History 60, no. 356 (April 1971).

Ward, R. E. Japan's Political System. Englewood Cliffs, N.J.: Prentice-Hall, 1968.

Weinstein, Martin. "Japan and the Continental Giants." Current History 60, no. 356 (April 1971).

_____. Japan's Postwar Defense Policy, 1947-1968. New York: Columbia University Press, 1969, 1971.

Welfield, John. "A New Balance: Japan versus China." Pacific Community 4 (October 1972).

White Papers of Japan 1970-71: Annual Abstract of Official Reports and Statistics of the Japanese Government. Tokyo, 1972.

Wohlstetter, Albert. "Security Politics of Japan as a Non-Nuclear State." Paper presented to the Peace in Asia Conference, June 1972, Kyoto.

Yiu, Myung-Kun. "The Prospect of Japanese Rearmament." Current History 60, no. 356 (April 1971).

Young, Kenneth T. "Japan and the U.S. in Pacific Asia." Pacific
    Community 4 (October 1972).

GENERAL

International Institute for Strategic Studies [previously Institute for
    Strategic Studies]. Soviet American Relations and World Order:
    The Two and the Many. Adelphi Papers no. 66. London: Inter-
    national Institute for Strategic Studies.

_____. The Military Balance. 1970-71, 1971-72, 1972-73. Lon-
    don: International Institute for Strategic Studies, 1970, 1971,
    1972.

_____. Strategic Survey. 1969, 1970, 1971. London: Interna-
    tional Institute for Strategic Studies, 1970, 1971, 1972.

Jukes, Geoffrey. The Indian Ocean in Soviet Naval Policy. Adelphi
    Papers no. 87. London: International Institute for Strategic
    Studies, 1972.

Millar, T. B. The Indian and Pacific Oceans: Some Strategic Con-
    siderations. Adelphi Papers no. 57. London: Institute for Stra-
    tegic Studies, 1969.

ABOUT THE AUTHORS

DOUGLAS A. ROSS is a doctoral candidate at the University of Toronto studying international relations. His academic awards have included the J. Reginald Adams Gold Medal in Political Economy (1970), a Department of National Defence Scholarship (1972), and Canada Council Fellowships (1973-75). He is currently writing his dissertation on Canada's involvement in Indochina 1954-73. Mr. Ross received his B.A. and M.A. from the University of Toronto, specializing in international relations, Canadian foreign policy, and strategic studies.

PETER G. MUELLER is presently on an extended trip through Europe and Asia. Mr. Mueller, in the past three years, has worked first as an analyst for the Ontario Government's Commission on Government Productivity and then as an independent management consultant. He received his B.A. and M.A. from the University of Toronto specializing in international relations and strategic studies. Prior to his departure in 1974, Mr. Mueller, acting as rapporteur, wrote Public Consultation on Population Questions: A Report to the Government of Canada for the Canadian Institute of International Affairs, one of the cosponsors of this extensive public survey.

RELATED TITLES
Published by
Praeger Special Studies

SINO-AMERICAN DETENTE AND ITS POLICY IMPLICATIONS
Edited by Gene T. Hsiao

CHINA AND THE GREAT POWERS: Relations with the United States, the Soviet Union, and Japan
Edited by Francis O. Wilcox

CHINA AND SOUTHEAST ASIA: Peking's Relations with Revolutionary Movements
Jay Taylor

SOUTHEAST ASIA UNDER THE NEW BALANCE OF POWER
Edited by Sudershan Chawla, Melvin Gurtov, and Alain-Gerard Marsot

THE NEUTRALIZATION OF SOUTHEAST ASIA
Dick Wilson

THE POSTWAR REARMAMENT OF JAPANESE MARITIME FORCES, 1945-71
James E. Auer

CHINA AND THE QUESTION OF TAIWAN: Documents and Analysis
Edited by Hungdah Chiu

JAPANESE PRIVATE ECONOMIC DIPLOMACY: An Analysis of Business-Government Linkages
William R. Bryant